DISSOLUTION

No-Fault Divorce, Marriage, and the Future of Women

by Riane Tennenhaus Eisler

toExcel
San Jose New York Lincoln Shanghai

Dissolution

Published by toExcel Press,
an imprint of iUniverse.com, Inc.

For information address:
iUniverse.com, Inc.
620 North 48th Street
Suite 201
Lincoln, NE 68504-3467
www.iuniverse.com

ISBN: 1-58348-029-3

Library of Congress Catalog Card Number: 98-88201

To my mother

ACKNOWLEDGMENTS

Wherever possible, specific acknowledgments have been made in the text or notes. Here I would like to thank all the others who have contributed their time and efforts to this book. These include the women and men who granted me interviews, especially those who were willing to share their personal stories, as well as my editors and typists. I also want to thank Sophie Schmidt, who made working on the chapter notes a far more pleasant task, Elizabeth Wahbe, who contributed much enthusiasm, support, and excellent work, and Billy Badstubner, who provided not only data, but also inspiration. Among the colleagues who gave me valuable suggestions and information are attorneys Albert Corske, Harry Fain, Georgia Franklin, Herma Hill Kay, Marvin Mitchelson, Sara Radin, and Lawrence Stotter. My particular gratitude goes to Professor Anette Ehrlich, Roberta Ralph, Esq., and Dr. Laurel Roennau for the generosity and intelligence of their help. Finally, I want to thank my daughters Andrea and Lori for their proofreading assistance, and above all, for their patient encouragement and support.

CONTENTS

PART III
Alternatives and the Future of Women

Divorce Checklist

Sample Marriage Contract

INTRODUCTION

Dissolution is a new word for divorce. Along with the new name have come fundamental changes in what once used to be a rare and socially unacceptable phenomenon, but which has today become a statistical commonplace.

This book is an analysis of the new and old family laws and of the social realities and values they reflect. Beyond this, the book is also about the dissolution of the traditional American nuclear family itself, and about the rapidly changing status of women. It is intended to give the nontechnical reader a working understanding of the whole legal system—from marriage and divorce laws to tax rules and constitutional principles—which governs the relationship between family and state. It is also designed to help people, particularly women, who are facing, contemplating, or already involved in the breakup of a marriage.

The events that take place in the courtroom, or in courthouse corridors and the offices of opposing lawyers, are only the most visible parts of a divorce. Nevertheless, the decisions made there will often determine the course of people's lives for many years. We are finally seeing some changes in this neglected field. This nation, and indeed most of the Western world, is being swept by a seemingly sudden, and in some ways revolutionary, movement toward family-law reform. But despite the fact that some of these new legal developments are more congruent with what is actually happening in people's lives today, not all the new laws are beneficial. In fact, particularly for women and children, it may well be that as much is being lost as gained.

In my work as an attorney practicing in the field of family law, I have seen the effects of both the old and the new laws firsthand. Time and time again women have come to me, disoriented and almost totally unprepared to accept the legal and economic facts of their divorces. Often just an explanation of what was legally in store for them enabled them to reassess their personal situations and to make positive contributions toward the outcome of their cases.

This book is an outgrowth of my professional experiences. Many of the ideas brought forth here have evolved from my research for courses I have taught on the social and legal status of women and children. Some of the most practical concepts emerged from my efforts to introduce new and socially responsive legislation and to set up programs to bring family-law services and information to women without means. On a more personal level, the book is also the result of my own experiences during the past decade, when my life, like that of millions of other women in this country, underwent major changes—when, as a housewife in the suburbs, I went back to law school, obtained a divorce, and became an attorney, a teacher, a lecturer, and then a writer.

In the course of preparing and writing this work, I spoke to many women and men, clients and colleagues, students, secretaries, housewives, and friends about the changes they, too, have been experiencing in their lives during recent years. I began to see recurrent patterns in the problems and obstacles these people encountered. Eventually, it became clear to me that our common personal experiences as well as the new and, as it turns out, often related developments in family law are all part of the vast changes taking place in American society today.

The armies of social scientists, journalists, and politicians studying these changes by no means agree as to where they will lead, but they do seem to agree that what is happening is of major proportions. According to futurologists studying present trends, we are in the throes of a major technological, economic, and social shift into a postindustrial age. This shift is as potentially dislocating as was the transformation of the basically religious, agrarian, Jeffersonian country we once were into the secular, industrial, urbanized America we are today. However, while the former process evolved over hundreds of years, we are experiencing today's accelerated changes within our own lifetimes.

In trying to make some sense out of these rapid changes, I have focused on our laws. It is my view that laws are more than just instruments of social control and devices by which personal and economic conflicts can be peacefully resolved. When examined in the context of technological, social, and economic developments, laws are major repositories of social values which affect our daily lives in far more subtle and ubiquitous ways than may at first be apparent. In essence, our laws determine how we may or may not relate to other people. Beyond that, and perhaps even more significantly, in their explicit or implied definitions, laws also help determine how other people shall view us, and even how we shall view ourselves. As social values change, so do laws. Therefore by examining new laws we can learn about much more than contemporary legal changes. Legal analysis can be a method of uncovering and discerning related and often less tangible social and economic trends. Laws in general can be seen as enforcers and reinforcers of cultural values, and new laws can be seen as signals or guideposts on the road to the future.

One recent legal guidepost is no-fault divorce—where grounds for divorce are no longer based on guilt or innocence. The first part of this book is an analysis of the new no-fault divorce laws and other trends in family law. About one-half of our states have already adopted some form of no-fault divorce. It has been the subject of violent legal battles that are still going on. Part I compares the older divorce laws with the new ones no longer based on marital fault. It also describes and analyzes other contemporary family-law developments and deals with the economic and personal mechanics of divorce. These include the division of property, alimony, child support, and child custody.

Part II consists of an in-depth analysis of both the laws and the institutions of marriage and divorce, as well as such related areas as welfare, illegitimacy, and birth control—with particular emphasis on their implications for women.

Part III explores possible alternatives, not only to divorce and marriage as we have known them, but alternatives to the social structures that are becoming obsolete.

Throughout the book I have included specific case histories, the stories of real people involved in and affected by the operation of our existing complex of family laws. I have also tried to supply some very practical suggestions which I hope will be useful to the reader in her or his personal affairs. In addition, I make some specific proposals for both short-term and long-range changes. I hope these will result in some modifications of our system, both in terms of attitudes and of laws, and that they will stimulate thinking about more creative alternatives.

Finally, Appendix 1 is a self-contained divorce checklist designed for easy access and use, containing concise, practical information and guidelines for those facing imminent divorce. Appendix 2 is a marriage contract. While originally prepared for a real case, it provides an example of the issues that arise when couples make their own marital agreements.

I

DIVORCE
AND
CHILD CUSTODY

1

Divorce: Past and Present

According to the U.S. Census Bureau, more than a million American couples were divorced in 1975.[1] This rate, which is more than double that of 1964, is the highest in American history.[2] What made it possible has been the steady liberalization of judicial and legislative attitudes toward divorce.

The contemporary trend toward more easily obtainable divorces is a significant departure from our earlier family laws which severely restricted the circumstances under which a marriage could be dissolved. In the course of Western history there have been a number of major shifts in the regulation of marriage and divorce. In ancient Rome, for example, the termination of a marriage was not even considered a proper subject for interference by the law. No court decree or other act of government was required for a divorce, since marriage was considered essentially a private social institution and not a legal one subject to regulation by the state.[3]

In the Middle Ages, under the influence of Christianity, with its emphasis on the sacramental nature of marriage, the institution ceased to be a private one and became a religious one, subject to the regulation of the Church.[4] In the view of the Church, a marriage could only be dissolved by God through death or by the Church through annulment. When Henry VIII and the pope had their famous argument over the king's desire to shed one of his wives, the English Church broke from Rome and the regulation of marriage became a British affair. Even so, divorces were almost impossible to obtain for a very long time. The only absolute divorce recognized in England was not only expensive, but extremely difficult to get—it required an act of Parliament or special law and usually cost more than a thousand pounds. The second method, the divorce *a mensa et thoro* (from bed and board), was not really a divorce at all in our sense of the word, since it did not permit the parties to remarry. Under the exclusive jurisdiction of the ecclesiastical courts, it was granted only upon proof of a spouse's adultery, cruelty, or unnatural practices. Again, because it usually involved a long and costly trial, this, too, was a remedy available only to the rich, and due to the inferior position of women in English society, primarily to men.[5]

For the poor, among whom matrimony was more the exception and cohabitation the rule even as late as the Victorian era, there was another method for terminating whatever marriages there were.[6] It was the sale or trade of wives, a practice apparently so widespread in eighteenth-century England that wives were sold like cattle at public auctions, and where, as one legal scholar put it, "apparently a consented-to wife sale did not ruffle the moral fiber of the English legal system, whereas gambling did."[7]

The English legal system did not assume jurisdiction over marriage and divorce from the religious authorities until 1857, when the Matrimonial Causes Act was passed. In America the transition from religious to secular family-law control came about much earlier, but very unevenly. Although some of the colonies granted magistrates jurisdiction to perform marriages almost immediately upon settlement, in many of them, particularly in the South, no effort whatever was made to grant courts jurisdiction over divorce. Some states allowed legislative divorces along the lines of the English parliamentary ones. In others, special equity courts, successors to the older chancery or ecclesiastic courts, had exclusive jurisdiction over family law, and in still other states, notably those in New England, divorce was handled by regular courts, either probate or common law. In addition, there was great diversity of grounds from state to state. In Massachusetts, only bigamy, impotence, or adultery would warrant an absolute divorce, whereas a divorce from bed and board could be obtained for cruelty. New York, even until very recently, had adultery as the only ground, while, as early as 1785 Pennsylvania permitted absolute divorce on the grounds of impotence, bigamy, adultery, malicious desertion, or a four-year unexplained absence, as well as a limited divorce for cruelty or intolerable indignities.[8] Despite these great diversities, until very recently (except for those states which permitted divorce for separation or insanity, and the Virgin Islands which have since 1933 allowed it for incompatibility) the general rule in America has been that a divorce will only be granted upon the proof of marital fault.

Then in 1969 a landmark event in American legal history took place. The legislature of the State of California decided to make a complete break with the past. The result was the California Family Law Act of 1970, the first divorce act in the nation to eliminate fault as the basis for divorce.

In the past, to bring an action for divorce, a husband or wife had to file a complaint alleging that the other party was at fault. The defendant could contest the action in only one of two ways —either by proving that the charges made against him or her were not true, or by establishing that the other party was also at fault.

In a divorce case, as in any other action, what is called the burden of proof—the responsibility for introducing enough evidence to make out a case—is on the party bringing the suit. In a criminal case that proof must be "beyond a reasonable doubt" and usually, unless a jury trial is waived by the defendant, it must convince the body the law calls "twelve reasonable men." A divorce action, however, being a civil case, requires that this burden be met only by "the preponderance of the evidence," and then just to the satisfaction of one person. It is the judge, who, in family-law cases, sits not only as interpreter of the law (the traditional judicial task), but also as trier of facts (the traditional function of the jury).

It is up to the attorneys for both parties to present this proof properly, in accordance with the rules of evidence. These rules determine both how proof is to be introduced (for example, by examination and cross-examination of witnesses versus their simply giving a speech), and what will and will not be admissible. "Hearsay" or evidence acquired secondhand, as for example the testimony of a witness who did not actually see or hear a particular event but was told about it by someone else, is not generally admissible as proof. There is, however, always the catch that unless the opposing counsel objects or a judge decides on his or her own motion to keep something out, even "legally inadmissible" materials can be sneaked in. There is the further catch that, even if a statement is "stricken from the record," it will of course have some kind of effect, once it has been made.

The attorneys also have the responsibility of helping the judge interpret the law by presenting legal briefs and arguments favorable to their sides. Even in fields like divorce that are based largely on statutory or code law, there are huge areas of interpretation contained, not in the code books, but in the cases themselves. However, the vast majority of cases tried and decided in the lower courts are almost never reported at all. Therefore it is important to emphasize that what in Anglo-American jurisprudence is known as case law is actually comprised of only a very small part of all existing cases, namely those appellate cases reported and printed in the official state and federal case-law books.

In the lower courts, especially in cases where there is little property and barely enough money to pay for even one court appearance, much less for an appeal, and where clogged calendars and limitations of time make lengthy legal arguments more the exception than the rule, all too often decisions are made quickly, and sometimes almost by rote. This situation is further aggravated by the fact that while for the principals a case is always unique, for judges who sit in family court day after day, even the most heartrending stories begin to lose their impact. After a while this becomes so even for those judges who truly care, as they realize that the underlying problems are really social and economic, and that, within the limitations of our institutions and many of the archaic laws and theories with which they must deal, there is often not much they can really do.

Before the introduction of no-fault divorce in California, one such archaic law (which is still in effect in some non-no-fault states) stated that if a defendant to a divorce action could prove that the plaintiff was also at fault, a judge would be precluded from granting the divorce.

The legal theory behind this rule is basically the old maxim that one must have "clean hands" to come to court and that where both the plaintiff and the defendant have committed some wrong, neither is entitled to any judicial relief. Later this concept was codified in American states under what has become known as the doctrine of recrimination, which was interpreted by many judges to mean that any ground for divorce constitutes a recriminatory defense.

In 1952, in the case of *DeBurgh* v. *DeBurgh*,[9] the California Supreme Court in essence threw out this theory. The case had originally been filed by Mrs. DeBurgh on the ground of extreme cruelty. Mr. DeBurgh cross-complained on the same ground. At the trial there was evidence:

> that defendant more than once inflicted severe bodily injury upon plaintiff; that after one severe beating plaintiff attempted to commit suicide by an overdose of sleeping pills; that defendant

often boasted in the presence of plaintiff and guests of intimate relations with other women and discussed their physical attributes in detail; that defendant was often intoxicated; that defendant frequently told plaintiff that her daughter by a previous marriage had loose morals; that defendant was insanely jealous of a former suitor of plaintiff and on one occasion seized an alarm clock given plaintiff by the suitor and threw it into the toilet; and that defendant lavishly tipped waiters and spent his money freely in public, but in private life refused to give plaintiff sufficient funds to purchase clothes suitable for her station in life. On the other hand, defendant's evidence was to the effect that plaintiff had invented false accusations against him; that plaintiff had deliberately attempted to ruin his business life by writing a letter to his partner falsely accusing defendant of dishonesty and homosexuality; and that plaintiff had announced her intention of writing similar letters to other business associates of defendant.

The trial court found that each party had been guilty of cruelty toward the other, that such acts of cruelty by each toward the other were provoked by the acts of the other, that each party had been guilty of recrimination and that *therefore neither was entitled to a divorce.*

In reversing that decision, Justice Traynor of the California Supreme Court wrote:

Much of the confusion concerning recrimination in California has proceeded from the erroneous discussion of the subject in *Conant v. Conant.* . . . It was stated in that case that this defense is based on the doctrine that one who violates a contract containing mutual and dependent covenants cannot complain of its breach by the other party. . . . The deceptive analogy to contract law ignores the basic fact that marriage is a great deal more than a contract. It can be terminated only with the consent of the state. In a divorce proceeding the court must consider not merely the rights and wrongs of the parties as in contract litigation, but the public interest in the institution of marriage. . . . Since the family is the core of our society, the law seeks to foster and preserve marriage. But when a marriage has failed and the family has ceased to be a unit, the purposes of family life are no longer served and divorce will be permitted. Public policy does not discourage divorce where the relations between husband and wife are such that the legitimate objects of matrimony have been utterly destroyed.[10]

On this basis it then became possible for a "guilty" party to get a divorce even before the California legislature enacted no-fault in 1969. The usual ground was cruelty, for which little more than a charge of the husband's lack of appreciation for his wife's cooking or a wife's constant criticism of her husband's golf stroke would be sufficient grounds.

I remember, with some embarrassment, how in the days before no-fault, especially in default cases, the stories of each plaintiff and her or his witnesses all had a peculiarly similar ring. Since clients were often reluctant to discuss their *real* problems in open court, a sort of stereotype had been developed for which the plot line ran something like this:

> ATTORNEY: Did your husband ever do anything to cause you mental suffering (or for variety, "grievous mental suffering")?
>
> PLAINTIFF: (With a deep sigh) Well, it was on the occasion of his birthday and I had gone to a lot of trouble and time and I had gone shopping all that prior day. . .
>
> JUDGE: (Interrupting) I don't think we need to know anything that happened the day before. Just about the incident.
>
> PLAINTIFF: (A little flustered and speeding up) Well, I gave him this surprise party and I invited all of the people I thought he'd enjoy and I made all kinds of fancy dishes and instead of thanking me for what I had done he humiliated me by criticizing my cooking right there in front of his friends.
>
> JUDGE: (To attorney, stifling a yawn) Do you have a corroborating witness?
>
> ATTORNEY: (Trying to rush things) Yes, Your Honor. (To witness after she's been sworn in and has stated her name, how long she's known plaintiff and defendant, and that she was present on the night in question) Did the defendant make any remarks to the plaintiff that you recall on that night?
>
> WITNESS: Well, he talked about his troubles with his secretary and. . .
>
> ATTORNEY: (Interrupting right away, but hamstrung by the rule that a friendly witness can't be led, in other words that a

lawyer can't put words in his own witness's mouth—one reason most attorneys "rehearse" their witnesses before putting them on the stand) Any remarks in connection with the plaintiff's cooking?

WITNESS: (A little snappish) Well, that's what I was just getting at. He said that as scatterbrained as his new secretary was, she could at least be counted on to make him a good cup of coffee and get him exactly the kind of sweet roll he asked for, while with all his wife's gourmet cookbooks and all her fancy recipes, it had got so that eating at home was a little like a game of culinary Russian roulette. (Corroborating or confirming the wife's story and making it possible for the judge to find "grounds" for a divorce.)

Under the new no-fault approach some of this courtroom dialogue has been eliminated, and witnesses are no longer needed to corroborate guilt. These changes have resulted not only in a saving of time, but have also brought some simplification and a little bit more credibility to the proceedings than the old legal fictions could permit.

Under the new California Family Law Act a marriage can be ended if a court finds that "irreconcilable differences" have led to its "irremediable breakdown." Although it is up to the judge to deny a divorce if this test is not met, there has not been a single reported case of such a decision to date. In effect, then, the new law has made it possible for Californians to end their marriages at will.

Since 1969, Arizona, Colorado, Florida, Iowa, Kentucky, Missouri, Michigan, Nebraska, Oregon, and Washington have also dropped fault from their laws and substituted irretrievable breakdown.[11] In addition, as of June 1, 1973, Alabama, Connecticut, Georgia, Hawaii, Indiana, and New Hampshire had added no-fault to their older statutory grounds. As of that date "incompatibility" was also a ground for divorce in Alabama, Alaska, Connecticut, Delaware, Idaho, Kansas, Nevada, New Mexico, North Dakota, Oklahoma, Texas, and the Virgin Islands.[12] In short, in less than four years, one out of every three American states had adopted some form of no-fault divorce, and all over the country legislatures are considering ways to incorporate this new approach into their laws.

West Germany has also instituted no-fault, Canada and Australia have revised their systems of family law, and in Italy the pope's absolute ban on divorce has finally been lifted. Even in England, divorce is now basically available by mutual consent.

What we are seeing all over the Western world is a fundamental shift in social attitudes and values. No-fault divorce laws are one legal manifestation of that shift. So is what appears to be a national trend toward lower and shorter alimony awards, as well as the increase in paternal and joint child custody.

These legal developments illustrate how changing social values become first more visible and eventually solidified as they are incorporated into laws. This solidification is a process that needs to be examined, as it has far-reaching and serious implications. Once shifting systems of values become part of a legal structure, they almost immediately become highly resistant to further change. That is why the current developments in family law must be studied and understood right now, before the legal language being drafted today becomes rigidified. For women and children, who have traditionally been powerless and who still have no real voice in the meetings of the attorneys and the legislative and judicial bodies that are at this very moment deciding what the new legal language will be, the issue is not one of theory, but of intense personal impact and immediate economic concern.

It has been said, sometimes even by the men drafting these laws, that no-fault is a product of women's liberation, or of what some people call the "male backlash." But the first no-fault divorce laws in this country were passed in California early in 1969, by an almost all-male legislature, before most people had even heard of the women's liberation movement; and at this writing, all over this country, the legislatures and bar associations that are considering proposals for divorce reform are with few exceptions nearly all-male.

The two principal proposals being studied are the Uniform Marriage and Divorce Act (UMDA), recommended as a model divorce law by the 1970 National Conference of Commissioners on Uniform State Laws,[13] and the Revised Uniform Marriage and Divorce Act (RUMDA), put forth by the Family Law Section of the American Bar Association (ABA).[14] The controversy between these two groups has been going on for years, and revolves around issues of public policy and economics. Basically, the Family Law Section of the ABA has taken the position that the UMDA, like the California law, makes marriage too easy to dissolve and that clearer definitions of "irretrievable breakdown" and stronger efforts to provide state conciliation services are required. The ABA also has been very critical of the UMDA's concept of marital property, one which would introduce a type of economic partnership theory into marriage, but only at the point where a marriage breaks down.

The UMDA and RUMDA are only the last in a long series of studies on divorce reform. Almost every one of the commissions and other official and semiofficial groups that have studied the subject have come to the same conclusion: that a new approach replacing the old, fault-based divorce is needed. Regardless of the exact legal language they recommend in its place, the consensus about fault as grounds for divorce seems to be, in the words of the Commissioners on Uniform State Laws, that it is "an ineffective barrier to marital dissolution regularly overcome by perjury... and an unfortunate device which adds to the bitterness and hostility of divorce proceeding."[15]

Curiously this reasoning is quite similar to that used by Archbishop Cramner in 1552 when he recommended in the Reformatio Legume Ecclesiasticarum that divorce be granted where there was "such violent hatred as rendered it in the highest degree improbable that the husband and wife would survive their animosities and again love one another."[16]

Why did it take until now for this concept of divorce to be accepted if, as we see, it was first proposed almost five hundred years ago? To answer that question one must look beyond the law.

Before the twentieth century divorce was rare. The rhetoric behind that fact may have been moral, but the realities were economic. Until the turn of the century, the family was still the place where clothing, food, and nearly all other necessities of life were produced—in other words, it was the major unit of economic production. Therefore, an intact family was essential. It was only after the turn of the century, when first the factory and then the corporation began to take over the former economic function of the family, that the divorce boom began.

Divorce has skyrocketed in all urbanized, industrialized Western societies. This development has been attributed to a variety of factors, from the gradual breakdown of religious sanctions and the increased mobility of population, to rising personal expectations for happiness and self-fulfillment, and simply to greater affluence. On a more fundamental level, it is undoubtedly related to underlying technological and ecological developments that are as yet not accurately understood, or even fully perceived. There is, therefore, no real basis for hope that the divorce rate will suddenly shrink or that the trend toward lower and shorter support awards will somehow reverse itself, particularly under present economic conditions. Neither is there any legitimacy to the currently voguish nostalgia for the past, nor to the recurrent moral and sentimental demands that women make everything right again by returning to their "natural" roles.

Social processes do not lend themselves to reversal, nor do they operate in simple cause-and-effect terms. One thing history has always taught us is that change is one of the few constants in human affairs. Throughout history, the structure and form of the family have continually changed and evolved. The recent dramatic changes are all reflections of evolving social and economic realities requiring new forms of social organization. For most of our grandparents and great-grandparents marriage was a lifetime sacrament. The word *family* meant parents, children, grandparents, and sometimes uncles and aunts, often living and working together on a farm. Today, we have most commonly the so-called "nuclear" family composed of a couple and their children, usually concentrated in urban centers of a million inhabitants or more. But just as the extended agrarian family was no longer viable in the urbanized industrialized milieu, the family form that succeeded it cannot be expected to remain static as vast technological, scientific, and social changes continue to occur.

Most women living today were brought up in a world where a woman's final destination in life was marriage. No matter what the new realities may be, it is very hard for them to give up the belief that marriage is the "feminine" woman's best and most fulfilling choice. Yet, while marriage is still being presented to us as an ultimate destination, it is clearly no longer a permanent one. Until just a few years ago, the millions of American women who had made marriage their full-time job knew they could not be legally fired without cause. They knew that if a judge thought they had done their job well, and their husbands had the means, they could expect good severance pay; and if they had enough tenure (and sometimes even after only a few years) a lifetime alimony pension. Some people said this was not fair, and that it penalized husbands. But fair or unfair, it was part of our laws. Today that is no longer the case.

 The impact of the new social and legal realities is perhaps felt most keenly by women and children in those states that have already adopted no-fault legislation. The impact is more visible and open there, partially because these are mainly more populous and urbanized states, where the incidence of divorce is at its highest, and also because the elimination of guilt and innocence has also taken away from divorce proceedings some of the weapons lawyers traditionally used to get better economic settlements for wives.

However, it is an oversimplification and indeed a gross distortion to assert, as some people do, that no-fault divorce is destructive. As a matter of fact, with the addition of certain safeguards, no-fault is in many respects an improvement over the older laws of divorce.

The dislocation in the lives of so many American women today stems from the traditional position of women in our culture —a position of physical, social, and economic dependence on men. The problems the traditional woman—the woman who has been or aspires to be a homemaker—faces in a divorce are comparable to those of the workers who in the past were displaced by mechanization or who today are being replaced by increased automation. Seen in such economic terms, what is happening is that as more and more women become unemployed as wives (that is, no longer supported by husbands), they are forced to find other jobs. Due to this and a whole complex of other socio-economic factors, vast numbers of women continue to be admitted, indeed forced, into the ranks of the "gainfully employed" where, despite all the new fair-employment laws, they still must work for little more than half the earnings of men. Simultaneously, the traditional labor market, particularly the lower segments to which most women are confined, is also shrinking. Consequently, an ever-growing number of these divorced women or "unemployed" housewives cannot and will not be absorbed into the general economy. For them, as well as for those who for reasons of age, the demands of child care, or health problems cannot find or hold jobs, the only recourse has been to join the swelling ranks of the nation's poor. Unfortunately, there is little recognition of the real nature and complexity of these women's problems, not only among the public, but also among the judges and attorneys who work with divorce.

I remember a conversation with another lawyer, where in

trying to negotiate for my client, a former actress who had just been traded in by her doctor-husband for a younger model, I referred to her as a social casualty.

"A what?" the husband's attorney wanted to know.

"Never mind," I said.

"You said a social casualty, didn't you? Well, I like to call a spade a spade, instead of using some of your high-sounding words, and I say that she's just a useless, spoiled," he hesitated, "bleached-blond, money-grubbing mess."

"Because she wants some remuneration for what, by our society's definition, were her best years?"

"You're damn right. Let her go out and find a job like everyone else."

"That's what she did," I said, hoping that just this once I might somehow get through. "She got herself the best job available to her, the job she was taught from childhood was the pinnacle of womanly success, the job of wife to a wealthy and successful man. And now she's been fired, admittedly and even legally for no fault on her part, and you think she's a gold digger and a bleached-blond mess. But if a man were to ask for good severance pay and the proceeds of a promised profit-sharing plan, you would only think it natural, even if he was one of those executives who took a huge expense allowance and really lived it up while he was employed."

Either my opponent did not want to hear what I was saying because it was not congruent with his position as counsel for the husband, or he really could not see it in that light; but to my mind the woman we were talking about is a social casualty, and even more so are the millions of less affluent, older, middle-class wives affected by the new divorce laws and the new social realities they reflect. And so are the young divorced mothers with little children, and beyond that, unless something is done to make them more aware of what is happening, the many teenagers who are today still aspiring to make marriage and motherhood their life's career.

Whether family law is the real key to the problem or not, it is certainly an essential component, if only because, as our divorce rates continue to climb, it is affecting more and more women every day. It is therefore imperative that we gain a better understanding of this complex subject. One obstacle to any understanding is the difficult technical terminology of the laws. Another problem is that although volumes have been written on the general subject of divorce, hardly any statistics comparing court awards in different states have been collected until very recently. What little data there are are mostly fragmentary and the few available studies are based on pitifully small samples.

The legal textbooks and summaries of cases are limited to reported appellate cases (cases appealed to higher courts and reported in the casebooks) which are of course in themselves far from random samples. The situation is further complicated by the legal changes of the last decade. Some states, like California, have completely scrapped grounds based on guilt. In others, the issue of fault can be by-passed by alleging that a couple have lived separately for a certain period of time, usually one year. Other states have retained some of the old guilt-based grounds in addition to no-fault, and in still others, while a marriage may be severed without resorting to allegations of guilt or innocence, fault may still be admissible in determining such economic issues as spousal support and the division of property.

But despite all this variety and complexity, in a very practical sense, family law has not really changed that much. It can still be summed up in one phrase: judicial discretion. Most criminal and civil proceedings are rather strictly circumscribed by relatively precise principles and rules of law. In criminal law, for example, a person must be found guilty "beyond a reasonable doubt." In most civil actions the trier of fact must find that the winning party has prevailed by "a preponderance of the evidence." The interpretation of the individual judge is of course always a major factor in the outcome of any case, but, at least in most fields of law, both statutory and case law are fairly clear as to where the legal boundaries lie. Family law, on the other hand, has traditionally been considered a field where, as attorneys and judges have often put it, there are so many emotional and intangible factors that decisions can only be made on a case-by-case basis. Consequently, both the old and new statutes in this field are full of phrases such as "the court shall award such sums as necessary and proper for the support and maintenance of the husband or wife...," "...having regard to the circumstances of the respective parties," or "the court may authorize...," and perhaps most frequently "...as the court, in its discretion, may deem equitable and just."[17]

Black's Law Dictionary offers a number of definitions for discretion. The first is "power or privilege of the court to act unhampered by legal rule," the language of an old Wisconsin case. Another is "judicial discretion is substantially synonymous with judicial power," and still another is "the equitable decision of what is just and proper under the circumstances."[18]

In practical terms, judicial discretion means that judges sitting in family-law cases have vast power. It also means that these judges do not have to be unduly concerned about their decisions being reversed on appeal, because, as the California Supreme Court and other supreme courts have so often put it, a divorce court's decision will only be reversed upon a showing of a "clear abuse of judicial discretion." Of course, family-law judges are supposed to exercise this discretion equitably. And it is precisely in connection with what is equitable that most of the problems in family law arise.

What is considered equitable is more an issue of social values than it is of law; of individual attitudes rather than of statutes and rules of legal procedure. In short, it is, more often than not, a function of the personal and social circumstances and background and sometimes even mood of the individual judge.

It may be that things are very much worse today for women and children all over this nation. It may also be that this is only so in certain states and for certain socioeconomic groups, such as middle-class women in California. It may also be that the problem has surfaced only because of the sharp increase in the rate of divorce and because women have become more vocal about their rights.

It seems to me that it really does not matter very much whether things are better or worse or the same as before. What does matter is that we have a social problem of vast magnitude, a problem that is causing a great deal of economic and psychological suffering to large numbers of people, and that we have to try to find some way of making our laws responsive to human needs.

2

The Economics of Divorce and
the Division of Property

The obvious place to start looking at contemporary divorce is California, where no-fault has been in effect longest and the divorce rate is high enough to provide sufficient material for analysis. California also illustrates what happens when radical new laws are tacked onto an existing legal structure based on different, and in fact, contradictory assumptions. Since 1970, the original bill introducing no-fault has been amended numerous times by the California legislature. This in turn has required its continuous reinterpretation by the courts.

For example, in 1972, Section 5118 of the California Civil Code was amended to provide that the earnings and accumulations of either husband or wife after separation are the separate property of each spouse. On its face the intent of the amendment was to equalize the situations of both spouses. Under prior law, in fact since 1872, the earnings and accumulations of the wife while living separately had been considered her separate property, whereas those of the husband were still considered community property until the marriage was dissolved by interlocutory judgment of divorce. One reason for this disparity was that the husband had the right to manage and control both his and his wife's earnings during their marriage.

The real impact of the 1972 amendment of Section 5118 on divorce proceedings did not become apparent until about a month after its enactment, when, at a professional meeting, California attorneys were given some rather startling advice. "From now on," they were told, "you should advise your husband clients that until a final decree of divorce is entered they are clearly entitled to use up the community property to satisfy any temporary court orders for the support of their wives and children, as well as any orders to pay debts, attorneys' fees, etc."[1] The reason for this advice turned out to be that when the legislature amended Section 5118 it failed to also amend Section 4805, which provides that in the enforcement of any decree or order for support or payment of fees under the Family Law Act, the court must resort first to the community property and only then to the separate property of the parties. It clearly followed, as the attorneys for husbands now argued, that when, during the pendency of a divorce action, a man was ordered to pay temporary spousal or child support, or debts, or attorneys' fees, he no longer needed to pay such fees out of his earnings, but could resort instead to savings or other property accumulated during the marriage. Many judges accepted this interpretation of Section 5118, until the legislature finally passed another amendment designed to correct the situation by requiring that temporary support orders be satisfied from current income.

Two other sections of the new California Family Law Act that have been subjects of great controversy are Section 4801, dealing with alimony or, as it is now often called, spousal support, and Section 4800, which sets down the ground rules for the division of property. The subject matter of these two sections, as well as that of Section 5118, illustrates how almost all of the controversies, both legal and nonlegal, about the new California Family Law Act have revolved around the same thing: money.

Indeed, except for the area of child custody (and we shall see that even here economics are sometimes involved), the main issues in divorces today are a question of dollars and cents.

The new procedures required in a divorce action in California are designed to handle the economics of divorce more efficiently. It used to be that a person who wanted to end a marriage filed a complaint, the way plaintiffs in most other civil actions still do. That document, along with a summons (a court order requiring a court appearance), would then be served on the other party or defendant, who could file either an answer or a cross-complaint. Under the California Family Law Act of 1970 there are no longer any plaintiffs or defendants and instead of complaints and cross-complaints there are now only petitions and responses. Unlike their predecessors, which were legal documents that only attorneys knew how to phrase, these petitions and responses are printed forms requesting concise statistical and economic information. The longest form is the financial declaration, which reads like a cross between a home-loan application, a tax return, and a statement of monthly expenses and income. This form requests the data central to what is the main business of a divorce—the division of the parties' property, the allocation of their debts, and, where appropriate, the award of spousal support, child support, and attorneys' fees.

In actual practice it is nearly impossible to isolate these various components from one another. I will, for the purposes of exposition, discuss them one at a time, but they are of course completely interrelated. This is so under both the old laws and the new, and it will be helpful for the reader to keep that in mind.

It may also be helpful to the reader to think of both marriage and divorce in contractual terms. The law usually imposes these contracts upon the parties, both in the case of marriages where few couples make their own, and in the case of divorces where even those couples that enter into negotiated property-settlement agreements usually do not give each other more than they think they would have to if a judge were to decide their case.

In that sense, divorce is the replacement of the marriage contract, be it explicit or implied by law, with a new contract between the former husband and wife. The terms of that contract are determined by the judgment or decree of divorce, which is in turn determined either by the express agreement of the parties or by a judge's interpretation of the laws of the state where they reside, or in some cases by combinations of the two. The custody and visitation of children, the division of property and the payment of child support, spousal support, and attorneys fees are all settled at the same time. In addition, a whole complex of mutual rights and responsibilities, such as inheritance rights and liabilities for each other's debts, must also be resolved.

In all cases, the parties must go to court for a divorce to take place. Cases where the wife's and husband's attorneys battle it out in court and the judge makes all the decisions are called contested cases. In default cases, one party does not appear, and usually the judge will grant (within limitations) whatever the appearing party asks. Child custody and visitation are always within the discretion of the court and many judges will make it their business, even in default cases, to quickly scrutinize the fairness of property division, support, and attorney's fees.

In many default cases, the two parties work out their own contract in advance. This marital-settlement agreement (commonly called the property-settlement agreement, although it usually deals with more than just the division of property) is signed by both husband and wife and then becomes part of the court decree. It involves not only all the technicalities of any other contract under the law, but is in addition governed by a host of special rules and regulations. Like all contracts, a property-settlement agreement must be clear, unambiguous, and capable of lucid interpretation in order to be binding. It must be properly dated and signed and must specify when it goes into effect. It must have what is known in law as consideration—essentially mutuality of promises and/or deeds—because otherwise it is not a contract but just a one-sided (and therefore a presumably inequitable) undertaking that the law will not enforce.

In addition to these and other general rules about contracts, which vary from state to state, there is a whole body of law dealing specifically with property-settlement agreements. This, too, varies from state to state and is extremely complex and involved. For example, there is the issue of at what point a property-settlement agreement becomes "incorporated" in the divorce decree, and whether that then means that the agreement is "swallowed" by the decree and is therefore no longer enforceable in civil court as a separate contract. Related and equally complex and technical is the area of case law that deals with whether an agreement is "integrated" or not. Central to this issue is the question of the court's power or jurisdiction to modify an agreement, particularly its provisions for spousal support. One solution to this problem is to state in an agreement explicitly whether it is the intent of the parties to make spousal support modifiable or not, and in California it has been the trend for attorneys to be explicit in this manner. Nevertheless, the issue of integration is still being litigated, particularly in connection with property-settlement agreements entered into before 1970. These actions are usually brought by husbands wanting to modify pre-1970 spousal-support orders, because judgments since that date have frequently been more favorable to husbands in both the size and duration of these awards.

A case in point is *Hayes* v. *Hayes*,[2] which also illustrates a number of other legal and economic issues under both pre- and post-1970 law. The case was originally filed in 1966, and although there have been more than half a dozen court hearings since then, it is still not resolved at this writing. It is a chronicle of the emotional and economic wrangles and the legal maneuverings and countermaneuverings that can go on in a divorce. What makes it somewhat unusual is that these have now been going on for ten years. The other factor that takes the case out of the ordinary is that Mr. Hayes is a man who has played a very special role in the history and development of contemporary family law. It was he, who, as a member of the California Assembly, authored and introduced the first no-fault divorce act in the United States in 1969.

Mr. Hayes's former wife, Janne, is a slim, soft-spoken woman of fifty-four. She was not quite twenty when she married James in 1941, after one year of college. Except for a two-week job in a department store during Christmas vacation that year, Mrs. Hayes never worked outside her home, before or during her marriage. They started to have children almost immediately, first two girls and later on two boys, and although Mr. Hayes was always very ambitious, some of those early years were rather lean. However, by the time of their divorce, about twenty-five years later, Mr. Hayes was already a fairly well known politician, and Mrs. Hayes and the two children who still lived at home had become accustomed to a certain standard of living.

The last years of the marriage were stormy, and, according to Mrs. Hayes, the main problem was Mr. Hayes's increasing absence from home.[3] But even after Mrs. Hayes finally decided to file for a divorce she held off getting her decree for three more years, until 1969. At that time, the property-settlement agreement worked out by their attorneys was approved by the court and made a part of their decree. Janne was given the family home and custody of the two minor children and James got the law practice that he was apparently still somewhat active in. Janne was also awarded $650 (per month) alimony until her death or remarriage and $175 child support until the two younger children reached majority. According to Mrs. Hayes, this settlement was reached after extensive negotiations by her attorneys, who allegedly told her to file for cruelty in order to get the best economic settlement, and that her spousal support could never be terminated or reduced.[4]

Nevertheless, three years later, on December 13, 1972, James Hayes, who was by then serving on the Los Angeles County Board of Supervisors, filed a petition asking that the courts terminate his obligation to pay Janne Hayes and his children any more support.

As is required under the new California Family Law Act, Mr. Hayes filed a financial declaration in support of his motion for a modification of the 1969 court decree. In it he declared his gross monthly income to be $3,032.75. After deducting income taxes of $704.57, Social Security of $157.50, union and other dues of $24.46, and a $200 retirement pension fund, his net monthly income came to $1,846.22.

On the expense side of his statement Mr. Hayes declared that he had monthly payments of $735 for his house mortgage, $125 for real property taxes, $100 for the maintenance of his residence, $260 for food and household supplies, $100 for clothing, $420 for auto payments and expenses and $250 for installment loan payments, and $385 for miscellaneous expenses, including insurance, entertainment, utilities, medical, and incidentals. This came to a total of $2,375 per month, or $528.78 more than his monthly net income, not taking into account his support obligation to Janne and the two minor children.[5]

The gist of Mr. Hayes's argument was that his financial situation was such that he simply could no longer comply with the original court decree. He argued that his remarriage had added to his responsibilities, that his new job as a supervisor required him to maintain a high standard of living, that his seventeen-year-old son was now staying with him rather than with Mrs. Hayes, that the second boy had taken his own apartment, and finally, that Mrs. Hayes should go out and get a job.

In California, as in most states, the general rule guiding support provisions of divorce decrees is that they are modifiable upon a showing of changed circumstances, provided of course that the court has jurisdiction to make a modification in the first place. This is ascertained in the following manner: If a divorce decree is based on a prior property-settlement agreement, the court will usually be devoid of jurisdiction, unless the portion of the agreement dealing with support is severable from (or not integrated with) those portions dealing with the division of property. Put another way, the legal theory involved here holds that if two parties make a contract where certain promises are specifically made in consideration of or in exchange for others, a judge who later interfered with an agreement that both parties originally relied on to be binding and final in its effect would be infringing upon the constitutionally guaranteed right of freedom to contract. In cases where an agreement is found to be integrated, regardless of how much the circumstances of one or both parties may have changed, the court simply has no power to make any modification of the divorce decree.

In the *Hayes* case integration was the issue to which the court had to direct itself before it could go any further. Mr. Hayes's position was that the agreement originally entered into between him and his former wife had not been meant to be integrated, and he cited certain passages and introduced certain letters to prove his point. Mrs. Hayes's attorney, on the other hand, argued that the agreement had definitely been intended as nonmodifiable, and he cited certain other portions of the contract which he said established his case and made it improper for the court to even admit extraneous writings like correspondence into evidence.

He also introduced the testimony and the financial declaration of Mrs. Hayes, but only as a second line of defense. In her financial declaration, Janne Hayes declared that her total monthly income was her alimony of $650, which, after deductions of $90 for taxes, left her with a net income of $560 per month. Her monthly expenses came to $892.23: $151 for the house mortgage, $150 for house maintenance, $50 for real property taxes, $130 for food and household supplies, $25 for clothing, $220 for auto installments and expenses, and $166.23 for all other expenses, including utilities, laundry, cleaning, medical, dental, entertainment, and incidentals.[6] She also stated in her testimony that she suffered from severe arthritis and asthma, conditions that would make it impossible for her to hold a job and furthermore, that she had no training or experience of any kind.

The judge did not make an immediate decision but "took the case under submission" instead, and asked for additional written briefs clarifying and expanding the legal arguments presented in court.

Mr. Hayes's brief included a quote from a 1969 Assembly Judiciary Committee Report on the proposed new California Family Law Act (which was introduced while he was chairman of that committee). Part of it read as follows:

> When our divorce law was originally drawn, woman's role in society was almost totally that of mother and homemaker. She could not even vote. Today, increasing numbers of married women are employed, even in the professions. In addition, they have long been accorded full civil rights. Their approaching equality with the male should be reflected in the law governing marriage dissolution and in the decisions of courts with respect to matters incident to dissolution.[7]

Mrs. Hayes's attorney directed himself to that quote in his brief:

> Counsel writes of the modern concern for women's equality. With respect to petitioner he is some 33 years too late. She was and is a housewife for some 30 years. Her husband provided the income for the family and she took care of that family—a situation which still prevails in most families today. To tell her that she has now attained equality which means that she must now go out and support herself is a cruel and inhuman joke and a perversion of the equality movement. If every wife is required to seek gainful outside employment to justify the "equality movement," respondent's current wife, a young, aggressive and well-educated woman should seek employment to supplement her husband's income.
> The court should recognize that respondent bears a substantial part of the blame for petitioner's current predicament. Until the divorce he was apparently satisfied for petitioner to remain a

housewife. During this time he provided for his own education and experience in the business world and politics, while she maintained the home. To deprive her of the only income she now has and is likely to get is like the politician who is turned out of office after many faithful years of service with the question "what have you done for me lately?"[8]

But when the decision in the case was finally handed down, in March 1973, Mr. Hayes's position prevailed. The ruling was that the agreement was modifiable, that Mr. Hayes's obligation to pay child support to Mrs. Hayes was terminated, and that Mrs. Hayes's support should be gradually decreased, first from $650 to $500, then to $400, and finally, commencing on October 1, 1974, to $300 per month.

Mrs. Hayes's attorney decided to appeal the decision to a higher court and, apart from the lengthy briefs and preparations such a step entails, there were no further legal developments in the case for a while.

But a year later Mr. Hayes was again back in court, where he once more asked that he be relieved from any further obligation to support his first wife. This time his financial declaration stated that his monthly expenses had increased to over $4,000 per month, largely due to the purchase of a new home, which, taken together with his country place, brought his total house payments alone to over $2,000 per month.[9] Mrs. Hayes's attorney countered that there should be no further litigation pending a decision in the appeal of the original modification case and that, in any event, Mrs. Hayes should not be deprived of what little support her former husband was still required to pay her.

Again, however, the court ruled for Mr. Hayes.

"Los Angeles County Supervisor James A. Hayes, 53, who earns $40,322 a year but complains that his expenses are nearly double his net income," reported the *Los Angeles Times*, "was successful Tuesday in his bid to reduce the alimony he pays to his first wife, Mrs. Janne M. Hayes, 53. Superior Judge Julius A. Title lowered the payment from $300 to $200 monthly and told Mrs. Hayes, who complains of asthma and back pains, to get a job."[10]

A few days after that decision, Janne Hayes applied for county welfare and food stamps. Questioned at a press conference about his reaction, Supervisor Hayes was quoted in the *Los Angeles Times* as follows: "This does not embarrass me at all. You're not able to control human behavior in life. She hasn't been my wife for 10 years."[11]

Finally, on October 3, 1975, the appeal of the original 1973 modification was decided.[12] In a thirty-one-page opinion the California Court of Appeal reversed the lower-court ruling on the basis that the Hayes property settlement was integrated, and therefore not subject to modification. In addition, the opinion went on to say that "had the agreement been modifiable, the reduction in support made by the trial court appears to constitute an abuse of discretion."[13]

Both the language and the ruling of the appellate case were unequivocal. Nevertheless, shortly afterward Supervisor Hayes was back in the L.A. county courthouse. This time, the action he brought against his former wife was to have the property-settlement agreement that the appellate court had ruled nonmodifiable declared a "mutual mistake," and to obtain an order to modify his payments. In March 1976, Mrs. Hayes's demurrer was sustained by Judge Charles Phillips on the basis that the question of whether there was a binding contract had already been resolved in prior court proceedings.[14]

According to Mrs. Hayes's attorney, Albert J. Corske, Mr. Hayes then engaged a new law firm to contend that since the appeal was only from the 1973 lower-court order reducing support to $300, the subsequent 1975 order reducing it to $200 remained unaffected by the appellate decision that the original property-settlement agreement is nonmodifiable.[15]

At this writing, Janne Hayes is still on food stamps, and Mr. Corske, who has already done a tremendous amount of legal work on the expectation of court-awarded fees, has just filed a motion requesting that Mr. Hayes's newest legal argument be disposed of without having to go through the time and expense of a second appeal.

As the *Hayes* case dramatically illustrates, both under the old law and the new, legal technicalities are a major component in the negotiation and adjudication of a divorce.

Beyond that, the case pinpoints some of the underlying financial realities behind the traditional marriage, where the basic economic contract is the trade of the woman's services as wife and mother for the husband's obligation of support.

As Mrs. Hayes's attorney pointed out in his brief, the problem is that our marriage laws are based on one set of assumptions and the new divorce laws on quite different ones. In the ideal middle-class marriage, it was considered dishonorable for a woman to work outside her home. Also, in this system of values a man's worldly success was at least partially measured by how decorative and attractive (pretty, well-dressed, and in many circles, young) a wife he could afford. Based on these premises, a realistic economic analysis would dictate that a traditional wife be viewed like the holder of any other depreciating asset and be compensated for the use of her "best years." In theory, this was the underlying, even if never clearly articulated, economic premise of divorce laws in the past. Today, when the trend is toward more "equal" marital settlements, the disparity between the earning power of husband and wife at the end of a traditional marriage must therefore be taken into account. Typically, during such a marriage (usually with the help of the woman's supporting services in providing for his physical needs) a man develops some kind of skill or career which, if he is successful, will provide him with higher and higher earnings as time goes on. On the other hand, the increased homemaking skills gained by the traditional wife are of little if any economic value. Married women receive no wages for these tasks (other than the minimal ones they can get if they go out and work as maids or babysitters), and as for a divorced woman getting another position as a wife, this is the one field where experience is more of a handicap than a help.

One approach to this problem is to develop a legal formula for including the relative earning power developed by each spouse among the assets to be divided at the end of a marriage, taking into consideration the relative contributions of each spouse toward the development of that power in the other. One argument always made against such a suggestion is that relative earning power is just too intangible to be measured. But the fact is that insurance companies use actuarial and other tables to determine precisely that, as do courts of law in personal-injury cases. And even in divorce courts today, judges are including pension rights and expectancies, anticipated insurance, and other commissions in the property that must be divided between the spouses. For example, in a recent California legal malpractice suit a wife recovered $100,000 in damages against her former attorney for his failure to obtain for her a share of her husband's pension and retirement funds.[16]

The increased judicial recognition of such less-tangible property rights is a new trend in family law. Another trend which has come along with the switch to no-fault is the treatment of the dissolution of a marriage less in moral or sentimental terms and more like the dissolution of a partnership. Consequently, the question of what assets that partnership owns is of crucial importance. As it stands today, the answer to that question still varies widely from state to state and even sometimes from one local jurisdiction to the next.

As a general system of classification, all states distinguish between two kinds of family-owned property. One is separate property, that which belongs exclusively to a husband or wife. The second is that property which by law or contract belongs to both spouses. Within that second category, however, there is a large disparity among those states that have a community-property system and those with systems modeled after English common law.

In eight states (California, Arizona, Idaho, Louisiana, Nevada, New Mexico, Texas, and Washington), all earnings and accumulations from earnings after marriage are community property. In the rest of the country, whatever a husband or wife earns or accumulates during a marriage is that person's separate property unless these monies or assets are also put in the other spouse's name.

In the community-property states, which derived their legal systems from either Spanish or French colonizers, the contributions of the wife as homemaker are recognized by law, at least in theory, and she owns one-half of the community property. In contrast, under the common-law system, a housewife who does not also work outside the home has no legal right to any marital asset, unless her husband puts it in her name or adds her to the title as a tenant in common or a joint tenant.

The reality of a wife's economic position usually does not become evident until there is a divorce, because it is only then that the property of the spouses is divided, and provisions for spousal and child support are made. It is here that the elimination of fault as one of the factors to guide the divorce court's discretion in making awards can make a very real difference.

One effect in community-property states is that under no-fault a judge is no longer empowered to "punish" a "guilty" spouse by decreasing or eliminating his or her share of the community property distributed upon divorce. Furthermore (and this is true in both community-property and common-law states), under no-fault, marital guilt can no longer be used as a bar to alimony.

But in most other respects, no-fault need not—and indeed has not—made that much difference in the division of property upon divorce. There are two other factors of much greater significance here. The first is whether we are dealing with a common-law or community-property jurisdiction. The second and even more important factor is the actual language of the statutory and case law dealing with division of property in any given state.

In a community-property state all earnings and property accumulated during a marriage (except by gift, inheritance, or as income or proceeds from property held by a spouse before the marriage) is community property and subject to apportionment upon divorce. In common-law states, the rules for the division of property vary widely from state to state. Approximately twenty-seven states provide that a judge has discretion to distribute property as "equity" and "fairness" require, regardless of how title is held. However, in approximately fifteen common-law states judges do not have such equitable discretion, and here as a general rule only jointly held property can be divided. In some states judges have limited equitable discretion. In some, personal property may be equitably apportioned, but real estate may not. In others, while the court has no power to divide separate property, it can order that an interest in such property be conveyed to the other spouse in conjunction with alimony.

What we have is a hodgepodge of statutory language and case law, lacking not only consistency, but clarity. The confusion is further compounded by the great latitude in judicial discretion, which even tends to dilute the difference between community-property and common-law states. For example, in some common-law states judges are empowered to dip into a husband's separate property if there is little or no joint property available for division. In others, these discretionary powers can be used to award a wife more support in lieu of more property. Because of its community-property system, California used to have the reputation of favoring women in a divorce. However, although there are no real statistics on the subject, it is probably true that since married couples frequently buy property in both of their names, wives in common-law states who were joint tenants with their husbands may actually have been in better legal positions because, until recently, in most community-property states, husbands had exclusive management and control of the community property by law.

But whether or not California wives once did get more property than women in other states, in 1970 the California law relating to the division of community property underwent a dramatic change. Strictly speaking, however, that change was not a function of the introduction of no-fault. Rather, it followed from the particular language of Section 4800 of the California Civil Code which requires that all community property be divided equally, unless the parties agree otherwise in writing or by oral stipulation in court.

This mandatory equal division of property has caused a lot of problems. Although Section 4800 goes on to provide that "where economic circumstances warrant, the court may award any asset to one party on such conditions as it deems proper to effect a substantially equal division of property," in many cases assets have had to be sold so that this could be done. Not surprisingly, another result has been to turn cases in which there is any property to speak of into valuation and accounting games, which in turn reduces the amount of property left for distribution.

Perhaps the hardest hit have been lower-income families. Cases in which there is not much property to divide are usually also the ones where there will be little, if any, spousal or child support. Before equal division became mandatory, a sympathetic judge could give a woman more of the property to compensate for lower support because under the old law California judges had the power to divide the community property "in such proportions as the Court, from all the factors of the case, and the conditions of the parties, deems just."

The language of the old California statute did not say anything about innocence or guilt as a factor in the division of property, and although the case law did, there was no real reason why, when California switched over to no-fault, the equal division of property had to become mandatory.

As a matter of fact, neither the Uniform Marriage and Divorce Act (UMDA) nor the Revised Uniform Marriage and Divorce Act (RUMDA)—the two proposed model acts for no-fault legislation—contain any such provisions. Both would basically continue to give judges equitable power to divide property, in the language of Section 307 of the UMDA, "in such proportions as the court deems just after considering all relevant factors."[17]

The drafters of the UMDA suggested that the following factors be considered:

> (1) the contribution of each spouse to the acquisition of the marital property, including the contribution of a spouse as home-maker; (2) the value of the property set apart to each spouse; and (3) the economic circumstances of each spouse at the time the division of property is to become effective, including the desirability of awarding the family home or the right to live therein for reasonable periods to the spouse having custody of any children.[18]

The drafters of the RUMDA did not feel this list of factors was adequate, so they substituted the following language:

> The court shall consider the length of the marriage, any prior marriage of a party, the age, health, stations, occupation, amount and sources of income, vocational skills, employability, estate, liabilities and needs of each of the parties, whether the property award is in lieu of or in addition to maintenance, and the op-portunity of each for future acquisition of capital assets and in-come; the court shall also consider the contribution or dissipation of each in the acquisition, preservation, depreciation or apprecia-tion in value of the respective estates, as well as the contribution of a spouse as a homemaker. It shall be presumed that each spouse made a substantial contribution to the acquisition of in-come and property while they were living together as husband and wife.[19]

But the main argument about Section 307 revolves around the concept of marital property proposed by the UMDA. In a con-troversy that has been going on for a number of years, the Family Law Section of the American Bar Association has taken the po-sition that that concept is totally unacceptable.[20]

The UMDA definition of marital property reads as follows:

all property acquired by either spouse subsequent to the marriage except: (1) property acquired by gift, bequest, devise or descent, (2) property acquired in exchange for property acquired prior to the marriage or in exchange for property acquired by gift, bequest, devise or descent, (3) property acquired by a spouse after a decree of legal separation, (4) property excluded by valid agreement of the parties and (5) the increase in value of property acquired prior to the marriage.[21]

In principle the concept of marital property is very similar to that of community property, except that, unlike community property, marital property only comes into existence in case of a divorce.

In their criticism of this concept the members of the ABA voiced two objections: first, that its introduction would create havoc in common-law jurisdictions; and second, that the courts should have power to divide and apportion "property and estates belonging to either or both, however and whenever acquired, whether the title thereto is in the name of the husband or wife or both," which is the language proposed by the RUMDA.[22]

At first glance that language would definitely seem to favor women. But if one remembers that it is basically the old statutory and case-law language of equitable discretion, which is already in effect in half the common-law states, a few doubts arise. The fact is that even in jurisdictions where fault is still a major factor considered by courts in the exercise of that equitable discretion, judges are very reluctant to award women any part of their husband's separate property, particularly if it was not acquired from earnings during the marriage. Would women then not be better off if a system of classification like that of marital property were adopted, wherein the judge is specifically directed to consider certain kinds of assets as the property of the marriage?

That has been my conclusion, and I am deeply concerned about the adoption of no-fault legislation in common-law states without at least the minimal safeguards that I believe marital property would provide. It is my opinion that a reasonable compromise of the UMDA and RUMDA positions lies in a combination of both,

that is, the adoption of marital property, with the additional provision that when circumstances warrant it, courts should have the
power to go beyond that property as fairness and equity dictate.

The UMDA and the RUMDA are of course only model law
codes. They serve mainly as guidelines, and it is up to each legislature to draft a particular state's law. Local bar associations or
individual judges or lawmakers frequently have greater influence
than model codes. It is therefore not only on the national, but
also on the state level that women must work if they are to exert
any influence on the new divorce laws.

The UMDA and the RUMDA offer many valuable suggestions
which I would like to see incorporated into our laws. For example, Section 307(d) of the RUMDA gives courts power to
impose a lien on the property assigned to a husband as security
for the payment of spousal- and child-support awards.[23] Equally
important for women who have performed traditional roles in
marriages of some duration is the language in both the UMDA
and RUMDA requiring judges to consider their contributions as
homemakers in making awards.

The inclusion of such provisions is particularly important in
conjunction with no-fault, since as we have seen, the elimination
of guilt as a factor can work to the disadvantage of women. In
my opinion this is not a necessary component of no-fault divorce,
but rather stems from a confusion about the meaning of what is
equitable and fair. In the past, divorce courts have tended to
equate doing the equitable thing with punishing the spouse that
is at fault. Consequently, as one divorcee put it, under no-fault
they seem to feel that if the husband isn't guilty, they should
punish the wife. Equity, however, need not involve wrongdoing.
It can and should be concerned strictly with fairness. That is why
it is so important to strip marriage and divorce laws of their
sentimental wrappers. It is only in economic and social terms
that a rational and systematic approach to the subject becomes
possible.

No-fault in its present form was a first step in discarding some of these false and misleading notions of marriage and divorce. However, it did not go far enough, for the social and economic issues underlying divorce go beyond innocence and guilt. One fundamental problem is that, fault or no-fault, we still have an adversary legal system where two professional opponents trained in the intricate procedures and technicalities of the law represent opposing clients. This system is based on the proposition that in the contest between two opponents justice will somehow emerge. But in most families the economic realities are such that for a fair resolution of a case neither party can really win, since each will end up with only part of the property and they will both have to reduce their standards of living. The failure to recognize this is one of the main reasons that no-fault seems to have made no major difference in eliminating interspousal hostilities.

When no-fault was first introduced there was a great deal of hope that the elimination of guilt would, as the National Conference of Commissioners on Uniform State Laws put it, cut down "the bitterness and hostility of divorce proceedings." One statistic often quoted by the proponents of the new law was the significant increase of defaults or noncontested divorces in the first year after its adoption. They cited this as evidence of decreased interspousal hostility due to the elimination of fault. However, the second year after the law was introduced the proportion of defaults leveled off again. It now seems clear that many of the people who flocked to court and got uncontested divorces during that first year did so because it had become simpler and cheaper to have an already defunct marriage officially pronounced dead.

For the majority of women in this country who have not participated in the management and control of money and property, our adversary system of law presents still additional problems. They rarely have the funds to pay their attorneys themselves, so except in cases of substantial community or jointly held property, the attorney for the wife is primarily dependent on a court award for fees, whereas the attorney for the husband usually gets paid up front or at the very least has the assurance of direct payment from the client. There are a number of consequences flowing from this situation. In lower-income families, the wife may simply not be able to afford a good attorney. This is especially true today in California because court awarded fees—those fees a judge orders paid by the husband or out of the marital property—have dropped. In higher-income situations, the problem is more subtle, since it usually involves the personal and psychological relationship between the two opposing counsels. If they are friendly or move in the same legal circles, the wife's counsel may, by gentleman's agreement, have little opposition from the other side about the size of attorney's fees. However, since the purse strings are under the control of the husband's counsel, there is a certain conflict of interests inherent in the situation which might set unconscious limitations on the effectiveness of wife's counsel.

As many proponents of family-law reform have said, a legal system of battle where two adversaries try to get the "best possible deal" for their clients only tends to exaggerate, rather than resolve, the emotional tensions of a divorce. But while no-fault does not overcome these problems, it does have the virtue of honesty in that it acknowledges and recognizes what is a legal and social fact, namely, that divorce can no longer be regarded as the court's punishment of the guilty party in a marriage. For women, who in many ways are "victims" of this new trend, the fundamental question is not really whether no-fault should or should not be adopted. While the issues are very complex, on the legal front they will require at the very least the adoption, along with no-fault or any other new divorce laws, of adequate safeguards for women, including certain interim measures to help the "traditional" housewife adjust to the unmarried state. But better divorce laws are only one end of the requisite legal reforms. Without also restructuring our system of marriage law, they can, as we have already seen, actually do as much harm as good.

3

Alimony and Child Support

In most cases, the economic settlement of a divorce involves not only the division of property but also, because they are simply different slices of the same economic pie, the award of spousal and child support. Except in those situations where there is a very short marriage or no children, alimony, or as it is often called today, spousal support, is still one of the major issues in a divorce. Much of the controversy surrounding the new developments in divorce law has centered around that issue, with no-fault opponents contending that all alimony problems are due to no-fault. However, as with the division of property, the situation is far from being that clear-cut.

Although each state has its own statute governing spousal support, and there is a great deal of variation in actual awards from place to place and even from judge to judge, the differences in statutory language between fault and no-fault states are typically minimal.

For example, in Illinois, where marital fault is still the only ground for divorce, the law provides that a court may "make such order touching alimony and maintenance of the wife or husband, as from the nature of the case, shall be fit, reasonable, and just."[1]

In Iowa, where fault is no longer material, the court may make such order in relation to "the maintenance of the parties as shall be justified."[2] In Michigan, where fault may still be material, the court is directed by the statute to award such alimony as it shall deem just and reasonable, having regard to the ability of either party and the character and situation of the parties and all the other circumstances of the case.[3]

According to the American Law Reports (ALR) treatise on the subject, the primary criterion for the award of spousal support is the financial situation of the parties.[4] The ALR survey, which unfortunately makes no attempt at any statistical or comparative analysis of the situation, goes on to point out that for a reversal in this field there must be a showing of a clear abuse of judicial discretion.

However, in reviewing the many examples from jurisdictions all over the country contained in the ALR discussion, it is impossible to find much consistency in what such "clear abuse of judicial discretion" might be. For example, in a 1962 Iowa case where the husband asked for a modification of spousal support and the trial court reduced it from $150 to $75 per month, the appellate court ruled that this amount was inadequate and increased it to $100.[5] In that case the wife worked as a registered nurse, earning approximately $200 per month, and the husband, who had remarried and had a child since the divorce two years earlier, was an anesthetist whose monthly income had dropped from approximately $900 to $710. However, that same year in Louisiana a lower-court decision awarding $150 per month to an unemployed wife who had received nothing from the parties' community-property estate (consisting of a home, furniture, automobiles, and the husband's medical practice) was held adequate.[6] The wife in this case had moved back to her father's home with the two minor children of the marriage (for whom she was getting $150 child support) and the husband was a physician with a net annual income of $13,000 out of a gross of $21,000. But in a Florida case involving another doctor with a $12,000 annual income, the appellate court ruled that the lower court's order, in which the husband was to pay $375 per month alimony plus $100 per month child support for each of his three children, was not excessive.[7] In addition, the court upheld the order awarding the use of the family home to the wife and requiring the husband to pay the mortgage and insurance, as well as attorneys' fees in the sum of $3,000.

But these examples show more than just the latitude of judicial discretion found in the field of family law. They are also to some extent indicative of the effectiveness of the parties' respective counsels in presenting their clients' cases to the court in the most favorable light, taking into account the idiosyncrasies of each particular judge.

In many ways, the California no-fault law was an attempt to replace social, moral, and personal attitudes as the bases for divorce awards with a less emotionally charged approach. Under pre-1970 California law, spousal support was awarded across the board to the "innocent spouse," "for his or her life, or for such shorter period as the court may deem just," so that a wife who was found guilty of marital misconduct could be cut off with no support at all while a man who was found guilty could be "punished" with an order to continue to support his wife.

Everyone knew that innocence and guilt were legal fictions. Still, these were the instructions of the statute and the terms in which divorces were considered by the courts. Furthermore, by social convention, the vast majority of divorces were filed by women. Usually the wife was the plaintiff and the husband was the defendant. The wife's complaint had to accuse the husband of some wrongful behavior. Even if in 90 percent of the cases the ground for the divorce was the catch-all "cruelty," the wife's attorney still had to put witnesses on the stand to testify as to specific acts of misconduct or mistreatment of the wife by the husband. This was required even in uncontested or default cases. In entering its decree the court had to find the husband guilty, or there was no statutory authorization to award the wife anything or even to grant a divorce. Although this procedure was a convention, and very often a farce, it still tended to affect the size of the award husbands were ordered to pay.

But gradually, as the number of divorces increased and the recitals of accusations and the corroborating evidence offered by the witnesses became more and more repetitive, it became increasingly difficult for judges and attorneys to continue to deal in terms of those legal fictions. If a man was not really guilty of anything, and if he and his wife were simply getting a divorce because they were not compatible, why then should he be "punished"?

This type of thinking was becoming more prevalent among judges and the public at large everywhere in the country. However, California was the first state to give it a legislative stamp of approval. When the California legislature voted in no-fault, it also struck the terms "innocent spouse" and "for his or her life" from the new spousal-support statute. Judges were told they now had to consider two specific circumstances in their awards: "the duration of the marriage and the ability of the supported spouse to engage in gainful employment without interfering with the interests of the children in the custody of such spouse."

There was nothing new about this language, since these were factors that California cases had long taken into consideration, along with such other criteria as the husband's earning power, the wife's needs and accustomed standard of living, her health, and her contribution to the marriage. However, since these latter criteria were not specifically mentioned in the new statute, attorneys for husbands argued that they should now be given less weight. The concurrent changing social attitudes about divorce began to show up in the courtroom, and after a while the burden of proof shifted to the wife to show that she could not find a job. By 1972, matters had become so bad that a few extreme cases were being reversed on appeal. One such case was *In re the Marriage of Rosan.*[8] It involved a marriage of seventeen years, with two children, born in 1953 and 1955. Mr. Rosan was

the sales manager for two jewelry stores, in which he held 15
percent of the stock, and earned a monthly income of $1,050,
plus commissions, bonuses, and an expense allowance of $150
per month. Mrs. Rosan had not been employed during the marriage, except for a short period in 1965 or 1966 when she worked
in a department store, a job she had to quit because of the emotional problems of one of the children.

In the divorce trial, Mr. Rosan was awarded part of the community property, including the business stock valued by the
court at $30,700, and $500 in insurance from the wreck of a 1963
Cadillac. Mrs. Rosan was awarded a $1,000 equity in a 1966
Buick, $6,790 from the sale of the family home, some furniture
and furnishings, a small trust account, and some low-income
rental property valued at approximately $10,000. To equalize
the division of property, Mr. Rosan was ordered to give Mrs.
Rosan a promissory note for $4,263, payable in forty-eight
months.

There was also a $150 support award for the fifteen-year-old
child in Mrs. Rosan's custody, and an order for three years of
spousal support as follows: $400 for one year, commencing on
January 1, 1971; $300 for the following year, and $200 for the
final year.

Mrs. Rosan appealed, alleging error in both the computation of
the value of the stock and the order for spousal support. Her first
contention was rejected, but the appellate court reversed the
automatic reduction and termination of spousal support as an
abuse of discretion, especially since Mrs. Rosan's future earnings
and earning capacity were completely unknown.
The court wrote:

We find nothing in the Family Law Act indicating any legislative
intent that a wife of a marriage of long standing whose attentions
have been devoted during the marriage to wifely and parental
duties and whose earning capacity has therefore not been developed should be, at a time when the husband is reaching his peak
of earning capacity, relegated to a standard of living substantially

below that enjoyed by the parties during the marriage or to subsistence from public welfare.

Cases like the above gave wives' attorneys a fresh legal argument, but as one judge put it at a recent family-law conference, the attitude of many California trial courts continues to be that "what they (divorcing women) need is to go to work, so they can get themselves liberated." This judicial attitude has been interpreted by some as the pendulum swinging the other way. But the pre-1970 statistics from around the country do not seem to bear this out.

According to a nationwide study of alimony and child support conducted by the Support Committee of the Family Law Section, American Bar Association, in 1965, alimony was even then awarded in only a small percentage of cases.[9] In higher-income situations, a particularly unrealistic and inflated picture of spousal support has been presented; in these situations child support is often shifted over into alimony, thus inducing the husband to make higher total payments. The catch is that alimony is deductible to the payer and taxable to the payee, while child support has no such tax consequences. At any rate, by 1972, according to the Citizens' Advisory Council on the Status of Women, the average spousal-support award was found to be insufficient for a person to live on.[10]

There are of course cases where divorced women have done extremely well, and in higher-income situations there will continue to be such cases. Nevertheless, in California, where divorce settlements were once perhaps a little better for women than elsewhere in the nation, they are now probably a little worse. The hardest hit have been older women and the mothers of small children. It is difficult for older men to get jobs. But for the older housewife who lacks skills and experience, it is almost impossible. Especially during periods of economic recession, the situation is precarious even for those divorced women who are employed, since women are traditionally among the first to be fired. In any case, the wages of women are typically much lower than those of men, and this is even more pronounced in the lower rungs of the labor ladder, so it is not surprising that many ex-wives of blue- and white-collar workers have had to seek welfare.

In community-property states the economic situation of former wives of either wealthy professionals or businessmen is eased by the possibility of a good property settlement. Since the Uniform Marriage and Divorce Act, in contrast to the revised version now proposed by the ABA, relies on marital property as "the primary means of providing for the future financial needs of the spouses,"[11] these are the women who would benefit the most from the adoption of that concept and the ones with the most to lose if it is not passed by the legislatures in their states.

Despite the legal technicalities involved in the awarding of spousal and child support under fault and no-fault laws, the problem is really more a practical one than a legal one. The manner in which support is actually awarded has always been guided more by mathematics than by guilt or equity. First, the judge takes a look at what the man earns and makes sure he has enough to live on. Whatever is left, he gives to the wife and children. If, as in the vast majority of cases, there is not much of a surplus, the wife and children simply do not get very much because, as most attorneys and judges will tell you, if you make a man pay too much, he will end up paying nothing at all.

However, according to a 1970 study of husbands who were in default on their court orders to pay child support, the size of the awards did not seem to be a factor. It also showed that, contrary to popular myth, the occupational distribution of nonsupporting fathers is similar to that of the entire male population. Five percent were professionals or semiprofessionals, five percent proprietors, managers or officials, eight percent craftsmen or foremen. There was not a predominance of low-income occupations and not a very high proportion of unemployed. Nor had these fathers disappeared. As a matter of fact, they usually were living in the same county as their children. Furthermore, the orders on which they had defaulted were not particularly large. The typical payment was $50 a month.[12] Researchers Winston and Forscher point out that many fathers who contribute nothing to the support of their children have incomes of $25,000 to $30,000 a year, and surprising numbers of physicians and attorneys have children on welfare.[13]

According to the Citizens' Advisory Council on the Status of Women, child support is also much more limited than is generally known, and enforcement is totally inadequate. Their statistics indicate that child-support payments usually do not furnish even half the support of children in divorced families. A 1965 survey of judges showed that 27 percent of them awarded 25 percent or less of the father's income, 34 percent awarded between 26 percent and 35 percent, and 25 percent, between 35 percent and 50 percent.[14] In 1969, the U.S. Department of Agriculture estimated that the average cost of raising a child in a two-child urban family ranged from $1,400 per year on a low-cost budget in the North Central area to $2,100 per year on a moderate-cost budget in the South.[15] With the recent inflation this cost has, of course, increased vastly. As the Citizens' Advisory Council on the Status of Women pointed out: "With the earnings of women averaging 60 percent those of men, women who work to support their children are contributing by and large more than their proportionate share, even when fathers comply fully with awards,"[16] and this of course does not take into account the fact that a mother receives no payment for her services in taking care of her child.

Although many fathers pay their child-support awards faithfully, there is evidence that others do not comply with support orders at all. According to a study conducted in 1971 by Nagel and Weitzman, within one year after divorce 20 percent of the fathers in their sample complied only partially and 42 percent made no payment whatever. By the tenth year, only 13 percent of the fathers were fully complying and 79 percent were in total noncompliance.[17] Whether the populations sampled in these studies are representative of the nation at large is not clear. Available data suggest that much of what we have been led to believe about the privileged position of women and children, even under the old divorce laws, is more fiction than fact. What is clear is that there is an urgent need for more research into both the size of awards and the degree to which compliance is enforced.

Almost all states have laws where husbands can be held criminally liable for the nonsupport of their wives and children. However, most states require that nonsupport be proved "willful" and that the wife or children be "in destitute or necessitous circumstances." But even in these cases law enforcement agencies are slow to act, and in some counties warrants for noncompliance just pile up and even traffic cases get higher priority.

In California and elsewhere, there has been an increased enforcement effort in cases where mothers are on welfare. In January of 1976, for example, the Los Angeles District Attorney issued warrants for five hundred fathers who were $720,000 delinquent in child support payments. "Our goal," he was quoted in the *Los Angeles Times*, "is to save the taxpayers $720,000 since the father's failure to provide has compelled most of the mothers and children involved to go on welfare."[18]

But the mother who is not on welfare must hire a private attorney and sue in order to collect her payments. Her attorney's fees will ordinarily run upward from $30 an hour, and any court awards she might expect for her legal expenses usually range only from $100 to $200. This is less than a third of the actual cost at going legal rates. Consequently few attorneys take these cases, unless the mother has other resources or the amount of child support is extremely high.

One would certainly not get this dismal picture of actual child support by taking our laws at face value. For example, according to Blackstone, one of the earliest and most influential commentators on English common law, "the duty of parents to provide for the maintenance of their children is a principle of natural law."[19] According to New York case law, a minor child is supposed to be entitled to support "according to the father's means and the child's needs."[20] A California case uses the phrase "in a manner suitable to the father's circumstances,"[21] reiterating the general rule of both statutory and case law that the primary responsibility for the support of children rests with their father. Furthermore, most states have adopted some version of the Uniform Reciprocal Enforcement of Support Act, providing legal machinery for the reciprocal interstate enforcement of child-support obligations where the child and the delinquent parent do not live in the same state.[22]

The problem here is not that we have inadequate laws. The basic problem, as with many other areas of family law, is social and economic. Of course, this is not to say that our laws themselves should not be improved. For example, pressure by organized groups of women in California recently resulted in the passage of a new law providing that child-support obligations may now be deducted from a delinquent father's wages by his employer and paid directly to his former wife. Not long ago a similar provision was adopted by Congress, making salaries of federal employees, including members of the armed forces, subject to garnishment for both child-support and alimony payments. The legislation, Public Law 93–647, is one of the most important efforts to date to strengthen the enforcement of family-support obligations. It also provides for the establishment of a federal service which locates parents delinquent in their support obligations, incentives to states to operate effective support-enforcement programs, and the collection of support by IRS under certain circumstances. In addition, the Secretary of HEW is imposed with greater responsibilities for leadership and direction to the states, and provision is made for federal aid to state courts and law-enforcement officials to help them collect from delinquent parents. These are all more reasonable and practical laws than the old approach of simply putting a man in jail for contempt.

Unfortunately neither the UMDA nor the RUMDA propose any really fundamental changes in the field of child support.

Under the UMDA, for example, the guidelines to be considered by courts in the award of child support are basically the same as those contained in existing state laws: the financial resources of the child and the custodial parent, the physical and emotional condition of the child, her or his educational needs, the standard of living she or he would have enjoyed if the marriage had not been dissolved, and the financial resources and needs of the non-custodial parent.

The UMDA does propose one significant change, namely that the word *minor* no longer be included in child-support statutes. The terminology suggested as a substitute is "a child of the marriage" to whom either or both parents owe "a duty of support." The Family Law Section of the ABA took exception to this change, pointing out that the word *minor* is universally found in all existing state laws, and it is true that the UMDA definition may be too vague.

The need for precision and clarity in this area of law was highlighted when in 1972 the California Civil Code was amended to provide that for most purposes, including the duty of parental support, the age of majority would henceforth be reduced from twenty-one to eighteen. A footnote to the statute provided that the word *minority* in court orders entered before the effective date of the statute (March 4, 1972) would also be deemed to mean eighteen, except within those orders affecting child support.[23]

Nevertheless, despite this specific exclusion of child-support orders entered before March 4, 1972, some California trial courts began to make it a practice, whenever a modification for a pre-1972 order came before them, to order its termination at eighteen. Finally, in 1975 the legislature enacted a special statute designed to end this practice by specifically providing that pre-1972 child-support orders could be modified "to increase and decrease the amount of such award" without terminating it at eighteen.[24]

As for awards made after 1972, it is still too early to determine the impact of the termination of the duty to support at eighteen.

Since in the past most young people have depended heavily on parental assistance to go to college, it would seem to have significant sociological and personal implications, particularly for children whose parents are divorced.

Another UMDA provision that has been criticized by the proponents of the RUMDA is that awards for both spousal and child support be modifiable only "upon a showing of changed circumstances so substantial and continuing as to make the terms unconscionable." The Family Law Section of the ABA objected to the word *unconscionable* on the basis that it places a very heavy burden on a petitioning spouse whose needs or circumstances may have changed radically, but who may not be able to convince a court that the situation is unconscionable. As an alternative deterrent to the use of modification proceedings to harass a former spouse, the RUMDA suggests that courts could award attorneys' fees and costs to the party subjected to harassment. This, however, is already a matter of judicial discretion in every case, whether or not this issue is involved. Perhaps a more practical alternative would be to direct judges to impose economic sanctions and/or injunctive orders prohibiting the bringing of further actions for specific periods of time in those cases where a pattern of harassment is proved.

This is a difficult area because motivation is difficult to pin down and prove, and also because it is certainly essential that people be able to use the judicial process to obtain economic and other help or to be relieved from economic obligations when circumstances so warrant. On the other hand there are times, particularly in the emotion-laden atmosphere of divorce, when motions for modification are used to continue the battle between a husband and wife.

One solution, as already discussed, is to make a marital-property settlement with nonmodifiable spousal-support provisions. However, the problem remains that it is hard to predict the future and therefore such agreements are a double-edged sword. An approach I have sometimes used has been to make spousal support nonmodifiable except in the event that either party becomes so physically incapacitated that they are unable to work. While such limited nonmodifiability provisions may not be appropriate in all cases, they do cut down the chances for continued conflict and litigation between the parties to a divorce.

Another attempt to reduce such bitterness has been the effort of judges and attorneys, from time to time, to establish actual economic guidelines for the award of child and spousal support. These guidelines are usually primarily a function of the noncustodial parent's income, and begin with the setting aside of a certain amount for that parent to live on. The number of children involved is also taken into account, although specific computations are seldom made for families with more than three children.

For example, in 1973 the supervising judge for the Family Law Departments of Los Angeles County proposed the following schedule:

Net Monthly Income*	Spouse Alone	One Child (More than one, not over amount in Column 6)	Spouse and One Child	Spouse and Two Children	Spouse and Three or More Children
$ 400	$100	$ 75	$100	$100	$ 100
500	200	75—100	200	200	200
600	250	100—125	300	300	300
700	300	100—125	350	350	350
800	300	150	375	400	400
900	350	150	400	425	450
1,000	375	150—200	450	475	500
1,200	450	150—200	525	600	600
1,500	500	200—250	600	700	800
1,750	600	200—250	700	800	900
2,000	700	200—250	850	950	1000
Above 2,000	⅓		⅓ plus 150	⅓ plus 250	⅓

* After deduction of taxes, Social Security, medical insurance, union dues, and retirement.

The judge proposed that "to encourage employment, if petition-ing spouse is employed, one half of net earnings will be deducted from the indicated spousal support." What this comes out to in practice is that in lower-income cases where there are no chil-dren, unless the wife has an extraordinarily low-paying job, she would end up with no spousal support at all. Furthermore, if the suggested deduction is applied to those cases where there are children, rather than encouraging women to try to rebuild their lives as independent individuals, it may actually discourage them since the net gain to the family may not be commensurate with the heroic effort required to earn enough for a decent standard of living, particularly if her skill level is initially low. In any event it is clear that it would not be possible for a single-parent family to maintain a standard of living comparable to that of the non-custodial parent on the suggested support levels. It is also clear, as the commentaries explaining the guidelines state, that "the unemployed spouse at the lower net income levels will require assistance from state or county agencies."[25]

There seems to be little question that some responsibility will have to be taken in this area by society at large. But what form this should take, and whether welfare is the best answer, is an-other subject, one which will be taken up in later chapters.

4

Child Custody

There are two circumstances in which custody of children becomes a legal issue. One is when a marriage is dissolved and a divorce court must determine which parent shall be awarded custody. The other is when the fitness of parents is questioned by the state, and a juvenile court must decide whether neglected or abused children should be removed from their natural parents. In both instances, the underlying premise is that the state is the ultimate guardian and protector of all children.

Whenever there is a divorce involving children, the award of custody is technically up to the court. In practice, however, the issue only arises when the parents themselves do not agree, and the ensuing contest for child custody must then be resolved. Up until the turn of this century when the common-law rule of father preference was first challenged, the law governing child custody in the event of a divorce had been that since the father was entitled to the services and earnings of his children as compensation for his duty of support and maintenance, he was also entitled to preference in the award of their custody. By 1925, however, this rule had been abandoned by every state in favor of statutes that directed judges to make the determination that "in their discretion" would be "in the best interests of the child."[1]

In order to decide what is in the best interests of the child, the judge evaluates the evidence introduced by the attorneys for each parent. Children, having no stand in divorce proceedings (or in any other legal action), do not have an attorney to introduce evidence on their behalf. The issue of who should have custody, in other words, to whom they shall belong after the divorce, is fought over and determined in the same manner as the disposition of any other disputed asset or liability.

Essentially, the courts make their awards by a process of elimination. On the basis of the evidence presented by each of the contesting parties, the judge determines if one of them has been shown "unfit," and gives custody to the more deserving of the two.

Today, in most states if a child is "of tender years" the law "presumes" that it will be in "the best interests" of the child that the mother be given custody. However, that presumption is rebuttable by proving that the mother is "unfit." In 1969 the California legislature rejected the proposal that the mother-preference rule be dropped and that the award of custody be based entirely on the best interests of the child. However, the Uniform Marriage and Divorce Act does contain that provision. This act also proposes that children in divorce proceedings be represented by their own counsel. Nevertheless, despite its support from the organized bar, to date no American state has adopted such a law.[2]

The recent changes in the area of child custody have been more visible in the courtrooms than in the legislatures. In California, as elsewhere across the nation, more and more fathers are being given custody of their children. This is due mostly to the changing attitudes of the parents themselves. For fathers, the change reflects an increased acceptance that their role is not merely economic and disciplinary and that it is all right for them to perform the intimate child-care functions that produce closeness. For mothers, there is increased recognition that not having custody of their children can still be compatible with being a good mother. Even so, women who do not fight for the custody of their children are still faced with strong social censure and a judicial attitude that frequently assumes the very worst about them. As a Cook County judge put it in a recent interview with the *Chicago Tribune*, "If the mother can't be bothered with her child, then the child is better off with a parent who cares. The law of the state is this: The fit parent gets custody of the child."[3]

In commenting on this judicial double standard, Dr. Pauline Bart explains it as a function of traditional attitudes:

> A man's role is defined by his job. His relationship to his family is often that of a visitor anyhow. If he continues to visit his children, that's acceptable. But a woman's identity traditionally has come from her role as a wife and mother. Our society has brought us up to believe that every woman has maternal instincts and a mother who would give up her children and reject those instincts is treated like a depraved monster.[4]

Also in keeping with some of the newer social attitudes are the increased number of cases where parents are splitting up custody of their children, or asking for joint custody, although, as with other innovations, there is still much resistance to these methods by both judges and attorneys.

There are only two really significant recent legislative changes in the area of child custody. Under both the new California divorce law and the proposed UMDA, judges must now take the wishes of older children into account when deciding who shall have their custody. Formerly the wording merely stated that judges "may" in their discretion do so. The other California change, which also seems to be something of a national trend, is that, just as with child support, the courts now have jurisdiction over child custody only until the age of eighteen.

In the area of child custody, the introduction of no-fault has made little if any difference. Although evidence of guilt or wrongdoing is no longer admissible in determining matters of property and support, this rule does not apply to custody. In a California

child-custody contest, evidence of immorality, bad character, in-
temperance, or any other behavior that would indicate "unfitness"
is still admissible. For the most part, the courts have interpreted
this narrowly and have tried to limit the evidence to acts of specific misconduct and to immoral acts committed in the presence
of or within earshot of the children. Also, standards of conduct in
urban centers are more realistic and less punitive than before.
Nevertheless, once this evidence is admitted, it tends to color the
whole trial. In addition, some counsels for husbands have been
accused of bringing up the issue of custody, not because their
clients wanted the children, but to introduce evidence of the
wife's "misconduct" so she will be awarded less support.

One of the great ironies of child-custody contests is that in
most cases they do not really settle much. A number of families
frequently end up in therapy anyway. Often, as children grow
older, they shuttle back and forth between their parents, never
really able to resolve the battle inside themselves as to which one
of them is "right." Another irony often encountered is that of the
father who ends up losing his bid for custody after a bitter and
ugly court fight and then hardly ever shows up to visit his children.

Increasingly, particularly in larger urban centers, judges refer
matters of child custody to psychiatrists for evaluation. This has
been of some help, and so has the now almost universal practice
of hearing much of the testimony, particularly that of the children, in the judge's chambers rather than in open court.

What is urgently needed is a massive analysis and reevaluation
of the whole area of child custody, along with the underlying
issue of the legal and social status of children in our society.
Neither the Uniform Marriage and Divorce Act nor the Revised
Uniform Marriage and Divorce Act have done this and, on the
whole, this field is the most neglected one in family law. Most
legal treatises on divorce devote only minimal attention to custody, and usually only to an analysis of existing case and statutory

law, rather than to any study of possible improvements and reforms.

An aspect of the field that often is entirely ignored in the literature is the legal contest, not between a mother and father, but between one or both of the parents and the state. These are cases where the state steps in to take a child away from the natural parents. Whether the court originally acquires jurisdiction because a child has been mistreated and abused by the parents or because of some antisocial act committed by the child, the issue the court must decide is basically the same as that in private custody cases; namely whether one or both parents are unfit. Only here the arena for the contest is that of juvenile rather than divorce court.

The American juvenile-court system did not come into existence until the early 1900s. Until then, even in criminal cases, children over the age of seven were treated the same as adults. In this new court system, intended as it was to help and rehabilitate rather than punish, the procedural safeguards that were being increasingly required for adults were deemed unnecessary. But finally in 1967, a major change in juvenile-court proceedings took place, when in *In re Gault*, the Supreme Court said that, where commitment to a state institution is possible, certain procedural safeguards such as notice of right to counsel, the right to confront witnesses, and the privilege against self-incrimination would henceforth also be required for the young.[5] Nevertheless *In re Gault*, although a landmark case, left a lot of problems unsolved. For example, in almost every juvenile-court proceeding there is a social worker or probation officer charged with making an investigation on behalf of the state, a report that will greatly influence the decision of the court. The quandary of the subjects of this investigation is whether to cooperate (and thereby perhaps make a few points) or to hire an attorney, as would any other defendant in a criminal case. In the proceedings to take children from the custody of their parents, where that investigation deals not with an offense the child has allegedly committed against someone else, but with an offense allegedly committed by someone against the child, these issues are even more complex.

As in divorce cases, the judicial determination of whether a child shall be removed from parental custody entails the evaluation of the available possibilities in order to decide which one will be best for the child. The basic difficulty here is that there may not be a really good solution. The root of the problem lies with the premise that the responsibility for children is a private one and that the state should intervene only when parents fail. Consequently, for the most part, our judicial and social system is primarily geared not to assisting parents and preventing problems, but to assigning guilt and meting out punishment. Furthermore, despite the many radical changes in family law, the fundamental legal status of children has changed little in the last hundred years. Our legal and social view of children still seems to be that they are property. Not only have children no legal standing to go to court themselves, but they can even be institutionalized under the juvenile laws of most states (sometimes for indeterminate sentences) if their parents assert that they are "incorrigible," that they "persistently and habitually refuse to obey," that they are "in danger of leading an idle, dissolute, immoral or lewd life," or simply that their behavior is "beyond their control."[6] In cases where custody is not voluntarily relinquished by parents, the issue of whether a child should be placed in the hands of the state is basically a question of judicial discretion. Frequently the outcome of these cases depends on the standards and attitudes of the judge.

The first job I ever had was that of a social worker in a small midwestern town. It was my task to look in on parents who had been reported for not taking adequate care of their kids, to try to work with them, and ultimately, if things did not improve, to help supervise the outside placement of their children. More often than not I dealt with women, usually very young, who for one reason or another were raising their children alone. These women were usually very immature, with many problems of their own, so much so that frequently they were as much in need of parenting as their kids. Many of them were only replaying with their children the events of their own lives. It was a tragic cycle of young girls who "slept around" out of loneliness and a need for love, imagining that if they could only find "that man," everything would be all right. If a child was accidentally produced, it then became the subject of another fantasy for the mother—at least she would now have "someone to love." Once born, these babies were needing and demanding as all helpless beings are; and rather than fulfilling a pleasant fantasy, they proved to be an additional responsibility for women who already could hardly contend with their own lives.

When I started that job, young, bright, full of theory and high standards, I was not very tolerant of the failings of the women I saw and it seemed to me only right and proper to have the state take their children away from them if they could not do a better job. But as time went on, and I saw more and more of the difficulties these children would have to face, I began to do some hard thinking about the realities of life.

I remember one child in particular, a little boy of five called Tod, whom I had to move from his second foster home to his third and how he sat in my car, clutching his suitcase, unwilling, despite all my kindness and efforts to make him feel better, to talk to me at all. "If he'd only quit seeing me as his enemy," I thought to myself, frustrated and upset that I was unable to give him the slightest help. And suddenly it hit me that from his standpoint that appraisal of me was not so far off—I was the agent of that power, that impersonal force called the state, that had taken him away from his mother (whether she had wanted to take care of him or not) and had shifted him around from one house to the next.

But in many ways Tod's case was not so bad, because he at least got to live with individual families, and if he was lucky, as

some children are, one of the families might work out for a
number of years or even until he grew up. I saw other children
like Tod for whom adoption was not likely because they were
physically handicapped or members of racial minorities. They had
spent most of their childhoods in institutions of one kind or
another, sometimes even in the same ones where our society
puts those other children we call juvenile delinquents. And
compared to them Tod was a very lucky boy indeed, for imper-
fect as they were, at least the foster homes where he lived somewhat resembled the social norm. In a society like ours, where
everything from TV programs to reading primers makes it very
clear to a child that the only "good" family is the "intact" two-
parent family, it is almost impossible for children whose en-
vironments do not conform to that norm to form healthy self-
images or any sense of their own worth.

I learned a lot in that job, about the differences between social
realities and social myths and what it means to grow up "different" in a success-oriented, affluent society. Some of the things I
saw I could not understand, like the power invested in the hands
of a small-town judge, in whose court the same attorneys worked
day in and day out. The power of that judge over the women
and children I was supposed to oversee was almost absolute.
And despite the constitutional and legal safeguards on our books,
the decisions handed down were very often more a function of
individual predilection or prejudice than of the law.

"Watch for the beer bottles," the judge would tell me, "that's
a sure sign that there's hanky-panky going on"; or, "Don't let
them soft-soap you with all those hard-luck stories of theirs.
They've all got one and they're always a mile long and what they
come to is one excuse after another for not shaping up and doing
an honest day's work."

And so children were taken away from single mothers on the
moral grounds that these women drank and ran around with men.
Having done what he considered to be the right thing, the judge

went home; it was then my job to go and pick up the children and remove them from their homes. So I learned some more about how human realities compare with social and legal myths and how, as I only later understood, the repetitive cycles of poverty and low self-esteem are perpetuated from one generation to the next.

It was a frustrating job, all the more so because none of the other people in my office saw matters the way I did. Years later, in the process of writing this book, I again had occasion to talk about these things to people in the social-welfare field and it was encouraging to find that with many of them, especially the younger ones, attitudes had really changed.

The sad thing though is that what they are still dealing with essentially are emotionally and economically deprived and damaged parents of another generation of equally damaged and deprived children. This is all in the context of a socioeconomic system that still tends to punish these people rather than offer them any real alternatives, much less dignity or self-esteem.

"They're just part of the reality of our society," I was surprised to hear one of the social workers I interviewed say. She went on:

> The economy is based on a certain percentage of unemployment and poverty because in what they call the free-labor market, the supply of workers always has to exceed the demand. Otherwise, or so economists tell us, either nobody would go to work or the cost of labor would be so high that all businesses would go broke. Anyway, these are the people in what is called the reserve labor force. In good times they do a little better and in a recession or depression they starve. But the fact is that neither the welfare system nor the court system nor any of the other institutions are really designed to get them out of that place, because if they did the whole economy would have to undergo fundamental change.

Sometimes, when I really face up to that I just want to throw in the towel and quit and maybe one of these days I will. But I haven't yet because it's better if these people have to deal with someone like me who at least doesn't judge and condemn them for not having "made a success" and also just maybe, every once in a while, I can really do something that actually does some good.

These are all marginal people I deal with. It's not just economically and socially that they're always on the outer fringes, but it's that way with their whole life and it certainly is that way when it comes to their kids. The women I deal with, they really do what they can and usually they really love their children. But they're just barely able to cope with living themselves.

She was a county adoptions worker in a middle-sized California city and I was interested to hear that a part of the agency's service was not only the placement of children, but also the counseling of pregnant women.

"We try to help them with whatever choice they make, whether it's to keep the baby or place it for adoption or to have an abortion instead," the worker told me, making me realize that at least in some ways things had really come a long way since my own days in that kind of work.

But at least in some places, very little has changed. In some small towns or even in some of the more conservative communities in large cities, women are still being "punished" by having their children taken away. Not so long ago I had a call from two single mothers who shared a small house in Orange County, California, telling me that they were being harassed because one of the neighbors had decided that they were lesbians and should not be permitted to raise their children by themselves.

Another case was that of a young mother, admittedly very immature and struggling with many problems of her own, who had decided she needed to get away from her responsibilities for a week. She left her children with a neighbor, only to find when she came back two days late that the police had been called to take them away. This might not have happened in another county, but in the conservative midwestern community where she lived the judge decided she had deserted her children, and they were placed in a foster home instead of being returned to her.

Much of the contemporary controversy about divorce and the attendant phenomenon of the single parent (which usually means the woman-headed family) has dealt with the contention that women alone are simply not able to raise their children. Where woman-headed families are depicted at all in the movies or on television, the focus is usually on the trials and tribulations of the mother as she searches for another mate or the problems of children who don't have a father in the home. Conversely, in TV series dealing with children being brought up by fathers, everything is usually just great fun.

In 1972, a group of Los Angeles women formed an organization for mothers who are divorced, separated, widowed, or who have never married. They called it MOMMA and started with the premises that single motherhood is more than just an unfortunate transitional period for women until they can find men to take care of them again, and that organizing would enable them to help themselves and each other deal with the many problems they had to face every day.

Some of their immediate goals were of course economic and educational and designed to improve their legal and financial status in the world, but their main thrust was and still is in the direction of self-help. Besides its regular meetings and rap sessions where single mothers can share some of their common problems and give one another moral and often practical support, the organization published its own newspaper, organized political and legal research groups, set up a housing exchange, and offered classes in everything from fixing your own car to workshops in self-defense. Some of the women in MOMMA have formed child-care cooperatives and still others have found that moving in together is helpful. Perhaps one of its most interesting offerings has been a series of courses called Parent Effectiveness Training. Based on the nonauthoritarian child-rearing theories and methods of Dr. Thomas Gordon, members of MOMMA have developed their own techniques adapted to the particular needs and problems of the family where a woman plays the role of both mother and father.

Karol Hope, one of MOMMA's founders, told me,

> We're treated like second-class citizens and there are lots of handicaps and pressures with which we must cope. But on top of all that, since obviously we don't fit into the ideal of mama and papa and the three lovely children and the dog of the standard television plot, there's also a lot that needs to be dealt with that's right inside of ourselves.
>
> Our society won't give it to us, so it's all the more important that we work on it ourselves. We've got to develop pride and self-reliance and self-respect, not just as former wives or as prospective wives, but as independent people with minds and lives of our own. We're not just "women alone," which is nonsense in the first place because all of us in MOMMA have kids. Even if society doesn't, we've got to see ourselves as not just marking time in our lives until another man finally comes around.

Today there is at least the beginning of a broader social and legal consciousness that children have certain fundamental rights. Organizations like Families Anonymous and Parents Anonymous are recognizing the problem of the battered child. The Children's Lobby and the Children's Defense Fund are dealing with child care, juvenile-court proceedings, schools, paternity, adoption, medical treatment, support, guardianship, and property rights. Now there is even a White House conference on children, and in the last few years, several books about children's liberation have appeared. But unfortunately, both in our courtrooms and outside there is still little if any consciousness of the real status and the real problems faced by children and women today.

A few years ago I had a case that involved both a contest between two spouses and the question of having the state take over custody and control. The scene of the legal battle that ensued was a courtroom in the Los Angeles Superior Court, Department 2. I had just put my client, a young woman of nineteen, on the witness stand.

> Q: Would you please state your name?
> A: Jane M.
> Q: How long have you been married?
> A: Three years.
> Q: And you have two children of this marriage?
> A: Yes. Dina, 2, and Charlie, 18 months.
> Q: You are asking custody of your children?
> A: Yes.
> Q: Where are your children now?
> A: In a foster home.
> Q: Who put them there?
> A: I did.

COUNSEL FOR HUSBAND: (Jumping up) Your Honor, in the interest of saving time, I would like to make a statement.

JUDGE: Well, it's somewhat out of order, but in light of the testimony of this witness, yes.

COUNSEL FOR HUSBAND: Petitioner has admitted that she put the children in a foster home. Our position is that she is an unfit mother, and that since she doesn't even have the physical custody of these children, she has no standing here to seek legal custody at this time. The court should just make these children wards of the court.

JUDGE: (To counsel for wife) Why doesn't she just come back to court when she's got the kids out of the foster home?

COUNSEL FOR WIFE: Your Honor, I'd like leave of this Court to put on our case first. The evidence—

COUNSEL FOR HUSBAND: (Cutting in) The evidence is that she got rid of her kids!

COUNSEL FOR WIFE: She's entitled, Your Honor, to present her case.

JUDGE: (Shrugs) Okay, go ahead with your case. But I don't see that there's much point.

COUNSEL FOR WIFE: I'd like to ask the Court to reserve that decision.

JUDGE: (Grunt).

COUNSEL FOR WIFE: (To the witness) Jane, when did you first place your children in a foster home?

JANE: The first time—four months ago.

Q: You were on welfare at that time?

A: Yes.

Q: How did you go about placing the children in a foster home?

A: Through my social worker. I asked her to help me find a good place for them. The Department of Social Welfare found a foster home for me.

Q: The Department of Social Welfare made the arrangements?

A: Yes.

Q: How long were Dina and Charlie in that foster home the first time?

A: Six weeks, until Chuck took them out.

Q: Your husband took them out?

A: Yes, he showed up and took them. I was told that there was nothing I or the Department of Social Welfare could do because there was no court order giving me custody, so he had the right to take them because he's their father.

Q: Where did he take them?

A: To his parents' house. He was living with his parents.

Q: How long were the children there?

A: Three weeks.

Q: Did you see them during that time?

A: No. Chuck's parents wouldn't let me see them. They said I was an unfit mother—that I—(upset) that they were going to go to court and take the custody of the children away from me.

Q: Then what happened?

A: Well, I got a phone call from Chuck and he told me that he was coming over with little Charlie and Dina. He said he couldn't keep them at his parents' anymore. That it was just too much for his mother and that he didn't have any way of taking care of them himself and that anyway the apartment house where his parents lived was for adults only. So he brought them over for me to take care of.

Q: Where are the children now?

A: They're back in the foster home.

Q: Jane, why did you put them there?

A: So I can get on my feet. So I can get myself together and get off welfare and take care of them.

Q: Are you working now?

A: Yes. And I'm going to school. Both Chuck and I were 16

when we married, so I didn't finish high school. I'm working as a box girl and I have to get my high-school diploma before they'll let me go to checker school.

Later, under cross-examination by her husband's attorney, Jane admitted that there had been times both during and after her marriage when she had felt totally overwhelmed. Her husband hadn't worked much during the marriage or afterward, so there had been very little money. They had lived on what she made and on gifts and loans from both sets of parents. But the problems weren't just financial—there were emotional ones as well. Yes, she had left the children alone in the apartment on two occasions. The woman who lived next door was supposed to look after them. No, she wasn't on drugs. She had prescription sleeping pills because of nerves. No, there certainly had been no immoral behavior, not in front of the children or anywhere else. No, she didn't want to get rid of her children. She just wanted to get on her feet. If she didn't go back to school, if she didn't work and save some money, she would never get herself together financially and emotionally, in order to make some kind of a life for herself and provide a good home for her kids.

"So, from your own testimony, Mrs. M.," counsel for husband concluded, "you admit you are at this time emotionally and financially unfit to provide a good home for your two infant children. I have no further questions of this witness, Your Honor. (To Jane) You may step down."

The next witness was Grace C., Jane's social worker. No, she wasn't here in an official capacity. Actually, she was here because counsel for wife had subpoenaed her. Reluctantly. Because she didn't want to get involved. It was against department policy. Yes, she had helped Jane place the children. The foster parents were nice people, the mother visited the children regularly and the children seemed happy.

Q: Who is paying the foster parents?
A: The County is. He (pointing to Chuck) doesn't have a job

and Jane is supposed to start contributing after she's promoted to a position as checker.

Q: How much is the foster mother getting paid?

A: $320.

Q: $320 per month. That's what she gets paid to take care of both children?

A: Yes.

Q: How much was Jane getting when she was on welfare?

A: $194.

Q: Per month?

A: Yes.

Q: That was for the three of them to live on, the two children and herself?

A: Yes. She was supposed to work part time—

Q: Jane was told she had to work part time?

A: Yes.

Q: Does the foster mother work?

A: Oh no, she can't. That's forbidden under the state law.

JUDGE: Wait a minute. How much did you say the mother was getting?

WITNESS: $194 per month.

JUDGE: And how much did you say the foster mother is getting?

WITNESS: $320 per month.

JUDGE: Do you mean to tell me that the Department of Social Welfare is willing to pay a stranger almost twice as much to take care of these children as it does to their natural mother?

WITNESS: Well, Your Honor—

JUDGE: What kind of a ridiculous system is that? Never mind! You don't have to answer.

Jane was given custody of her two children with the provision that they were to stay in the foster home without any further interference from their father until such time as Jane, in the opinion of her social worker, and herself, was emotionally and financially able to provide for them on her own. As Jane's attorney, it was rewarding for me to know that we had made a judge more sensitive to the inequities that women and children have to deal with. He simply had not known.

II

THE SOCIAL
AND
LEGAL CONTEXT

5

Women, Marriage, and the Law

Divorce- and juvenile-court proceedings are only the last act in the dissolution of families. As in any other drama, what happens at the end is, to a very large extent, a function of what went before. In order for us to fully understand the ramifications of women's status in divorce, we must first ask some questions about the underlying assumptions behind our family laws, and in particular the ideals of the institution we call marriage.

In 1970, at an international symposium on the family, Dr. Nicholas Tavuchis, a sociologist from Cornell, took scholars in his field to task for "the extreme circumspection of social scientists and their inability to propose or evaluate experimental or alternative social structures that might serve as competing models for conventional marital and family patterns" and "their tendency to equate social change with problems and social pathology, rather than with tactical and strategic opportunities for new ways of meeting human needs."[1]

It is not surprising to find these problems in the approach to such an emotional-laden subject since social scientists, too, are products of this society, where the value of marriage and the family is not to be questioned. One researcher who has addressed

73

herself to these basic assumptions is Dr. Jessie Bernard. Her book, *The Future of Marriage,* is an analysis of sociological work about marriage, going back over a period of some forty years. On the basis of these earlier studies and her own work in the field, Bernard came to the conclusion that marriage has very different meanings for men and for women, and that "his marriage is far better than hers." In comparing married and unmarried women, Bernard found that the unmarried woman has more self-confidence, less self-consciousness, and fewer psychological problems than the married one. But that was not all. While for women marriage and the family were a liability as far as the job market was concerned, for men they were assets to careers and earning power. For married men, the suicide rate was almost half that of single men, and both the mental and physical health of the married man was statistically much superior, particularly after middle age. On the other hand, Dr. Bernard found that single women suffer far less than single men from neurotic and anti-social tendencies. Finally, even when Bernard compared *married* men and *unmarried* women, she found that unmarried women seem to be much better off insofar as psychological distress symptoms are concerned. This suggested to her, as Ashley Montagu had already observed, that women as a sex may start out with an initial advantage,[3] but marriage then reverses it. This seems particularly true for the woman who stays home. Dr. Bernard reports that being a housewife literally makes women physically sick and that, according to the National Center for Health Statistics, the mental health of working women is far superior to that of housewives.

A more recent research project on "singlehood" conducted by sociologists Elmer Spreitzer and Lawrence Riley sheds some additional light on Bernard's conclusions. It is significant that singlehood was a term the researchers had to coin, because, as they put it, "the dearth of social-scientific literature in this area is reflected in the fact that we do not have a nomenclature with which to conceptualize the status of persons who never marry."[4]

As Spreitzer and Riley also point out, the strong social pressure toward marriage is one of the main reasons for this dearth. Because this pressure is greater for women and also because of the differences in ascribed roles associated with sex status, they hypothesized that the predisposing factors associated with singlehood may also be different for females and males. Their findings corroborated this theory in a number of respects. For example, while predictably there was a relationship between negative childhood family experiences and later propensities not to marry, these were far more significant in the case of males. The findings concerning children of families with less authoritarian and more democratic orientations also indicated an association with singlehood, but in the opposite direction for males and females. Males from democratic families were the *least* likely to remain single, whereas comparable females were the *most* likely to do so.

Their study also verified earlier findings that the concentrations of single people occur primarily at the lower and higher ends of the socioeconomic scale. This appears to be connected with the fact that middle-class values have less influence on people in these groups. Also, at the lower socioeconomic levels, women are discouraged from marrying men who cannot provide support, while for women at the higher levels marriage is not an economic necessity. The researchers also found that there was a strong correlation between singlehood and education. But perhaps most interesting was the finding that not only was there an inverse relationship between educational level and singlehood, with women on the higher educational level being far less likely to marry than their male counterparts, but that among males, those with the highest level of intelligence were the *least* likely to remain single, whereas females with the higher levels of intelligence were the *most* likely to do so.[5]

The picture that emerges from these studies is certainly far from the popularly accepted one. If anything, it is men, not women, who are typically depicted as complaining about marriage, saying that it ties them down too much, and that although they may end up by doing the proposing, it is rarely their idea in the first place. And in the popular literature, in the movies, and on television, it is always the woman who wants to "catch" a man. Furthermore, even in real life, most women want to marry and despite some recent trends, the vast majority of them still do. The obvious question that arises in the light of the findings of Bernard and other social scientists, is why.

Again this is a very difficult question, one that involves extremely complex biological, psychological, economic, sociological, religious, and political issues. To answer it fully would require an analysis of comparative family forms and child-rearing, of the entire socialization process through which women and men are channeled into assigned social roles, and of the way in which the different institutions of a society interrelate; and such an in-depth analysis is beyond the scope of this book. Nevertheless, if we are to understand the institution of marriage there must be at least some discussion of the social and economic considerations involved.

It is clear that economic factors are central to the institution of marriage. This is true with respect to both the relationship between the family unit and the larger society of which it is a part and to the relationship between the individual members of that unit themselves. It is also clear that, in economic terms, the traditional marriage is basically a private employment contract, where a woman exchanges her sexual and homemaking services for her husband's support.

As recently as 150 years ago in this country, marriage was very often the only real, and certainly the only socially acceptable, means of survival for middle-class women. Effectively barred from every economically advantageous job and profession by both social convention and the inaccessibility of the requisite education and skills, and thoroughly conditioned to aspire to nothing else, women were like commodities competing with one another in a marriage market where the luckiest and prettiest got the well-to-do men. If a woman married a man who could not or would not provide for her—in other words if she made a bad bargain—she, like many poor women, would have to hold down two jobs. She would have to work as a wife and mother inside her home, but she would also have to get a second job on the outside, usually as a domestic servant or as a spinner or weaver or sewing-machine operator in a sweatshop or a factory, or, if she was really fortunate, as a teacher or clerk. In the jobs where women earned cash wages their pay was much lower than that of men, but even this money was legally not their own. In most American states marriage was regulated by laws modeled after those in England. These laws provided that a married woman could not work outside her home without her husband's permission and that when she did, her husband was entitled to her wages. Like a single woman, she also could not vote, hold public office, or practice law. In addition, unlike a single woman, she could not manage property, including property she had brought into the marriage, or make contracts without her husband's consent. A married woman could not be sued and neither could she sue anyone, not even for injuries inflicted on her body. And the law even regulated her personal relationship with her husband by legally subjecting her to "domestic chastisement," which simply meant that if a wife did not perform her services to her husband's satisfaction he had the legal right to beat her.[6]

Today, under the laws that are still on the books of most states, the husband is still legally defined as the head of the household, as the spouse who has the legal right to choose his wife's and children's domicile, to file for homestead, and to give them his name.

Although the rule that a woman must take her husband's name when she marries seems to be based more on convention than specific cases or statutes, bills that have been introduced in state legislatures in recent years to give women the right to retain their names after marriage have usually been laughed out.

In 1945 an Illinois woman sought a court order to compel the Board of Election Commissioners to permit her to vote although she had not registered under her married name. The Illinois appellate court held against her, not on the basis of any statutory or case laws, but because under the "long-established custom, policy, and rule of the common law among English-speaking peoples a woman's name is changed by marriage and her husband's surname becomes as a matter of law her surname."[7]

In Massachusetts a woman was not permitted to recover for her injuries when a train hit her car because she had failed to register the automobile under her married name.[8] And despite the old common-law rule that anyone can change her or his name simply by adopting and using a different one as long as it is not with the intent to defraud, a United States federal court refused to issue citizenship papers to a married woman in her maiden name, despite the fact that she was a professional musician and had never stopped using that name after her marriage.[9] Even after a divorce, a time when many states allow women to reclaim their old names, most states expressly deny women that right if there are still any minor children of the marriage.

Although most states provide that a wife may acquire a separate domicile if she is living away from her husband "for cause," in over one-third of American states if a couple live separately by mutual agreement the wife's domicile still legally remains that of her husband. Women in these situations, or women who simply marry men who are residents of different states, cannot vote or run for office in the state where they live. Other practical consequences have been higher out-of-state college and university tuition fees, ineligibility to receive welfare assistance, and sometimes higher real and personal property tax rates.

These are but a few examples of how the simple fact of being or having been married affects women. When we go beyond this and examine the legal rights, duties, obligations, and responsibilities of the individual members of a family to one another and those that regulate the relationship between families and the state, a far more insidious truth becomes evident: The assump tions behind our family laws conspire to deprive women of their most basic rights.

For example, at the turn of this century, in the *Wickes* case, the California Supreme Court justified the rules denying a married woman the right to have a different domicile than that of her husband as follows:

> The subjection of the wife to the husband was not the only reason for the rule. Parties marrying contract to live together. The husband obligates himself to furnish a proper home for his wife and to maintain her there in a degree of comfort authorized by his circumstances, and they mutually agree to live there together. It is a matter of great public concern that this should be so. In this association there can be no majority vote, and the law leaves the ultimate decision to the husband.[10]

Over fifty years later in *Carlson* v. *Carlson*, the Arizona Supreme Court quoted that decision with approval and added:

> The law imposes upon the husband the burden and obligation of the support, maintenance and care of the family and almost of necessity he must have the right of choice of the situs of the home. There can be no decision by a majority rule as to where the family home shall be maintained, and the reasonable accompaniment of the imposition of the obligation is the right of selection. The violation of this principle tends to sacrifice the family unity, the entity upon which our civilization is built.[11]

But in *McGuire* vs. *McGuire*, one of the few reported American cases where a wife actually went to court to get an order for a husband to perform this obligation "to furnish a proper home for his wife and to maintain her there in a degree of comfort authorized by his circumstances," not one of these cases or rules of law was cited by the court.[12] The action had been brought in 1953 by a Nebraska housewife, the wife of a well-to-do farmer. She alleged in her complaint that she had been married thirty-four years, had worked in the fields, did outside chores, cooked and attended to her household duties, raised as high as 300 chickens, sold poultry and eggs, and used the money to buy clothing and groceries," that she lived in a house without a bathroom, had to get water from a well, and was driving a 1929 Ford without a working heater. She claimed that although her husband had the means to do so, he refused to fix the house or the car, and that in the last four years he had hardly given her any money.

The Nebraska Supreme Court threw out the case. They said that "to maintain an action such as the one at bar, the parties must be separated or living apart from each other," and, beyond that, "the living standards of a family are a matter of concern to the household, and not for the courts to determine," and that is so, "even though the husband's attitude toward his wife, according to his wealth and circumstances, leaves little to be said on his behalf."[13]

Indeed, it is true that a husband's legal duty to support a wife will only be judicially defined in divorce court. Almost every state has laws that make it an offense for a husband not to supply at least "necessaries" for his wife. However, these statutes, as well as those providing that a wife must support a husband who is likely to become a public charge, are designed primarily to protect third-party creditors who have supplied goods or services to the family. Regardless of what services a wife may be rendering to her husband and family, our courts will not impose a clearly defined financial duty of support or payment on the husband while a marriage is "intact."

In his book *Women and the Law*, Leo Kanowitz tried to explain these legal contradictions on the basis that if a husband and wife have reached the point where their obligations instead of being based on "mutual affection" have to be taken to court to be enforced, "their marriage in all likelihood consists of no more than an empty shell."[14]

In 1915, Blanche Crozier advanced another theory to explain why a husband has the legal duty to support his wife, but why that obligation will not be interfered with by the courts except in the case of a divorce or on behalf of third parties. The underlying problem, wrote Crozier in the *Boston University Law Review*, is that our laws view wives as the property of their husbands. "This is precisely the situation in which property finds itself," she wrote. "It may be overworked and underfed, or it may be petted and fed with cream, and that is a matter for the owner to decide."[15]

Shortly before Christmas of 1971 the advertisement on page 82 appeared in the *Los Angeles Times*. It drew a good deal of public attention to some of the laws that govern the relationship between California husbands and wives.

Many women—and men—were surprised and outraged that contemporary family laws should so blatantly discriminate against women. Nevertheless, until very recently the U.S. Supreme Court refused to rule that differences of sex, like differences of race, religion, and national origin, do not justify unequal treatment under the law.

In October 1970, the Western Center for Law and Poverty and the Los Angeles Women's Center Legal Program submitted an amicus curiae, or friend-of-the-court, brief* to the Supreme Court challenging the Arizona counterpart of the California statute that gave the husband exclusive management and control of the community property solely on the basis of his sex.[16]

The brief was filed on behalf of Emma Perez, an Arizona housewife. Emma's husband, Adolpho, had been in an automobile accident. A civil suit for negligence was filed against him, and on October 31, 1967, Emma and Adolpho were required to pay a judgment of approximately $2,450. However, they had no insurance, no money, and no assets. On November 6, 1967, they filed a voluntary petition of bankruptcy, and the judgment was discharged. Shortly thereafter, Emma and Adolpho Perez received a notice from the Arizona Department of Motor Vehicles advising them that both their driver's licenses had been revoked

---

* A brief submitted by an individual or organization not a party to the suit, but concerned about the issues involved.

Give your wife
EQUALITY
for Christmas

We are presenting this message as a public service.

The laws of the State of California provide that the *husband* has management and control of community property. This means that although the husband and wife share equally in the ownership of their joint property (except real estate), the husband is by law given the right and power to sell, transfer, convey, or mortgage that property without the wife's consent or even her knowledge. The *only* limitation is that he cannot give it away without receiving something in return. The wife has no legal power to change or limit her husband's decision, even if she completely disagrees. And it's her property as much as his! The law also gives the husband exclusive power to choose where the family will live, and the wife *has to* agree.

Community property does not insure equality to both spouses. Until 1951, even a wife's separate earnings were under husband's complete control. And today, once a wife's separate earnings are mixed in the same bank account with her husband's earnings, she loses all control over what she herself earned.

If you, as a husband, trust and respect your wife as a truly equal marriage partner, you should want to change a situation which gives her 50% of the ownership but not even 1% of the joy and responsibility of control. We are presenting this message as a public service —to husbands who want to do something very special for their wives this Christmas. If you write to the address indicated below, we will send you a simple form which a husband and wife can execute in the privacy of their own home (all you need do is fill in your names, sign it, and put it with your other important papers) to give your wife an equal voice in deciding how to use the property which is hers as much as yours.

We must ask you to enclose one dollar with your request, to cover our mailing and printing costs. The greatest gift a woman can receive for Christmas, 1971, is EQUALITY.

Write to: WOMEN'S EQUALIZATION COMMITTEE, P.O. Box 48638,
Los Angeles, Ca. 90048
9601 Wilshire Blvd. (Suite 22), Beverly Hills

for one year, for failure to carry liability insurance or otherwise pay the judgment.

Adolpho could no longer drive to work. Emma could not go to the market or drive her children to the doctor. Finally, they found a lawyer who took their case free of charge and went to court to try to get their licenses back. The attorney tried to convince the court that what it came down to was that these people were being penalized for being poor. But the judge did not agree. The attorney then argued that at least Emma should be permitted to drive. She had not been driving. The car was not registered in her name. And on top of everything else, since under Arizona law her husband had the exclusive management and control of the community property, she could not have bought liability insurance, even if there had been any money to do so in the first place. She really had no connection whatsoever with the accident. Certainly *her* driver's license should not be revoked. Again, neither the trial court, nor, later on, the District Court of Appeals for the 9th District agreed.[17] The appellate-court opinion read in part:

> The statutory and decisional law of Arizona make the husband what might be termed the managing agent of the wife in the control of the community automobile. We might well say that the Arizona community property law was written into and became part of the marriage contract between appellants. . . . With married couples in Arizona, the driver's licenses of both husband and wife are an integral part of the ball of wax, which is the basis of the Arizona community property laws. . . . The fact, if it be a fact, that Mrs. Perez could not use the community property to purchase casualty insurance is beside the point. Her driver's license was issued subject to the financial responsibility law. The loss of her driver's license is the price an Arizona wife must pay for negligent driving by her husband of the community vehicle. . . .[18]

The case was appealed to the Supreme Court of the United States. Paula Chernoff, for the Western Center for Law and

Poverty, and I, for the Women's Center Legal Program, wrote a friend-of-the-court brief, urging the highest court of the United States to strike down the law that gave Mr. Perez exclusive management and control of the community property:

> We ask this Court to rule that the suspension of Mrs. Perez's driver's license and the expropriation of her right to share in the management and control of her own property, based, as they are, on her sex, amount to a denial to her of the equal protection of our laws. We ask this Court to clarify the legal status of women and to overturn the discriminatory and discredited rule that sex is a reasonable basis for legislative classification. . . .
>
> Sixteen years ago this Court stated: "Classifications based solely upon race must be scrutinized with particular care, since they are . . . constitutionally suspect." Last year this Court said: "A careful examination on our part is especially warranted where lines are drawn on the basis of wealth or race. . . ."
>
> Like race, sex is determined not by choice, but by birth. Like race, sex has in the past been used to deprive individuals of important civil rights. Just as racial differences do not justify differential treatment under the law, there is scientific and sociological proof that classifications based on sex are equally unreasonable.
>
> . . . Individual variations are far more significant than generalities about ethnic, racial or sexual characteristics. In the case of women, these variations must also be held the only permissible basis for classification, inasmuch as there is no factual basis for the classification of women as incompetent or inferior. It was, however, precisely on that basis that Mrs. Perez was deprived of two fundamental and important rights.
>
> This Court has held that a classification that penalizes the exercise of a basic constitutional right is unconstitutional and invidious discrimination "unless shown to be necessary to promote a compelling governmental interest." It is hard to imagine what interest a state might have in depriving wives of personal and property rights. It has been said that the domination of the wife by the husband is necessary to the stability and protection of the family, but such an argument is totally untenable in the context of contemporary democratic society, and in the light of our standards of what is just and equitable. The notion that the family can only be preserved by maintaining wives in an inferior and

economically dependent status is repugnant to all current ideas about familial affection and mutual responsibility.

There is no compelling state interest, in fact, no interest at all, in perpetuating and continuing an outmoded and unreasonable method of legal classification. We respectfully urge that the Court extend to Mrs. Perez and to 110 million other American women the equal protection of our laws.[19]

On June 1, 1971, the United States Supreme Court handed down its decision. It held in favor of the Perezs, on the grounds that the Arizona financial responsibility law was in conflict with the federal bankruptcy act, and therefore unconstitutionally applied under the supremacy clause of the United States Constitution. However, the Supreme Court never dealt with the constitutionality of the Arizona community-property management and control statute, and it has not done so to date.

However, since then three states, first Texas, and then Washington and California, have amended their laws. In Texas each spouse now has "the sole management, control and disposition of the community property that he or she would have owned if single," as long as the property is not mixed. If the spouses mix their community property, then it is subject to their joint management, unless they provide otherwise by power of attorney or agreement.[20] In Washington either spouse acting alone may control the community property, except for the conveyance or lease or mortgage of real property, the sale of certain types of personal property, and a number of other transactions that require the consent of both.[21] In California too, since 1975, either spouse has had management and control, except for the sale, lease, or conveyance of real property, gifts of community property, or the sale or mortgage of furniture and wearing apparel where the consent or joinder of both is required. Also, specifically exempted is "a spouse who is operating or managing a business or an interest in a business which is community personal property," and under these new laws such a spouse continues to have "the sole management and control" of such a business or interest.[22]

In California, this is the latest in a long list of legislative amendments enacted since 1848, when California acquired, along with its territory, the Mexican system of community property. From the beginning, the theory of community property was that marriage is a partnership. But for California women it was *only* a theory. Before the California Civil Code was amended in 1891 to preclude husbands from making a gift of the community property,[23] the only way a wife could be sure she would get any of it was if her husband died before she did, provided, of course, that he had not given it all away before his death. In 1901 the law was again amended, so that the wife's written consent was required before the husband could sell or mortgage the household furnishings and the wife's and children's clothes. Sixteen years later, legislation was passed requiring that the wife join with the husband in any deed or contract to sell or mortgage real estate or lease it for over one year.[24] In 1923 California wives were given the right to dispose of their half of the community property by will,[25] and in 1951 the law was amended to permit wives to manage and control their own outside earnings, so long as they didn't "commingle" them with their husband's, in which case they again came under his exclusive control.[26]

The new laws providing for equal management of community property have come about after much pressure from feminists and in anticipation of the adoption of the proposed Equal Rights Amendment, which would require an end to legal discrimination based on sex. Nevertheless, there is still immense resistance to real joint management and control. Many legislators, judges, and attorneys argue that a real partnership between husbands and wives who often know little if anything about business and money management would result in mass bankruptcies. But this argument, which is not without foundation, has been met in California by excluding businesses from the provinces of the new community-property laws. The fundamental opposition to joint management and control stems from certain traditional notions and stereotypes about sex-based roles and unwillingness to give up traditional male powers.

In a recent article in the journal of the California State Bar two Los Angeles attorneys speculated on the real implications and effects of the newest amendment to the California community-property law. "Although the statutory changes might at first impression appear to be quite revolutionary," they wrote, "it is difficult to imagine that the new law will have a significant effect on most households."[27] They then went on to make a few suggestions as to how attorneys might work with the new law. "For those couples who desire to circumvent the new law in order to facilitate dealings with community property by one spouse," they wrote, "several alternatives may be available." The most obvious one, they went on,

> is a written agreement. . . . Two other means of avoiding the new law are a power of attorney from one spouse to the other and a funded revocable trust with one of the spouses acting as sole trustee. Presumably, a power of attorney is subject to less judicial scrutiny than an agreement because the power is normally revocable by the granting spouse. Likewise, a properly drawn revocable trust funded with community property will permit either spouse to revoke the trust as to the community property.[28]

At first glance it seems a little shocking to find an article advising people how to "circumvent" and "avoid" our laws in the official journal of the state bar. But as Professor Herma Hill Kay, an authority on family law, points out, the big hurdle facing the new egalitarian family laws is that of implementation:

> One trouble is that these laws are capable of a number of interpretations both judicially and practically. For example, if the statutory language is that either has control, in a sense that's left to the spouse who is more aggressive. When you've drafted legislation as long as I have, you know that that's not where the problems end. You've got to look at what a court can do.[29]

Also concerned about what the courts can do is Los Angeles attorney Roberta Ralph, who made the following comments on California's new law:

> First, philosophically, I prefer "joint management" as I feel that a more viable marriage partnership can be achieved only by both parties having full knowledge of the assets, liabilities and plans for these assets and/or liabilities as to usage, indebtedness, etc. "Equal management" though, is better than the husband's having absolute control and can work IF there is a joint understanding between the parties—otherwise it could be a disaster of another sort."[30]

The problem underlying the whole issue of management and control is, of course, the judicial resistance to fundamental social change. Therefore, as Professor Kay and Attorney Ralph point out, there is the possibility that the new Washington, Texas, and California laws and even the Equal Rights Amendment might simply lead to a family-law version of separate but equal. Conceivably, common-law states would remain as they are, while community-property states would revert to a similar system where a husband and wife each have "equal but separate" management of their own earnings, in essence doing away with the whole partnership concept underlying community property.

As with any other law designed to correct social injustices and imbalances of power, there is the problem of bringing the social and psychological realities in line with the provisions of the new laws. However, there are ways to provide for these readjustments without sacrificing the essence and indeed the basic intent of the legal reform. For example, the new community-property laws should clearly spell out what procedures and actions one spouse can take against the other for failure to abide by the requirement for equal or joint management and for mismanagement of the community property as well. In addition, guidelines for revisions of existing commercial documents and agreements should also be spelled out, so that third parties dealing with married couples can protect themselves and at the same time abide by the new egalitarian requirements of these laws.

Although I believe that the new "joint"-management statutes may be preferable to those giving "each" or "either" that right, in both cases it is essential that the standards for mismanagement be clarified. The recent California statute provides that each spouse shall act in "good faith" with respect to the other spouse,[31] which should certainly give rise to a cause of action for intentional mismanagement. But an older code section,[32] dealing with agreements between spouses respecting community property, imposes the much stricter "fiduciary duty" standard legally required of a trustee toward the beneficiaries of a trust. This standard gives rise to a cause of action for negligent mismanagement in situations where ordinary "good faith" would otherwise be a sufficient defense. I believe that this is the test that should have been specifically written into the new law, in order to discourage husbands from simply continuing their exclusive management of the community property without any participation by their wives, and also to encourage more responsibility on the part of both spouses.

Certainly wives and husbands deserve from each other the same treatment strangers receive from bankers and other institutional officials who serve as trustees. In any event, if a husband found the stricter accountability test excessive, his alternative would be simply to share the management and control with his wife, since she would then be precluded from complaining that he was negligent.

While it would be possible for individual judges to adopt this approach in interpreting the new management and control laws, it is far preferable that legislatures actually put this standard into the statutory law of their particular states. There is a big difference between laws that are legislatively enacted and those that arise through judicial interpretation. While many of our finest laws have come about through the latter method, the problem is that when new courts composed of different judges hear or re-hear such cases they may come to different conclusions. Perhaps the most dramatic manifestation of this phenomenon takes place in the U.S. Supreme Court, where in recent years we have felt the influence of the Nixon appointees in the massive reversals of precedent in criminal justice, the rights of indigents, and civil rights in general.

These radical shifts occur despite the theory of stare decisis, the hallowed and long-standing bulwark of Anglo-American jurisprudence, which provides that the policy of our courts shall be to stand by precedent and not to disturb settled points. Nevertheless, judicial shifts do take place with changing times, and with what some legal theoreticians have called advancing standards of morality.

It would seem that the best protection against this type of legal instability in the field of family law is to have the individual state legislatures adopt clear legislation protecting the rights of wives. As a start, I would suggest that model legislation like the Uniform Marriage and Divorce Act be revised to include an expanded concept of marital property applicable not only after a marriage is dissolved, but while it is still functioning. This marital property should be under the joint management and control of both spouses, who shall be held accountable to each other by a fiduciary standard of care. Further, both the commercial mechanisms for implementing that standard in the business community and the legal remedies for its breach should be explicitly spelled out. This would be an important first step, urgently needed to balance the introduction of no-fault divorce and the trend toward shorter and lower spousal-support awards, by preventing one spouse from siphoning off the other's share of the property accumulated during the marriage. Such a higher standard of care will also afford protection to men who are concerned that egalitarian laws will allow their wives to mismanage and dissipate marital assets. Additionally, joint-management laws would promote the mutual responsibility and cooperation on which every workable partnership must be based.

6

Women and Employment

In light of the rigid social, economic, and legal constraints on women it is not surprising that their training traditionally centered on the acquisition of the "feminine" skills that would enable them to make a good marriage bargain and perform satisfactorily as wives. The value set upon the acquisition of these skills is intrinsically connected to the masculine desire for the *indicia* of wealth and status that signify worldly success in the eyes of society. This has been true since the late eighteenth and nineteenth centuries when the newly rich burghers began to aspire to the luxuries that until then had been the exclusive prerogative of noblemen and kings. Along with large houses, fine clothes, culinary delicacies, and elegant carriages, these men also wanted to possess the purely decorative and nonfunctional women that formerly only the nobility could afford. These earlier prototypes of the modern "sex object" were the courtesans and mistresses of the rich, but the Puritan ethic and the great bourgeois emphasis on conformity demanded the evolution of a different type of woman. This was the more genteel and respectable "lady" who played the piano, wore fine jewelry and lace and velvet gowns, embroidered, and delivered charity to the workers in her husband's mines and factories. Besides being moral, domestic, and virtuous, her main job was to squeeze her body and indeed her soul into the shape and form that would please the man who kept her. According to the pulpit, the bench, the politicians, the writers, and even the women's magazines of the 1800s, all women aspired to this ideal. Nevertheless, the vast majority of men continued to be poor and could not afford such luxuries; so their wives continued to work.

The peasant and working-class women worked in their homes, as servants in other people's homes, and as shopgirls and whores. As the industrial revolution progressed, more and more women also worked in textile mills and sweatshops, and even in quarries and mines. They became office workers and were employed increasingly as teachers and nurses. By 1890 one out of every six workers in the general labor force was a woman.[1]

But even from the beginning women rarely got jobs as good as those men had, and almost as soon as women became widely accepted in a particular occupation, both its pay and prestige declined. Even in the "outside world" of the general labor market women were confined by the rigid boundaries of what Caroline Bird has called the "sexual job map" of the employment world.[2] It segregated women into the wifely roles of secretary, nurse, schoolteacher, waitress, helper, and assistant, where, just as in the home, they almost invariably worked for a male. Even the women who worked alongside men in factories, shops, and offices were usually confined to the lower-paying and less responsible job classifications, or again simply to "women's jobs," such as electronics and other close assembly work for which women presumably had "more patience" than men. As for the woman who would not let herself be so confined, there were all kinds of other labels, the kindest of which was "exception."

Beyond its social implications, the primary impact of this phenomenon has been economic, resulting in a wide disparity between the earnings of women and men. Economist Isabel Sawhill relates this phenomenon to the great growth of the female labor force. She points out that smaller families and the wider availability of labor-saving devices in the home may actually be consequences, and not just causes of women's working outside the home, since they do not coincide with the timing of the greatest upsurge of female employment.[3] She suggests that the increasing demand for women workers appears to be the dominant factor in the situation, and that supply has adjusted itself to demand, a conclusion also reached by Valerie Oppenheimer in her study of the growth of the female labor force, concentrating on the twenty-year period after 1940.[4]

The growing demand for women in the labor market was largely the result of the sex typing of certain industries and occupations as female, with savings in labor costs. It would seem then that, to a large extent, more permissive social attitudes and even the pressures and demands of women have not really been so much the cause as the effect of the changing labor market.

There is little evidence for the proposition that the wider participation of women in the general labor market *is* due to the passage of new laws. For example, it is true that the adoption of the Married Women's Acts in the nineteenth century made it more feasible for women to work outside their homes, since these acts repealed many of the severe restrictions of the earlier common law. But it is also true that the passage of these laws (which freed married women from some of the economic controls formerly exercised by their husbands and permitted them to enter into employment contracts legally and to keep their own earnings) coincided with the increasing demand for cheap female labor. Other dramatic changes in laws affecting women came during both the First and Second World Wars, when a series of equal-work-for-equal-pay laws were passed. As Bird points out, these were periods of national crises when women were required "to do the work of men," particularly in heavy industry. In the postwar periods, however, there was no further use for "Rosie the Riveter." Women workers were again sent home, and whatever equal-employment legislation had been obtained was no longer enforced either by the men who owned and ran the places of employment or those who administered the laws.[5]

Dramatic changes in our employment laws have only come about in recent years. It is generally assumed that they are responsible for both the acceleration of women's entry into the general labor market and for the significant improvement in their status there. However, Elizabeth Duncan Koontz, the Director of the U.S. Department of Labor Women's Bureau, took a different view in 1971. "Occupationally," she wrote in the introduction to the U.S. government pamphlet *Underutilization of Women Workers,* "women are more disadvantaged, compared with men, than they were 30 years ago."

There has been an enormous increase in the number of women in the labor force in the last few decades—from 16.7 million in 1947 to 29.2 million in 1968. However, while in 1940 women held 45 percent of technical and professional positions, by 1969 they held only 37 percent of such jobs. During the same period, the proportion of women in the bottom rungs of the labor ladder increased spectacularly, while the percentage of men who were lower-paid clerical, service, and sales workers declined by almost 20 percent. And in 1969 it was the men who constituted 99 percent of all engineers and federal judges, 97 percent of all attorneys, 93 percent of all physicians, and 91 percent of all scientists.[6]

The most extraordinary thing about these statistics is that, as Koontz points out, these were the years when women made their greatest gains in labor-legislation reform. While as early as 1923 the Civil Service Classification Act provided that federal employees receive equal pay for equal work, it was not until 1963 that the U.S. Congress enacted the Federal Equal Pay Act, requiring that all businesses engaged in interstate commerce have pay schedules that do not discriminate on the basis of sex.[7] In 1964 the landmark Title VII of the Federal Civil Rights Act became law, prohibiting any type of discrimination, be it in hiring, promotion, or pay, on the basis of not only race, color, and creed, but also sex.[7] Furthermore, according to Koontz, during these years, when women were doing worse and not better in the labor force, it was not because these two federal statutes were not being implemented. Underpayments of more than $17 million to more than 50,000 employees were disclosed under the equal-pay legislation by April of 1970, and during 1969 alone approximately 2,700 sex-based complaints under Title VII were investigated by the Equal Employment Opportunities Commission.[8]

Nevertheless, today women are the fastest-growing group in the American labor market. According to Sawhill, while the long-run historical data shows little variation in the total proportion of the population in the labor force, it shows increasing rates of employment for women and decreasing rates for men. This is so despite the fact that in 1971, among year-round full-time workers, men earned an average of $9,399 while women earned $5,593—or only 60 percent as much.[9]

Since the evidence shows that sex discrimination in employment usually leads to job segregation rather than to unequal pay for the same tasks, it is unlikely that the equal-pay laws can be expected to do much. Legislation of equal-employment opportunity is of much greater importance as protection against overt acts of exclusion and discrimination. The most significant laws have been the federal executive orders, particularly 11246, as amended by 11375 in 1968, prohibiting discrimination by federal contractors, and requiring that affirmative-action programs be developed and carried out under the threat of contract cancellations.

The affirmative-action portion of these orders requiring employers not only to desist from discriminatory practices, but also to take concrete steps in recruiting and promoting minorities and women for all types of jobs, has been the most effective enforcement device to date. In the last few years it has resulted in significant changes in the in-training and hiring policies of most major U.S. corporations with respect to minorities and women, and equally important, it has led to major jumps in the enrollment of minorities and women in professional schools.

But just as these new developments began to gain some momentum the economy stopped growing and so did hiring, particularly at higher levels, with the result that few of the new jobs earmarked for women and minorities were filled. By 1973 according to Dr. James O'Toole, chairperson of the Special Task Force that prepared the report, *Work in America*, for the Department of Health, Education and Welfare, the affirmative-action program had virtually come to a halt.[10]

There are trends in the current economic situation that seem to cast serious doubts on the future economic security of women in our society. According to the Bureau of Labor Statistics, by 1980 the percentage of the labor force in manufacturing will drop to 22 percent, and according to a Rand study, by the year 2000 only 2 percent of the population will be required to turn out all necessary manufactured goods.[11]

As a matter of fact, if an industrial society is defined as a goods-producing society in which manufacturing is central, then the United States today may no longer be such a society. According to some economists, more than 50 percent of our labor force is already engaged in services, working in some branch of what Daniel Bell calls "tertiary" industry (transport and recreation), "quaternary" industry (trade, finance, insurance, real estate) and "quinary" industry (health, education, research, and government).[12]

A related phenomenon which is also having a major impact upon employment is the shift from the goal of unending economic expansion to a philosophy of lower, and according to some, zero economic growth. The accompanying slowdown in economic expansion is resulting in fewer new jobs, less hiring, and fewer promotions—in short, in an increasingly static labor market where individual opportunities for both entry and advancement are substantially curtailed. By January 1975, our unemployment rate had reached 8.2 percent of the work force (about one out of every twelve),[13] and despite subsequent economic upswings, even the more optimistic government sources caution that the unemployment problem will be with us for some time to come. Although available government statistics do not provide a breakdown by sex, it is not unreasonable to assume that the percentage of women out of work is higher than that of men, since the female unemployment rate traditionally has been a good deal higher than the male (4.7 percent versus 2.8 percent in 1969 and 6.9 percent versus 5.3 percent in 1971).[14] It is also likely that with current economic uncertainties there will be a tendency toward less stringent enforcement of antidiscrimination laws, so that in the short run women can probably expect even further setbacks in the scramble for jobs and survival.

Underemployment is another fundamental problem of our labor market. According to Columbia's Ivar Berg, while education is still being held out as a sure ticket to the better life, 80 percent of America's college graduates are taking jobs that previously were filled by workers with lower educational credentials.[15] On the other end of the scale, a 1967 survey in San Francisco found that 17 percent of employers required a high-school diploma for unskilled jobs.[16]

For women, who are already overrepresented in some of the worst jobs in the economy, and for whom this gap between educational qualifications and job availability is nothing new, underemployment poses additional problems. For example, if, as the Department of Labor has predicted, between 1972 and 1985 over twenty-two million people with college degrees will compete for about eighteen million openings for high-status jobs,[17] how will this affect the future of the increasing number of women who have finally gained entry into professional schools?

In 1974, in a speech to the graduating class of Ohio State University, President Ford made public mention of the problem of underemployment. He and other officials have offered a simple policy response: a return to the nineteenth-century emphasis on vocational training.[18] Others have suggested that a number of more basic changes will be required—redesign of existing and emerging jobs, greater worker autonomy, increased profit sharing, as well as better job and skill matching. The need for fundamental changes in our educational system toward a less competitive and more integrated lifelong learning approach, no longer geared to the assembly and production of a well-regimented industrial work force, have also been stressed. One component of this new educational approach would be mid-career retraining, during which workers would be given a government stipend while they learned new skills or even professions. At the same time these workers would, at least temporarily, be removed from competition within the work force.[19]

Perhaps in the long run some of these proposals will be adopted, but for the immediate future most observers agree that the prospects for the American labor market look grim. And yet, it is precisely now, when nothing seems certain except that there are hard times ahead, that the relative proportion of women in the labor force continues to increase.

Most women work out of economic necessity. This is so not only for single, widowed, and divorced women, but also for married ones (e.g., according to *Work in America*, 86 percent of all working wives have husbands earning less than $10,000 per year).[20] It makes no sense, therefore, to suggest that women not enter the labor market. Furthermore, as we have seen, the job that women have traditionally held, that of wife and mother, is also in a great state of flux, with many dislocations of its own.

Whether in the general labor market or at home, the issue is not and never has been whether women should work, but at what occupations and professions and for what rewards. The crux of the problem is the low economic and social valuation of whatever women do in a patriarchal society, where, by definition, men are at the top. Yet the shift from industrial to postindustrial society raises a number of immediate and urgent questions relating to women's position in the work force. For example, will they continue to be confined to the least socially desired sectors of the labor market, and, as has consistently happened in the past, will the economic and social value of occupations be lowered as soon as they are reclassified as "women's work"? Equally important, will homemaking and child care continue to be excluded from the gross national product, or will they be redefined to compensate those who perform these services with direct pay, retirement pensions, and all the other fringe benefits of jobs our society classifies as economically productive?

The whole issue of work, its economic and social ramifications, what it is and what it should be, has become one of the most important subjects of our time. There seems general agreement that the Puritan work ethic, which holds that those who do not work shall not eat, is no longer economically viable, and it has been suggested that the answer lies in some form of guaranteed income for all. Such measures may be necessary, but the fact remains that people derive from work not only economic sustenance, but also a great part of their sense of personal identity, and that any redefinition of work must consider psychological and sociological factors as well.

While some futurologists predict only gloom, others contend that, on the contrary, good times are on their way. The English Nobel Prize winner, Dennis Gabor, maintains that in the mature society of the future, work will no longer be interpreted solely in terms of production. He further states that our concept of leisure as simply free time will have to be redefined as an activity outside the realm of necessity which is both freely chosen and rewarding.[21]

But Gabor soon makes it plain that his ideas do not apply to women who, despite all his visions for the future, he continues to see in patriarchal terms:

> Those women fit for it must be encouraged to give all their time to their children in their formative years, instead of unloading them on nurseries. An advanced technological society has no need of the productive work of all young women. There is no

need for them to rush back to their machines or typewriters. After the children have grown up, there is no necessity to fill the great emptiness with routine occupations learned before the first child was born. The great emptiness will be better filled by the first course in adult education, by preparing for a new profession, or by absorbing that "useless" culture which the young girl may have judged "irrelevant." The mature woman of 30 to 45 may be ready for it.[22]

For women the real issue—whether they work in the labor force or at home—is whether the patriarchal system of values under which we have lived for so long can finally change. Central to that system of values is the traditional belief that women are meant to be economically, physically, and psychologically dependent on men, both in the home and outside. The corollary to that belief and one that has been largely translated into fact is the powerlessness of women, which is the cornerstone of patriarchal social organization.

We see the manifestations of that powerlessness everywhere, in the corporate board rooms from which women are excluded, in military conferences, in high political caucuses, on the Supreme Court, in short, in all the places where important decisions are made. On the familial level, we see it in our fundamental religious and social attitudes, as in St. Paul's command, "Wives, submit yourselves unto your husbands, for the husband is the head of the wife, even as Christ is the head of the church,"[23] and in the laws that still accord husbands that status in contemporary democracies, pointing up the fact that the real basis of patriarchal marriage is dominion rather than, as we have been led to believe, romantic love.

Like any other powerless group, most women have lived out their lives according to the value system of the dominant group. The successful socialization of women is a prerequisite for the continued functioning of patriarchy. But in the same way that feudalism broke up when serfs no longer accepted their rulers, and kings had to give up absolute power when their subjects no longer saw them as divinely ordained, the patriarchal control of men over women will no longer be possible when women reject the value system of the dominant group and define and value themselves, not according to somebody else's characteristics, but their own.

When reduced to its most basic level, however, the reason for the powerlessness of women in patriarchies is that women are barred from access to any of the instruments of force. Patriarchal societies are based on the institutionalization of hierarchical and power-centered social relationships. To ensure that men remain in control of these hierarchies, women have to be confined to rigidly prescribed roles. Traditionally this has been done by denying women access to the outer, public, or "man's" world, and by confining them to the home.

However, the increasing entry of women into the general labor market will not necessarily change that situation. Neither will the contemporary loosening of traditional family bonds. As we have seen throughout recorded Western history, social institutions can change, they can incorporate and coopt new and even larger segments of the population into the top echelons, and they can even evolve new forms, without losing any of their basic characteristics.

Despite the many bloodlettings, the violence and the revolutions, despite the periodic takeovers of control by one group from another, and even despite the trend toward broadening the bases of power, all patriarchal societies have one thing in common. Their actual leadership effectively excludes women (even in those few countries where there are women heads of state), and their social institutions have remained hierarchical, vertical, and based on power.

The patriarchal family has always been a microcosm of the particular patriarchy in which it functions. In Nazi Germany, where the lines of control were sharp and tightly drawn, the father's power in the family, like the Führer's in the nation, was supposed to be unchallengeable and absolute. In our country today, when political power is supposed to be derived from and representative of the people, and where there has recently been much dislocation and reshuffling in high places, the dominance of the male is far more subtle and less official, and the family is going through many dislocations and reshufflings of its own.

And yet, at the same time that the traditional constraints that confined women to their homes are breaking down, and more and more women are being permitted to participate in the "outside world," a new patriarchal family form is developing. It is less personal and less intimate and is no longer bound up with sex or affection. But it is paternalistic and rigid and very strict with its women and children, and again, it is run by men. It is an increasingly prevalent familial structure where the authoritarian figure is no longer the individual patriarch, but the government and its bureaucracy. Most people on the outside call it welfare. Most people on the inside call it "the system" or "the man." And despite its severe problems and shortcomings, it is already becoming firmly entrenched in our laws and institutions.

7

Women and Welfare

The American welfare system is one of the most complex legal and bureaucratic systems in the world. It consists of a combination of federal "enabling legislation," which sets out the general rules for federal policy and funding, an intricate system of state laws with significant variations both in social policy and monetary stipends, and an immense body of local county rules and regulations, which again are different from one locality to the next. Its complexities and variations are so great that it is almost impossible to summarize except to say that, despite prevalent assumptions, far from providing "free handouts" for anyone who does not want to work, the existing welfare system actually provides assistance to certain specifically defined segments of our population—the totally disabled, the blind or partially blind, the aged, and families with dependent children. Furthermore, despite the occasional well-publicized cases of fraud, welfare payments at best provide only minimum subsistence incomes. According to HEW statistics, in January 1973 the national average payment to a mother and 2.5 children was $168 per month or $2,016 per year. Even the state with the highest payments, New York, gave only $284 per month or $3,408 (this during a year of high inflation).[1] It should be clear from these figures that welfare payments are not enough to take a family out of poverty.

According to a United States government study conducted in October of 1971, of the 13.6 million Americans then drawing public welfare payments, less than 1 percent were "able men."[2] Using census figures, *U.S. News and World Report* compiled a report on U.S. poverty the following year. The findings indicated that more than 80 percent of the 26 million poor in this country were children, the elderly, or women, and more than one-half of the 12.5 percent of our nation officially classified as poor were people in families without a male head of household.[3]

By far the largest single group of people on welfare in 1971 were the 10.6 million women and children on Aid for Dependent Children (AFDC).[4] According to *California Women: A Report of the Advisory Committee of the Status of Women*, the number of woman-headed families on AFDC in California doubled from 1968 to 1970,[5] and in 1971 the California State Social Welfare Board Task Force on Absent Parent Child Support reported that 85 percent of the almost 1 million children on California's AFDC case rolls were receiving no support whatever from their fathers.[6]

Another one and a half million of those on the welfare rolls are elderly women on Old Age Assistance. According to studies done by Ralph Nader, not only does the social and sexual value of women drop sharply with age, but so does their economic status. Despite all the myths about women controlling our wealth, women over the age of sixty-five are the single poorest segment of our population. While only the most destitute are eligible for welfare, millions of old, unmarried women survive on Social Security benefits averaging 82.5 percent of what their husbands would have received had they outlived them, and over one-quarter of all unmarried women over sixty-five have no assets at all.[7]

It would seem then that poverty in America is largely a problem of women and children. Of the women who are on welfare, the highest proportion seem to be unemployed housewives, either widows unemployed by death, or divorced and separated mothers. In his book *The Politics of Guaranteed Income*, presidential adviser Daniel P. Moynihan reported that in the midsixties the AFDC rolls, particularly in large centers like New York, suddenly swelled to monumental proportions. Moynihan said there was no apparent reason for this, but that where one New Yorker in thirty had been on welfare in 1960, by the 1970s the city's Human Resources Administration submitted a budget providing for one person in six to be on welfare. "The essential mystery," wrote Moynihan, "is that in the midst of great economic prosperity the number of penniless persons began to soar."[8]

If Mr. Moynihan had taken the available data one step further, he might have solved his "essential mystery." Some of the welfare increase in the urban sectors was of course due to the migrations of the poor who were now more visible than they had been in the past. But more significantly, during the 1960s when the divorce rate soared, so also did the numbers of families on welfare.

In 1969 the median income for families headed by women was $4,000—compared to a median of $11,600 for two-parent families. The discrepancy in incomes between these families was greater for whites than for nonwhites, partially due to the greater poverty of nonwhites of any marital status. Looking at the higher end of the income distribution, only 9 percent of woman-headed families had incomes of over $10,000, compared to 55 percent of two-parent families.[9]

Nevertheless, there is increasing evidence that so many woman-headed families are poor not only because they were poor before divorce, but that divorce is an important cause of that condition. This has been the conclusion of a number of recent studies showing that the poverty of divorced mothers is determined largely by contemporary circumstances and not by their socioeconomic origins.[10]

Much of this downward mobility of divorced mothers can be related to the problems of child support as well as to the general economic discrimination against women and the lack of facilities for daytime child care. Besides a former husband's support payments, or her entry into the labor market, the only institutionalized form of income available to a divorced mother is public welfare. Still, despite the massive problems of child care and the enormous burden of working at a job and taking care of a home and children alone, 62 percent of divorced mothers with preschool children, according to a 1971 study, had outside jobs and many of those who went on welfare did so only for short periods of time.[11]

One reason that many poor women do not even apply for welfare is the great social stigma associated with being "a public charge," and, in addition, there are the many difficulties of qualifying and of meeting agency requirements for continued help. Beyond that, as Lee Rainwater, one of the experts in this field, points out, there is evidence that the welfare system, as currently constituted, is actually damaging to the women and children who depend on it for support.[12] The crux of the problem is that since our society labels the members of welfare families as unproductive, its members themselves doubt their own social value; since they are denied access to the conventional means of achieving identity, deviant avenues such as juvenile delinquency and drug addiction are then pursued. It is in an effort to find some kind of validating identity that welfare mothers often speak of themselves as working hard to raise their children and assert that this activity merits compensation. But, as Rainwater writes, "there is a fictive quality to that stance, exactly because they recognize that society does not value their children very much and does not really care whether they are raised well or not."[13]

Since work provides not only economic resources but day-to-day evidence that one has something to offer in return, Rainwater argues that the absence of a validating work role for women on welfare is very damaging, both to them and to their children, and one way to deal with that problem would be to designate mothers not supported by husbands as unemployed workers, and to provide for their families a system of unemployment insurance.[14]

The economic problems of woman-children families are rooted in the same patriarchal double standard that characterizes the attitude of judges, attorneys, and law-enforcement officials. Although judges continue to see women as primarily responsible for their children after divorce, support awards have kept going down during the same years that divorces and prices have both soared. Sometimes these men have rationalized low awards on the basis that they were only temporary, until the woman could find somebody else to take care of her. Other times their rationale has been that it is not good for a woman to be dependent, or that wanting liberation, this is what they deserved, and in any case, it was not equitable or practical to burden a man unduly. The end result, as the Citizens' Advisory Council on the Status of Women has found, is that the average child-support award covers less than half of the expense of supporting a child, even by the most minimal of standards. Furthermore, minimal or not, a great many of these awards are not even enforced. Consequently as the laws of divorce become more liberal and as more and more couples split up, more and more women and children find they have no other choice but to seek public welfare.

It is not that women do not want to go out and get jobs. As a matter of fact, the Labor Department statistics on women workers indicate that the vast majority of unemployed housewives have been absorbed into the general labor market, where they work for a median wage of 60 percent of that of men.[14] According to a 1971 HEW study, even then the major problem was that of job availability. Taking into account the higher unemployment rates for women, the government estimated that only 34 percent of mothers then on welfare would be able to find any jobs.[15]

Thomas C. Thomas of Stanford's Center for the Study of Social Policy points out that the American economy has barely been

able to absorb the yearly increases in labor force due to population growth. Since the private sector, being profit based, has
built-in limitations beyond which it cannot expand, in recent
years the public sector of employment has been growing at an extraordinary rate. It already employs about 13.1 million bureaucratic workers (2.6 million in the federal government, excluding
the armed forces, and 10.5 million in state and local government).
Thomas estimates that to accommodate 10 million welfare recipients would mean a 75 percent increase in total government
employees, which, even if it were possible, is certainly economically unsound and socially extremely unwise.[16] Nevertheless, the
solution to the "welfare mess" that is most frequently presented
to the media by public officials is "getting recipients out to work."

But even beyond that, assuming a level of full employment,
for welfare mothers there is still another major obstacle to working at outside jobs, namely, the problem of who will take care
of the children. According to the report of the California Advisory Commission on the Status of Women, in 1971 more than
one million California children needed child care because their
parents worked. However, all the state's licensed and supervised
child-care facilities, private and public, profit and nonprofit,
could only accommodate 125,000 children.[17] This was the situation before former Governor Reagan's lower budget for child care,
the HEW cutbacks, and new federal revenue-sharing regulations
giving states control over child-care eligibility standards resulted
in the closing of many publicly funded centers and the removal
of thousands of already placed children from the eligibility lists.

On the national level, where the lack of child-care facilities
is even more acute, President Ford's veto of the bill that would
have enacted federal aid to child-care centers and his decision
to provide no new social-service programs in the foreseeable
future have been a severe blow. Not only did his 1976 budget
propose no new initiatives for early childhood programs, but it
actually included cutbacks of $127 million from the 1975 allot-
ment for existing programs, the termination of the $33 million

special food-service program providing school lunches, and a hold-the-line policy for most other HEW programs. There has been much criticism of Mr. Ford's budget priorities, particularly his proposal to increase defense spending by $9 billion while cutting social programs and at the same time proposing a $6 billion tax reduction for business. Although at this writing it is not certain how many of Mr. Ford's budget ideas Congress will accept, even among our legislators child care does not seem a top priority. For example, the three-year bill to upgrade child-care services introduced in 1975 by Senator Walter Mondale and Representative John Brademas, the leading daycare advocates in Congress, was for $1.8 billion, substantially less than the $2.5 billion, two-year measure passed by the Senate in 1972.[18]

In vetoing that bill, former President Nixon said he was not going to commit the "vast moral authority of the national government to the side of communal approaches to child rearing over against the family-centered approach." He said he had nothing against daycare for the poor and that indeed he wanted to do everything possible to allow poor mothers to "leave the welfare rolls to go on the payrolls." But to make the services of child care available to nonwelfare mothers was something else, because the President said it was necessary to "enhance rather than diminish both parental authority and parental involvement with children—particularly in those decisive early years when social attitudes and conscience are formed and religious and moral principles are first inculcated."[19]

The plan Mr. Nixon vetoed would of course not have made child care compulsory. It was designed to operate on a sliding scale with parents paying according to their means. It was intended to provide some kind of a place for the six hundred thousand children, who in 1973, according to the Day Care and Child Development Council of America, were left to care for themselves completely on their own by their working parents. It was also intended to try to find better care for the more than 70 percent of the nation's preschool children of working parents, who are left in unlicensed facilities, or with friends, neighbors, or older children.[20]

In one sense, it is not surprising that child care has been such a low priority for our legislators and makers of social policy, since they are the same people who made the laws that define work in strictly economic terms and exclude homemaking services from our gross national product.

As Thomas points out, the distinctions between work and welfare, producer and nonproducer, worker and nonworker are arbitrary. Work occurs when an individual contributes something to society and not just when policymakers include or exclude that effort from the GNP. Logically then there is no reason that housewives should not be paid wages and their contributions not be included in the GNP. Indeed, if one housewife goes to work in a child-care center and another one is thereby enabled to come and clean the first one's house, cleaning and child care suddenly become part of the GNP.[21]

But logic does not seem to be the governing factor in this field. For example, in looking over the reasons former President Nixon gave for his veto, it is somewhat difficult to understand what he had in mind. Did he mean that it was all right for the children of welfare recipients to do without their mothers' help in the formation of those all-important "religious and moral principles?" Did he mean that only the children of the well-to-do were entitled to "parental authority and involvement?" Or did he simply mean that for nonpoor women the only place is in the home with their children, but that these same rules do not apply to the poor?

These differences in ground rules are very apparent in the welfare system, which subjects poor women and their children to what under any other circumstances would be considered unlawful invasions of personal privacy. In order to determine both initial and continuing eligibility, government officials are entitled to probe into the economic, personal, and even sexual details of the recipient's life. The welfare mother must of course make complete disclosure of any assets and income in order to qualify, and she is required to report any changes right away. In addition, her job activities will be strictly monitored since they affect eligibility, and for the welfare mothers who work part-time, they will determine the size of each check. A woman's homemaking activities are also policed, since she is required to meet certain standards in the environment and care she provides for her children. And even her social and sexual life is not her own, since the state presumes that if a woman has a relationship with a man he is providing her with support, which could then terminate her eligibility for welfare payments.

The situation of the welfare mother has been compared to that of a traditional wife, whose husband will "let her" do certain things and "forbid" her others, since men are, at least in theory, supposed to exercise authority and control over the families they head. But, except for those wives with really despotic husbands, the welfare system imposes economic, social, and sexual controls which are much more overt, and of course, far more impersonal.

Many husbands will put their wives on living allowances or household and personal budgets, but usually these are not as meager, rigid, or complicated as the ones welfare workers must work out for their clients. Wives of jealous husbands are exposed to many indignities, but very rarely do these include inspections such as the welfare departments' practice of showing up in the middle of the night to see if there is a man around, and in the bargain, also to check whether the sheets are clean.

While husbands rarely institute criminal proceedings against their wives or testify in such actions, welfare workers do just that against their clients. For example, in a 1968 Maryland case,[22] after complying with the state's requirement that she initiate paternity proceedings against the father of her illegitimate child in order to qualify for welfare eligibility, a woman was prosecuted for criminal and civil neglect of her children. The court decided that the disclosure of illegitimacy indicated the children were living in an unstable moral environment and that they were therefore neglected. The case was reversed on appeal, on the basis that, under Maryland's statute, illegitimacy was only one, but not the sole consideration in determining whether a mother is unsuitable. But in a 1967 Connecticut case,[23] the conviction of a welfare mother for "lascivious carriage" was upheld on appeal. Here, too, the information that the mother was having an illicit relationship was originally given to the state by the welfare authorities.

Of course there also have been cases where welfare workers have tried very hard to help recipients, and even some where they have lost their jobs in the attempt. In a 1967 California case,[24] a social worker was discharged for refusing to participate in early-morning mass raids deliberately staged by the welfare department. The worker sued for reinstatement and won on the ground that "governmental welfare agencies ferreting out fraud must be cognizant of the recipient's constitutional rights. . . ." But most workers have neither the economic ability nor the personal fortitude to take such steps. There is evidence that many welfare workers really care about the people they deal with. However, the welfare system seems to demonstrate that it is the structure of an institution, its policy, its rules and regulations, and its internal organization and not the quality or the wishes of its personnel that determine how it operates.

The immense and costly administrative machinery of the welfare system does offer a number of auxiliary services, such as helping recipients utilize community, state, and federal health-care programs, child-protective services and foster-home placement, and in some counties family planning, daycare placement, and personal counseling. However, the bulk of its activity is concentrated on determining qualifications, policing continuing eligibility, and working out the excruciatingly complex formulas according to which benefit payments are computed.

A mother's AFDC payments are supposed to be a function of the family's income after certain allowable deductions, considering "actual and reasonable needs," and a "minimum basic standard of adequate care." However, the courts have consistently upheld the state and local regulations that in practice override any statutory ideals of need and care,[25] and welfare benefits continue to be computed according to such convoluted formulas that one must be an expert in both welfare regulations and mathematics to figure them out.

Despite all of these problems, it was not until the 1960s that any real public attention was given to the welfare mother's Kafkaesque world. During that decade many former members of the middle class found themselves on public assistance. They were not used to being required to report to social workers the intimate details of their lives, or to endure raids where beds were checked to see if there was a man in the house. It was probably their increased numbers, as well as the raised consciousness of minorities and the other traditionally poor during that same period, that gave impetus to the national rise of welfare-rights organizations. These groups, founded and organized by AFDC recipients or "welfare ladies" as they asked to be called, were primarily concerned with helping welfare mothers make sure they were actually getting the benefits authorized by law. Law students, recipients, and other volunteers were trained in the intricacies of the welfare regulations so they could catch errors in the allotment of benefits, and find local or state policies which were contrary to the federal rules. There ensued a number of lawsuits challenging the constitutionality of many common welfare practices, including the midnight bed-checks, which were declared unconstitutional searches without warrants in a number of states, including California and New York.[26] At first, these actions met with some success. But after Mr. Nixon's new appointments to the Supreme Court, here, as on other legal fronts, the tide began to turn.

In 1971, the nine men who have the final say on the laws of our land handed down their decision in a case called *Wyman* v. *James*.[27] Barbara James, a New York woman with a five-year-old son, applied for AFDC in 1967. After the usual preliminaries, which included an investigation of her home, her request was granted.

For two years she and her son received public assistance. In May of 1969 Ms. James received a notice that a caseworker would be visiting her home. She phoned the Department of Social Welfare and told them that she would provide them with any information that was "reasonable and relevant" but that she did not consent to a home investigation. Thereupon her public assistance was terminated.

Ms. James argued that her refusal did not justify AFDC termination since the entering of her home without a warrant was an unconstitutional search of her home within the protection of the Fourth Amendment to the Constitution. The Supreme Court of the United States agreed that "the right of the people to be secure in their persons, houses, papers and effects is basic to our society" but it held against Ms. James.

In the ten-page majority opinion, Justice Blackmun said:

> One who dispenses purely private charity naturally has an interest in and expects to know how his charitable funds are utilized and put to work. The public, when it is the provider, rightly expects the same.
>
> The home visit, it is true, is not required by federal statute or regulation. But it has been noted that the visit is "the heart of welfare administration."
>
> The visit is not one by police or uniformed authority. It is made by a caseworker of some training whose primary objective is, or should be, the welfare, not the prosecution, of the aid recipient for whom the worker has profound responsibility.
>
> It seems to us that the situation is akin to that where an Internal Revenue Service agent, in making a routine civil audit of a taxpayer's income tax return, asks that the taxpayer produce for the agent's review some proof of a deduction the taxpayer has asserted to his benefit in the computation of his tax. If the taxpayer refuses, there is, absent fraud, only a disallowance of the claimed deduction and a consequent additional tax. The taxpayer is fully within his "rights" in refusing to produce the proof, but in maintaining and asserting those rights a tax detriment results, and it is a detriment of the taxpayer's own making. So here Mrs. James has the "right" to refuse the home visit, but a consequence in the form of cessation of aid, similar to the tax-

payer's resultant additional tax, flows from that refusal. The choice is entirely hers, and nothing of constitutional magnitude is involved.[28]

Three judges used rather strong language in disagreeing with the six-man majority. In their joint dissenting opinion, Justices Marshall and Brennan wrote:

> It is argued that the home visit is justified to protect dependent children from "abuse" and "exploitation." These are heinous crimes, but they are not confined to indigent households. Would the majority sanction, in the absence of probable cause, compulsory visits to all American homes for the purpose of discovering child abuse? Or is this Court prepared to hold as a matter of constitutional law that a mother, merely because she is poor, is substantially more likely to injure or exploit her children?
>
> Second, the Court contends that caseworkers must enter the homes of AFDC beneficiaries to determine eligibility. Interestingly, federal regulations do not require the home visit. In fact, the regulations specify the recipient himself as the primary source of eligibility information thereby rendering an inspection of the home only one of several alternative sources.
>
> Despite the caseworker's responsibility for dependent children, he is not even required to see the children as a part of the home visit. Appellants offer scant explanation for their refusal even to attempt to utilize public records, expenditure receipts, documents such as leases, non-home interviews, personal financial records, sworn declarations, etc.—all sources which governmental agencies regularly accept as adequate to establish eligibility for other public benefits.
>
> We are told that the plight of Mrs. James is no different from that of a taxpayer who is required to document his right to a tax deduction, but this analogy is seriously flawed. The record shows that Mrs. James has offered to be interviewed, anywhere other than her home, to answer any questions and to provide any documentation which the welfare agency desires. The agency curtly refused all these offers and insisted on its "right" to pry into appellee's home. Tax exemptions are also governmental "bounty." A true analogy would be an Internal Revenue Service requirement that in order to claim a dependency exemption, a taxpayer *must* allow a specially trained IRS

agent to invade the home for the purpose of questioning the occupants and looking for evidence that the exemption is being properly utilized for the benefit of the dependent. If such a system were even proposed, the cries of constitutional outrage would be unanimous.

Even if the Fourth Amendment does not apply to each and every governmental entry into the home, the welfare visit is not some sort of purely benevolent inspection. No one questions the motives of the dedicated welfare caseworker. Of course, caseworkers seek to be friends, but the point is that they are also required to be sleuths. The majority concedes that the "visitation" is partially investigative, but claims that this investigative aspect has been given "too much emphasis." Emphasis has indeed been given. Time and again, in briefs and at oral argument, appellants emphasized the need to enter AFDC homes to guard against welfare fraud and child abuse, both of which are felonies.

In deciding that the homes of AFDC recipients are not entitled to protection from warrantless searches by welfare caseworkers, the Court declines to follow prior caselaw and employs a rationale that, if applied to the claims of all citizens, would threaten the vitality of the Fourth Amendment. This Court has occasionally pushed beyond established constitutional contours to protect the vulnerable and to further basic human values. I find no little irony in the fact that the burden of today's departure from principled adjudication is placed upon the lowly poor. Perhaps the majority has explained why a commercial warehouse deserves more protection than does this poor woman's home. I am not convinced; and therefore, I must respectfully dissent.[29]

Justice Douglas wrote his own dissent:

We are living in a society where one of the most important forms of property is government largesse which some call the "new property." The payrolls of government are but one aspect of that "new property." Defense contracts, highway contracts, and the other multifarious forms of contracts are another part. So are subsidies to air, rail, and other carriers. So are disbursements by government for scientific research. So are TV and radio licenses to use the air space which of course is part of the public domain. Our concern here is not with those subsidies but with grants that directly or indirectly implicate the home life of the recipients.

In 1969 roughly 126 billion dollars were spent by the federal, state, and local governments on "social welfare." To farmers alone, over four billion dollars was paid, in part for not growing certain crops. Almost 129,000 farmers received $5,000 or more, their total benefit exceeding $1,450,000. Those payments were in some instances very large, a few running a million or more a year. But the majority were payments under $5,000 each.

Yet almost every beneficiary whether rich or poor, rural or urban, has a "house"—one of the places protected by the Fourth Amendment against "unreasonable searches and seizures." The question in this case is whether receipt of largesse from the government makes the home of the beneficiary subject to access by an inspector of the agency of oversight, even though the beneficiary objects to the intrusion and even though the Fourth Amendment's procedure for access to one's house or home is not followed.

The applicable principle, as stated in the case of *Camara vs. Municipal Court*, as "justified by history and by current experience" is that except in certain carefully defined classes of cases, a search of private property without proper consent is "unreasonable unless it has been authorized by a valid search warrant." In *See vs. City of Seattle* this Court added that the "businessman, like the occupant of a residence, has a constitutional right to go about his business free from unreasonable official entries upon his private commercial property." There is not the slightest hint in *See* that the Government could condition a business license on the "consent" of the licensee to the administrative searches we held violated the Fourth Amendment. It is a strange jurisprudence indeed which safeguards the businessman at his place of work from warrantless searches but will not do the same for a mother in her home.

Is a search of her home without a warrant made "reasonable" merely because she is dependent on government largesse?

Welfare has long been considered the equivalent of charity and its recipients have been subjected to all kinds of dehumanizing experiences in the government's effort to police its welfare payments. In fact, over half a billion dollars are expended annually for administration and policing in connection with the

Aid to Families with Dependent Children program. Why such large sums are necessary for administration and policing has never been adequately explained. No such sums are spent policing the government subsidies granted to farmers, airlines, steamship companies, and junk mail dealers, to name but a few. The truth is that in this subsidy area society has simply adopted a double standard, one for aid to business and the farmer and a different one for welfare.[30]

The cost of administering the welfare system is huge, perhaps as high as the total benefits paid out. As Alicia Escalante, a former welfare mother who is now working full-time in the Chicana Welfare Rights Organization, has suggested, it might be cheaper to pay welfare mothers a minimum wage. Giving welfare mothers economic recognition and positive personal identification through their work would also result in another great saving. As Escalante points out, the human cost is never considered in the computations of the cost of welfare:

> It's in terms of the children that the cost of the present system is the highest. It's the human cost—many diseases that occur, the nonfunctioning of the children in the schools. It is not lack of attention or mental retardation. A lot of times those kids go to school without breakfast, and what they're doing now is cutting back on school lunches as well. They're raising the prices on them. And the amount of money that is being allowed on the welfare food budget is totally unrealistic. It's still sixty-five cents per meal. What can you buy with that, especially now?
>
> But people expect the child to have three balanced meals a day and if the child doesn't, they blame the welfare mother. What people don't seem to understand is what it's really like to be a welfare mother. The typical day could be getting up and you're going to send your kids off to school. Breakfast can be a bowl of oatmeal or a cup of coffee and toast. If you're lucky, it's the first week that you got the check so you have food for that week. But still, you limit yourself because you learn very quickly on welfare to cut out the goodies. Meat, fruit, even whole milk, are goodies. You usually try to get yourself to a second-day bakery so you can buy your bread from a couple of days before and that way get it cheaper. If you don't have the transportation,

and most mothers don't, then you're stuck with the neighborhood market that has fantastic prices.

When my children were small, I lived in a housing project, and the market was a good twelve blocks away. To get there we had to start off pretty early. We couldn't get on the bus, because it meant taking all of my children, and if I ended up by paying for all of us I couldn't afford it. For the welfare mother to board a bus, she thinks of the thirty or forty cents per person that she's going to spend, and she decides that she can't because she would rather buy milk for the kids.

And with all that, the welfare mother is the whole head of the family, the sole leader of the family. She manages to survive, to sustain, and to keep going, and this is amazing, and it just makes no sense to say that a woman like that doesn't deserve "government handouts" because she doesn't work or that she should "plan better," because there is just no way.

I have learned the politics of welfare and I know the way it is set up is really to keep people on welfare because our economic system requires a certain percentage of unemployment and a reserve labor force. You have no opportunity, no chance of getting past that. And if you're poor it takes all of your energy just to survive. That's why there's a cycle of poverty. It's something that it takes a really tough woman to fight against, to learn from and to do something about. You feel a lot of defeat. You feel a lot of hopelessness. And besides everything she has to go through, everybody looks down on the welfare mother. Even our own people tend to look down on the welfare mother.

8

Illegitimacy and Birth Control

In March of 1972, the State of California Department of Social Welfare issued a position statement on illegitimacy.[1]

> It is the position of the State Social Welfare Board that appropriate legislation should be enacted so as to amend Section 232 of the California Civil Code to provide that a rebuttable presumption shall arise that a mother is, in fact, morally depraved upon the birth of the third child out of wedlock and the appropriate public agency be directed to commence legal proceedings under Section 232 to terminate the relationship of parent and the third illegitimate child and any subsequent children so conceived so that said child may be placed for adoption.[2]

In leading up to its proposal the State Social Welfare Board pointed out that it was concerned not only with "considerations about the welfare of the children born out of wedlock," but with "the economic impact on the public assistance payments to this group." According to the statistics quoted by the board, in December of 1970 (the last date cited) there were in California 234,623 illegitimate children aided under California's AFDC-FG program, representing 26 percent of the total case load.

Nevertheless the board went on to make it clear that it was

concerned, not only with people on welfare, but with "welfare and non-welfare children alike." "It is evident," they wrote, "that the increase in births out of wedlock is not a phenomenon peculiar to the welfare case load. The little recognized but startling fact is that, according to the United States Public Health Service, illegitimate births in the United States more than doubled between 1950 and 1967."

The board then cited a number of additional statistics such as the rise of illegitimate births for women under nineteen (in 1967 almost as many as for all other age groups combined), and the great acceleration of the illegitimacy rate in the later 1960s (in California, from 25.6 illegitimate births per thousand unmarried women in 1966 to 27.2 in 1967, figures which according to the report were actually "under counts") and the fact that in that same period illegitimate births had risen from 9.4 percent of all live births to 10.4 percent, indicating an overall rate of increase of at least 1 percent per year.

In carrying out its statutory function, the board then proceeded to make a number of additional recommendations as "initial steps" in dealing with the issue of illegitimacy. Among these was the recommendation that mothers age sixteen or younger should be considered as falling within the definition of "incapable of providing support as set forth in Section 232 of the California Civil Code... so that the child born to the unwed minor 16 years or younger may be placed for adoption." Furthermore, in order to reduce the public assistance rolls, the board urged the immediate enactment of legislation requiring the "mandatory establishment of paternity within 6 months of the birth of the child except when the child is relinquished for adoption," and that "the legislation should provide that the mother's failure to cooperate is evidence of her lack of concern for the child's welfare."[3]

Although anthropologists and historians have not directed themselves specifically to the issue, one possible index of the strictness of a particular patriarchy could very well be the degree of punitiveness of its laws about illegitimacy. In some Polynesian Islands, where before the arrival of Western missionaries the position of women seemed to be very similar to that of men, a child was considered the child of the tribe regardless of whether the father was known or not. Even when the father was unknown there were no legal or social sanctions against the mother or her offspring.[4] By contrast, in a strict Moslem patriarchy like Saudi Arabia, a woman who becomes pregnant out of wedlock still can be stoned to death for her crime.[5]

In the Christian West, the treatment of illegitimacy has been more related to social class. In polite society an unwed mother, like other unpleasant phenomena, was placed out of sight, sometimes in a convent where she frequently stayed for the rest of her life. In poorer circles, unwed mothers usually did what they had to. They kept their children and brought them up.

Under English common law, an illegitimate child was one that was not born in "lawful wedlock" or within a "competent time" afterward.[6] Even if the parents later married, a child born out of wedlock could not later be made legitimate. Illegitimate children had no right to inherit property from their parents or from anyone else. Furthermore, according to the older cases, there was no parental duty to support such children, and it was not until 1576 that the first statute was enacted providing that both parents could be charged with the payment of "money weekly for the relief of such child."[7]

Today all American states have laws that require parents to support their children. In the case of illegitimate children, most states offer a woman the legal mechanism of the paternity suit, where she can bring a man to court and try to prove that he is the father of the child. Most of these laws provide that the court can order that the mother and her child and the defendant submit to one or more blood-grouping tests, which while they do not determine if the man is the father, can be used to rule out that possibility.

Of course, even where a woman prevails in such cases, the

most she can hope for is some measure of economic support so that at least she and the child will not have to seek government help. There is no judicial or, for that matter, extrajudicial pressure on fathers to assume any share of the noneconomic responsibilities for their children. Until very recently, even those fathers who wanted to do so had no such legal right. However, in the case of *Stanley* v. *Illinois*[8] the Supreme Court held that a natural father has a right to the custody of his illegitimate children superior to that of the state. The case was brought by a man whose common-law wife had borne him six children before she died. He challenged the right of the welfare authorities to take the children away from him on the basis that while their mother was alive he had been providing them with financial support.

The *Stanley* case has created a national furor in both public and private adoption agencies. Until now, in illegitimacy cases only the consent of the child's mother to adoption has been required by law. The theory was that by not even giving the child his name, the natural father demonstrated that he was unfit, or at least uncaring, so society could move ahead without his involvement in making other provisions for his child. Now, however, the *Stanley* decision has made this issue the subject of heated debate. The result will probably be a rule that a natural father is legally entitled to at least notice of a proposed adoption, so he can avail himself of the opportunity, if he chooses, to assume responsibility for his child.

Most contemporary laws dealing with illegitimacy discriminate, not so much against the parents, but against the children themselves. For example, in some states, even in those cases where paternity is judicially established and, further, even where paternity is established voluntarily, illegitimate children do not have the same inheritance rights as legitimate ones. Here again there are recent cases that would seem to indicate that these laws may be on their way out. In 1968, in *Levy* v. *Louisiana*[9] the Supreme Court held that to deny illegitimate children the right to recover damages for their mother's death, where legitimate children have such a right, violates the equal-protection clause of the Fourteenth Amendment, and in a related decision, the Court overturned a Texas case that had held a mother could not collect damages in the wrongful death of her illegitimate son.

But the case that will probably have the greatest impact on illegitimacy was handed down in 1973, when in a seventy-nine-page opinion the Supreme Court held that, at least in the first three months of pregnancy, the decision to have an abortion was a matter between a woman and her physician.[10] The implementation of this decision has since been watered down in a number of local courts and has also spurred a massive counterattack by the Catholic church and other antiabortion forces. Nevertheless, it represents a radical turning point in our laws. Until 1973 most American states either severely restricted or completely outlawed abortion. At least until the recent public consciousness about overpopulation, most men took little or no moral or practical responsibility for the prevention of births. The unmarried pregnant woman who did not use birth control or whose birth control failed had three choices: she could get married (according to the National Center for Health Statistics one out of every three brides is pregnant),[11] take the risk of death or maiming through illegal abortion, or bear an illegitimate child. For almost 150 years, from the pulpit and the government, from scientists, writers, and the media, women have been told that abortion is a heinous crime, akin to murder. But in fact, as Professor Cyril Means[12] pointed out in his report to New York's Governor Rockefeller in 1968, under early American common law women had the right to abortion at every stage of gestation. Even when, in 1830, the first American abortion laws were passed, it was not to protect the fetus but to protect pregnant women from the danger of a surgical procedure which at that time had a death rate ten to fifteen times greater than childbirth at full term. With Lister's introduction of antiseptic techniques in 1867, patient mortality in both childbirth and abortion dropped sharply. Today, according to the most recent figures available, deaths due to physician-performed legal abortion in the first twenty-four weeks of pregnancy are 88 percent lower than deaths from childbirth.

Nevertheless, until now the official message to women has been that abortion is illegal and immoral. To married women, who, according to researchers, constitute over half of the women who seek to terminate pregnancies, this message also included the rationale that, since children are necessary for the continuation of society, women must not place their individual desires above the common good.

Today "responsible" men are still telling women what they must do. As Professor Garrett Hardin put it in an editorial for *Science*, it is still necessary, in fact imperative, that women place "community needs" over "individual goals."[13] However, his message is that women must now be required to stop having children in order to reduce the burgeoning birth rate. While he concedes that persuasion should be tried first, he goes on to say that "in the long run a purely voluntary system selects for its own failure."

"It should be easy to limit a woman's reproduction by sterilizing her at the birth of her n'th child," editorialized Dr. Hardin in the professional journal published by the American Association for the Advancement of Science. "Is this a shocking idea? If so, try this 'thought-experiment': let $n = 20$. Since this is not shocking, let n diminish until population control is achievable."[14]

Unlike Dr. Hardin, as Mary Petronowich, Director of the Los Angeles Women's Clinic pointed out, there are still those who find the idea of compulsory sterilization of women shocking, regardless of the value assigned to n, and who see other alternatives to the problems of population control. Petronowich suggests that if Hardin were a woman he would know how preposterous his premise that "in every nation women want more children than the community needs" really is.[15]

It is men, not women, who passed and enforced the laws against birth control. It is men, like the Catholic pope, who have decreed breeding a religious duty. It is men who have told women that their highest mission and noblest destiny is to be mothers. It is men who control both government and science and who have denied women effective birth control. And it is men who write, as does Dr. Hardin, that "the Women's Liberation Movement may not like it, but control must be exerted through females."[16]

If it were true that this control is necessary because "in every nation women want more children than the community needs," why is it that every year thousands and thousands of women have maimed and killed themselves in desperate efforts to achieve abortions which the men in control have made unlawful? Why is it that it was not men but women like Margaret Sanger who led the crusade for the development of birth control and wrote impassioned pleas for the right of women to control their own bodies and gave massive financial and organizational support to the post–World War II research in hormonal anovulants? And why is it that free elective abortions and unhampered access to birth control have been two of the major demands of the women's liberation movement? And why is it that even today, when "more responsible men" would no longer force us to carry out our duty to breed but would just as forcibly require us not to breed, that men like Governor Reagan still veto legislation that would make birth control available to girls under sixteen?

In a recent study by the Princeton Office of Population, researchers found that one-third to one-half of the population growth in recent years was probably the result of unwanted births. Considering how socially unacceptable it still is for people to admit that their children were unwanted, these figures are probably very conservative.[17] Nevertheless, between 1830 and 1970 women in this country reduced their average number of births from six to three. Since during most of those years, not only abortion, but any form of birth control was a crime in our country, what this means is that since the beginning of feminist legal and educational reform, massive numbers of women have defied and disobeyed our laws and our official population policy. According to Petronowich, it is Catholic Latin America with its strict laws and mores against birth control that has the highest infanticide and maternal mortality rate from self-induced abortion. "And in this country," she writes, "the wide acceptance and continued use of the pill, even though there are many side effects, known and unknown, demonstrates how strong the desire of women is to protect themselves from conception."[18]

In his editorial, Dr. Hardin wrote, "Divorce and remarriage play havoc with assigning responsibility for birth control to couples or to men."[19] That men don't really want to be bothered with that problem is clear from another man's comment, which while somewhat cruder, is straight to the point. "Nobody," he said when someone suggested the development of chemical contraception for men, "is going to mess around with my sperm."

But at the same time that men will not accept responsibility, they also refuse to give up control. Even when the Supreme Court officially turned around our population policy, it did not leave the decision to the woman alone, but to her and her doctor, and of course, her doctor is almost always a man.

The professionals of medicine and of law and of science and politics are today as before mostly men, and their premise is that women do not know what is good for them. In the past, the men who controlled medicine and science were reluctant to develop new techniques for birth control, and even when these were finally known and available, they still refused to help their patients with them. They did this on the grounds of social policy and to protect the lives of unborn children. In the same way, in the future, these men could refuse to develop new vaccines or deny access to already developed vaccines to certain segments of the population, also on the grounds of population control and social policy and to protect the lives of unborn children from death by slow starvation or some other ecological catastrophe.

The unwillingness of the men in power to let women determine what happens to their own bodies is part of what Kate Millett has called sexual politics, wherein men preserve their power by controlling women. That control is exercised in every sphere of life. Most critically, it is exercised through male control of technology, not only the technologies of production and destruction, but also of reproduction, and through dominance of the major instruments of social control—police, army, law and culture. The laws and myths that were once used to forbid birth control, like those that may in the future be used to forbid birth, the whole complex of laws and myths about marriage and divorce and legitimacy and illegitimacy, are all part and parcel of a social system called patriarchy, wherein, as Dr. Hardin and the California Social Welfare Board both recognized, all the important decisions about women and their children are to be made by men.

III

ALTERNATIVES AND THE FUTURE OF WOMEN

9

Social Inventions and the Status Quo

When science-fiction writers describe the world of the future—a world of interplanetary travel, life on other planets, and astonishing technological inventions—it is usually still a world where the traditional patriarchal notions of heroic male dominance and seductive female dependency prevail. These notions seem to have become so deeply rooted in our collective unconscious that most of us treat them as inalienable and unalterable truths. There is further reason for such a limited vision of the future: we have become so accustomed to the status quo that we take for granted a society, indeed a world, that is rich in technological inventions and almost bereft of social ones.

Dr. D. Stuart Conger has defined social inventions as new laws, organizations, or procedures that change the way people relate to themselves or to each other, either individually or in groups.[1] Schools, jails, and churches, jury trials, strikes, and laws against cruelty to children are all examples which fit Dr. Conger's definition.

Social inventions are not abstract ideas, ideals, or goals. They are concrete means for dealing with human needs and social priorities. Their form varies from place to place and from time to time and their creation alone does not bring about social change. However, it is characteristic of social inventions that they tend to alter a society substantially once they are adopted. After a social invention has become part of the laws, institutions, or procedures of the society, it tends to become so ingrained in the thinking habits and reality perceptions of the members of that society that it becomes invisible. It is as though, once it has taken hold, it is no longer thought of as a human creation or invention, but as part of human nature, either divinely or instinctively ordained. By the same token, once adopted, these laws, procedures, and institutions and the people who run them are extremely resistant to the introduction of any new social inventions that might displace or replace them.

One of the earliest known social inventions is the institution we call the city. According to most historians it was invented around 3700 B.C., in the Fertile Crescent of Asia Minor. It is still with us. A later European institution known as feudalism was developed in the Middle Ages and has since disappeared from our Western world along with other social inventions once considered essential for the preservation of orderly society such as slavery, trial by immersion, and public execution.

As Dr. Conger points out, most social inventions in use today are ancient. While some are still functional, most are not. Yet largely because we continue to ignore the fact that our institutions, laws, and social procedures are simply inventions that can and should be improved, and replaced as necessary, we fail to develop or accept new and better alternatives.

In the last one hundred years, despite enormous technological advances, the number of social inventions adopted in our society have been extremely few, and when compared with the accelerated rate of technological inventions, infinitesimal. For example, it is clear that the virtual monopoly on child-rearing once held by the church, the school, and the family is breaking up. While this phenomenon is subtle and not always measurable, the staggering statistic that the American family spends over seven hours per day in front of the television set[2] is concrete evidence that in this country the corporately controlled media have already begun to move into the vacuum with a highly impersonal form of socialization. The dangers of this kind of socialization have been graphically portrayed in a new genre of literary and scientific work like Orwell's *Nineteen Eighty-Four*[3] and Ellul's *Technological Society*,[4] but the fact is that unless alternatives are found, the existing vacuum will ultimately be filled by the institutions now in ascendancy or control.

While the specter of direct governmental control of our families is for most of us still only a subject for intellectual debate, for the millions of families now dependent on the government for economic survival, it is an immediate reality. Ironically, some of the most gallant supporters of the traditional concepts of womanhood and motherhood, and indeed, those who most often staunchly advocate the American principles of independence, liberty, and freedom from governmental control, seem to be the least concerned about the ever-increasing encroachment of our state and federal agencies into the lives of those who depend on welfare. One reason is that many of these people subscribe to the tenets of a Puritan ethic that views poverty as something to be frowned upon and punished. But it is also possible that there is another fundamental reason for this apparent paradox in attitudes: most of the burgeoning population on welfare rolls are "only" women and children.

As our old world breaks up, as we continue to shift from industrial to postindustrial society with all of the attendant economic and social dislocations, as no-fault divorce makes marriage disposable, as the population crisis increases, and as test-tube babies and laboratory developed life may ultimately make the female uterus replaceable, there is little question that the entire role and function of women must undergo a radical change. That this has already begun is evident if we examine the contemporary family.

Marriages are being terminated by divorce with such numerical frequency that, from a social standpoint, it can be said the phenomenon is not just quantitative, but qualitative. Since the turn of this century, the divorce rate in this country has increased by 700 percent. It doubled in the decade between 1964 and 1974, and according to the latest National Center for Health Statistics figures, it is still increasing steadily. In 1975 it was 4.3 percent higher than in 1974[5] and the combined number of divorces for January and February of 1976 was 6 percent above the number reported for the same months in 1975.[6]

Millions of divorced, widowed, separated, and single women are no longer dependent on men for support in nuclear patriarchal families. However, in terms of patriarchal models and modes, not much has changed. The women who earn their livelihood outside their homes work primarily for male bosses, who pay their wages and tell them what to do. As we have seen, the basic situation of the woman who has to seek public assistance is also not very different from that of the traditional housewife. She is still dependent and, as the Supreme Court stated in *Wyman* v. *James*, she does not have a right to support either for herself or for her children. Whatever she receives is a privilege she has to deserve. In order to be granted this "privilege" of support, she has to depend on the good will or largesse of the person or group dispensing it, and she knows that privileges can easily be withheld or taken away. Since the new social inventions of sequential marriage, no-fault divorce, and welfare are still patriarchal, the vast majority of American women—whether they are married or on public assistance—are still dependent for their survival on the good will or largesse of men.

In the last few years, more and more women have begun to realize, or at least suspect, the real nature of their position. Yet, after their initial shock, anger, and bewilderment, many cling even more desperately, indeed frantically, to the past. Capitalizing on women's fears, entrepreneurs like Helen Andelin, author of *Fascinating Womanhood*, have advised them that if they want to keep their marriages, they will have to understand that "nothing gives him [man] a more enjoyable sense of power than does his supremacy," and that the only prescription for marital bliss is that "the husband's word should be law."[7]

But history, like time, will not stand still and the historical moment for the nuclear patriarchal family has already come and gone. Throughout history there have been many kinds of families.[8] The Western word *family* is derived from the Latin *familia*, a unit that originally included a male Roman's children, wife, and slaves. The modern nuclear family of mother, father, and children is basically a product of urbanization and industrialization and is only a recent arrival on the scene. Historically and cross-culturally, it is the larger or extended family that prevails.

The only bond which universally appears in each of these forms of the family is that between the infant and its nurturing adults.[9] More often than not—both historically and cross-culturally—that bond has been between the infant and a number of older members of the society, who share the responsibilities of feeding, protecting, and caring for the child. Historically, family forms are largely determined by the economic needs of the type of society within which the family exists. The extended family met the economic needs of agrarian society by producing food and clothing, pots and pans, beds and houses, and just about everything else that its members needed for survival. As industrial society developed, with its concomitant requirements for a more mobile work force, the smaller more isolated nuclear family became economically more functional and the only thing it produced was children. In the society of the future the family will inevitably take still other forms. Some of these alternative arrangements have already begun to emerge in the first stages of postindustrial society—companionate pairing marriages for those without children, communes, and intentionally extended families, where the responsibility for rearing children is taken on, not just by the biological mother and father, but by a number of related or nonrelated adults.

Sequential marriage, the ability to divorce and remarry ad infinitum, represented the first step in the revolution of the family which we are now witnessing. The incorporation of this social invention into our legal system led eventually to the radical change in family law we now know as no-fault divorce. For the divorced woman with small children or the older unemployed housewife, the introduction of sequential marriage has created a severe economic crisis. At a time when women earn approximately half as much as men in the labor market and support awards are being cut back radically, these women face severe competition in the remarriage market. Generally, the competition for successful men comes from younger women who still believe that marriage is the most secure and lucrative career for an ambitious female. It is that economic reality—not just ignorance and a continued social channeling of girls into conventional roles—which also probably accounts for the findings of a 1971 survey of teenagers conducted by the California Advisory Commission on the Status of Women. The survey showed that the vast majority of California girls were still planning to make marriage their life's career.[10]

Yet despite the very real economic incentive to marry, more and more women are opting not to remarry, or not to marry at all. A recent Los Angeles television special polled several hundred divorced people at random.[11] When asked whether they wanted to remarry, almost twice as many women (18 percent) as men (11 percent) said no; to the question, "If you had to do it over again would you have tried harder to save your marriage?" more men (19 percent) than women (15 percent) said yes, but the vast majority of both sexes—82 percent of the women and 79 percent of the men—said no. Despite social attitudes and prejudices that still view divorce as a tragedy, the overwhelming majority of those polled said they and their children were better off and happier since divorce.[12]

Today we are witnessing experiments with alternative family

forms on a scale unprecedented in recorded history. The intentionally extended family, communes, collectives, and single-mother households all provide children with world views and models of life not dominated and controlled by all-powerful father figures. In addition, open-structure schools, encounter groups, radical and other group therapies, and hundreds of community-based self-help groups from Parents Anonymous to MOMMA and Re-Evaluation Co-Counseling offer alternative models of behavior. They show people how to relate to one another and themselves in ways not based on dependence and reliance upon traditional patriarchal control.

It is still far from certain that these new social inventions will replace our older institutions or that, if they do, they will not be so altered in the process that, in the end, only appearances will have changed—the old forms will remain. This possibility is a familiar historical phenomenon, one that sociologists have labeled "co-option." It is a complex process whereby a limited number of dissident ideas and individuals are permitted into a society's power structure and themselves become instruments for perpetuating the status quo. During the cultural upheavals of the sixties and early seventies, women made significant strides toward awakening their own consciousness, and, to some extent, that of others, to the sexism of our society, so that more women obtained entry into the male establishment. But as we have seen, socially and economically, women are still very much the second-class sex.

Since we have all been socialized in a patriarchal culture, we have all, in varying degrees, learned to see ourselves and others in its terms. Even our fantasies and our dreams are molded by patriarchal values and goals, and the only family that is sanctioned—be it extended, nuclear, or sequential—is one in which the male is the strong and dominant figure and the woman and children are his dependents.

When, in the forties, French philosopher Simone de Beauvoir

wrote her comprehensive analysis of the historical and contemporary situations of women in Western culture, she called them the "second sex." In that same sense, there is a "second family" system in this country, the "unmarried families" headed by women who are divorced, separated, widowed, or who never married.

According to the U.S. Census, in 1970 approximately one out of every ten American families was headed by a single parent, and in over 85 percent of those families that parent was the mother. Between 1955 and 1973 the number of families in the United States headed by a woman increased by 56 percent—from 4.2 million families in 1955 to 6.6 million in 1973. During the decade from 1960 to 1970, the number of such families increased by about one million. *And during the first three years of the present decade, the number has again increased by another million.*[13] Although these numbers are sizable, statisticians indicate that the real figures may even be higher because census takers often show absent fathers as still heading their families. In addition, census questionnaires and procedures reflect strong social bias against naming females as heads of families. One couple was threatened with federal arrest for giving false information on their census forms because they had listed the wife as head of the household.

Until very recently, this bias against women-headed families has been strongly reflected in our sociological literature, where research on one-parent families has focused almost exclusively on the absence of the father rather than on the remaining parent. These older studies characterize the female-headed family as pathological ("broken," "disorganized," "disintegrated"),[14] and proceed from the assumption that there is a cause-and-effect relationship between father absence and juvenile delinquency or other antisocial childhood behavior. But the results of these studies have been very mixed, and the hypothesis has never been proved. Moreover, a recent survey of father-absence literature has increased doubt about the validity of these older studies, concluding that only a small fraction of them were methodologically and statistically sound.[15]

A major weakness of the absent-father approach lies in its failure to examine the psychological and behavioral implications of the frequent downward economic and social mobility of the mothers and children left behind. Often the families have to move to poorer accommodations in poorer neighborhoods where there is more juvenile delinquency, less personal safety, and less than adequate schools. It is hard to see how these changes could not have severe repercussions.

Another assumption in these earlier studies—that single-parent households are only temporary and will be "normalized" as soon as the mother finds another man—has resulted in what is perhaps their most fundamental weakness, their failure to investigate what factors might lead to the successful establishment and equilibrium of such households.

The fact is that for some divorced women and their children the single-parent family has provided an infinitely more satisfactory way of life than the two-parent family did. For still other single women and men, who are today voluntarily bearing or adopting children on their own, the single-parent family is functioning in a stable and gratifying way. Furthermore, a healthy minority of these families are headed by women who are able to provide their children with a good standard of living—often they are women who have made exceptional personal and career achievements. This is all the more remarkable considering the enormous social and economic pressures they have to contend with.

Since the institution of the family functions as both a social model and a microcosm of the larger society, feminists have always perceived that no real change in the status of women is possible unless the patriarchal family is replaced. But it is precisely because the whole structure of patriarchy rests so heavily on the institution of the family that any challenge to it is perceived as a fundamental threat. The patriarchal family is protected by a formidable alignment of religious dogma, legal sanction, and economic constraints, so that while it receives support from practically every existing social mechanism, alternative family forms are considered "abnormal" and receive no support at all.

For example, the American cultural and social framework has structured housekeeping and child care so that they are to be performed without pay by women; any alternative social arrangements such as daycare centers meet violent opposition despite the fact that today millions of mothers have full-time jobs. In Washington, D.C., the welfare department formerly provided home-making services for single fathers, but permitted mothers to use the same services only if they were mentally incompetent, chronically ill, or physically disabled. Unwed motherhood is still considered by many to be a disgrace. The general social status of single mothers is so low, one recent study found, that even when such women go to hospitals, churches, and guidance clinics to receive the very services ostensibly designed to provide them with help, the aid is frequently "accompanied by actions or comments injurious to their self-esteem."[16] There is ample evidence to support the view that our institutions are designed to discourage "deviant" family forms. Most available housing, for example, provides only for the nuclear family. Few housing developments or apartment complexes have space suitable for daycare centers, and the U.S. Office for Child Development recently refused to fund such a center in a proposed single-parent housing project on the ground that "the mothers might become too dependent on such housing."[17]

The depth of institutional resistance to alternative family forms is clearly and explicitly apparent in our laws. Every conceivable and inconceivable statute, rule, and regulation makes it clear that the only "good family" is the patriarchal one. For example, in almost every American state, work loss due to pregnancy is specifically excluded from both unemployment and disability coverage. Implicit in this is the idea that if a woman is pregnant she has a man who is legally responsible for her care and support.

If she does not, or if the man is too poor or otherwise unable to provide for her, she must seek welfare.

In the tax arena, deductions allowed for child care, although significantly raised in 1971, are still inadequate. Under the new law a maximum deduction of $400 per month is allowed single persons, persons with incapacitated spouses, or working couples who itemize their personal deductions, provided that total income does not exceed $18,000.[18] If it does, the deduction is reduced by fifty cents on the dollar. If total income exceeds $27,600, the deduction is completely eliminated. Under the double standard of our labor market, very few women can make over $27,600. However, since the vast majority of people who need child-care deductions are working mothers (many of them supporting children on their own), the implied message of this law is that even where women can earn such an amount, they shouldn't.

So deep is our system's commitment to supporting and strengthening the patriarchal family structure, that our tax laws penalize those who do not want to enter into a traditional marriage and favor those marriages where one spouse, presumably the husband, brings in all the income. Despite popular misconceptions, a couple with a double-income marriage in which each has good earnings is taxed at a higher rate than single people with the equivalent income. Again, the message to both sexes is that the equal-career marriage is to be discouraged. Under our tax laws, a man is encouraged to marry a woman who will be financially dependent on him, since he will then be eligible for the savings of a joint return. However, if these same two people share the same household without marrying, they will be taxed individually and there will be no allowance made for the fact that one is providing all of the other's support.

Similarly the effect of head-of-household tax rules is to discourage nonrelated people from supporting one another. For a person to qualify as the head of household under the Internal Revenue Code, the individuals to whom support is provided must be children or "dependent relatives."[19] A member of a commune, collective, or intentional extended family who provides more than 50 percent of the other members' support is thus denied the savings of the lower tax rate.

Common-law marriages are not recognized in the vast majority of American states. While a lot of people are now more willing to accept this type of union, American laws have steadily become less permissive. Although the Uniform Marriage and Divorce Act would allow those few states where common-law marriages are still recognized the option of continuing that policy,[20] the American Bar Association voted against that provision and unanimously recommended that common-law marriage be abolished.[21] Nevertheless, in the past decade more and more young women have chosen cohabitation over marriage. What these women may not realize is that when these relationships break down, they will have no legal protection in the vast majority of states. They will have no property rights, nor will they be entitled to support. Their children will be illegitimate, and their only legal avenue for obtaining child support will be to file paternity proceedings.

These women could try to protect themselves by entering into written partnership agreements with the men with whom they live. They run the risk, however, that such agreements will not stand up in court, on the basis that they violate "public policy."

Traditionally our courts have also invoked "public policy" to strike down prenuptial agreements which explicitly provide for the contingency of divorce, on the ground that "an agreement in contemplation of divorce" is against the public policy in support of marriage. In many cases this has helped women who had inadvertently contracted away marital property rights—those, for example, in community-property states who agreed that all of the husband's earnings and acquisitions after the marriage should still be considered his separate property and go to him in the event of a divorce. However, the public-policy rationale has also been a judicial device to limit private agreements and to force compliance with existing marriage and divorce laws. Today most of the new egalitarian marriage contracts entered into specifically to skirt laws that discriminate against women could be struck down on the same basis.

A related public policy that also perpetuates male dominance in the family is overtly expressed by police officers when they refuse to protect women from beatings by their husbands, former husbands, and even boyfriends, on the basis that they "can't interfere in family affairs." Such open and systematic bias on the part of law-enforcement personnel is not unusual and is practiced by many public agencies. Local school systems that fail to meet federal requirements in making lunches available to children at school on the ground that "it's the mother's job" are another obvious example.

Indeed, to a very large degree, it is not only the presence of certain laws but the conspicuous absence of certain others that serves to perpetuate existing sexual stereotypes and roles, both inside marriage and out. Inadequate child-care legislation is a case in point. The absence of rules in our public school system prohibiting the portrayal of the "intact" patriarchal family as the only acceptable form serves a similar purpose. So, too, do the absence of laws providing a minimum wage for housework, the denial of homeowner's insurance to single women because "there won't be a man to mow the lawn or do odd jobs," and the continued existence of public and private retirement, pension, and disability plans which provide the wife with only reduced and derivative benefits.

Legal changes are obviously necessary and horrendously overdue in the areas outlined above. Unfortunately, however, replacing discriminatory laws with fair, nonsexist ones will not in itself guarantee a resolution of the problems of which such laws are mere indicators. To be successful, legal changes must correspond and interact with the technological, natural, social, and personal contexts within which they operate.

In the physical and biological sciences it has long been understood that form or structure is a determinant of function. There is increasing evidence from the social sciences that this same principle applies to the relationship between human behavior (function) and social organizations (form). When seen in that context, it becomes apparent that the basic issue is not one of women against men. The goal of feminism cannot be a bigger slice of the existing social pie for women or a reversal of roles so that men rather than women become the second-class sex. Both sexes lose in a system of social organization based on power-centered, hierarchical relationships designed to perpetuate mistrust and fear. We see the effects of this type of social structure not only in the tension that exists today between women and men, but in any antihuman social invention (such as war) that involves the exercise of power for its own sake. It appears that nothing short of a radical overhaul of our entire social and cultural structure will provide any real relief, and that what is required, for both women and men, is a different system of values along with technological and social inventions required to bring it alive.

The institutional odds look pretty grim, and yet every day more women—and men—are beginning to realize that the old patriarchal values and patterns of behavior are no longer socially functional, and that, on a more personal level, they never were. Today millions of people are questioning and challenging these values and the social inventions that affect and perpetuate them, not only in courts, institutions of learning, and churches, but in the way they are living their daily lives. Some social observers have called this a new type of revolution, a revolution of lifestyles and of human consciousness, and it may well be the greatest hope we have of actually breaking through the seemingly impenetrable patriarchal barriers. I, too, share this hope, because I believe that the basic agent for institutional, legal, technological, and even natural change is always the individual, and that in that sense, all change, and indeed all revolution does begin at home.

10

Three Case Histories:

A Single Mother: Gail N.
An Intentional Family: Lisa T.
A Marriage Contract: Jennifer R. and Gregory S.

Social inventions do not just spring up full blown. They are the end product of experimentation, trial and error, and probably as much failure as success. Usually they are developed not by the well-adjusted, content, conventional members of society, but by the rebels, the dreamers, and the malcontents. Therefore, if it is indeed fact and not patriarchal fiction that women today are less satisfied (not just more vocal) than they have previously been, it can be assumed that women will now take an even more active role in bringing about social change.

Throughout history every powerless group has been kept powerless by a social ideology that has been intricately woven into the institutions of the prevalent social structure. Such was the case with serfs under feudalism, and blacks in the preindustrial South. Not only has the larger society traditionally accepted the lower status of these people as inevitable, but with the exception of the "troublemakers," so have the powerless groups themselves. It is not surprising, therefore, that women in patriarchal societies have always been forced to live out their lives confined to roles which they themselves have not determined. Nor is it surprising, although remarkable, that there have always been women who fought against the myths and institutions which conspire to keep them powerless. Today all over the world there are millions of women who, in one way or another, are striking out on their own. They may not be liberated, because that presupposes a world of free and open alternatives, but in their internal retooling, in their new consciousness, and above all, in their new patterns of behavior, these women are trying to create new choices, new social inventions, new models for nonpatriarchal institutions, and with that, new social and personal realities.

We have all met some of these women, as well as men with the same aspirations. Some live in communes or what they call intentional families. Others, in or out of wedlock, have chosen one-to-one relationships, but instead of striking up the bargain traditionally implicit in such a relationship, they have made their own personal contracts. Still others have simply gone their own ways, either out of a sense of rebellion or with an intuitive recognition that the well-trodden roads are not for them.

A Single Mother: Gail N.

One such person is a thirty-two-year-old woman I shall call Gail N. Here is what she has to say:

> When I was fifteen I was absolutely positive I was going to get married immediately after high school. I guess I didn't when I saw what happened to my sister. She got married when she was barely seventeen and right away they had a baby and I saw her change from a very sparkling, whistle-clean, happy, high-school girl to somebody with straggly hair washing diapers with pins in her mouth and cooking dinner constantly.

There was a lot of pressure on me to get married over the years. My great-aunt Thordis, who was also my legal guardian when my parents died, used to send me Christmas cards and say "Merry Christmas, Happy New Year, and I hope this year you catch yourself a good man."

But I just couldn't tolerate any of the men I had known for any length of time because they'd play power trips on me, expected me to do things I thought they were able to do as well as I, like emptying the trash or doing the dishes or cooking dinner, things like that, things that women are complaining about these days. I lived with a man for eight months. It never would have occurred to him to vacuum the rug. Or pick up his own clothes for that matter. Or take them to the laundry or anything else. What did he do before I got there? I don't understand it. Most men I know are like that. They put you in a slot and there you stay or it confuses them. And when they are confused they get angry. Their anger is also something that startles me and I am afraid of because they are so strong and can be so violent and so nasty. Being an independent person, I knew that these drills that men run you through was something I could never tolerate.

So at twenty-seven when I found that I was pregnant, I thought I want this child and I'm going to have it. I considered moving. Then I thought I'm already pregnant, and I'm going to need the job I have. It's very difficult to find jobs.

When I was about seven months pregnant and really showed it I told my bosses. I worked for eight men and I got eight different pieces of advice from them and eight different pieces of advice from their wives. Have it and adopt it. Have it and keep it. Don't have it. Have an abortion. They went from periods of being so nice to me and so charming, sending gifts and being concerned about my health, to going "you're mad, you're out of your mind, what are you doing?"

One day one of my bosses called in three lawyers from a very large law firm in downtown Los Angeles that we work with in our brokerage business. They were in the conference room and he called me in. I thought they wanted me to take something in shorthand. I took my little pad in and sat down and he goes, "Gail, I've been discussing your situation"—they always referred to it as "my situation"—"and these gentlemen here would like to talk to you and maybe we can think about some way that we can get that rascal." I just sat there dumbfounded. They were all lined up on the other side of the table, asking me questions, most of which I would not answer, like his name or where he worked or where he lived. I was so upset I started to cry. I just sat there. I didn't believe this was happening. They were big lawyer-types, you know, and I didn't want to do anything to upset them after they had been brought over especially to consult with me on this thing. I didn't want to offend them, and yet I thought they were being terribly offensive to me.

About two weeks before Lisa was born I finally told my Aunt Thordis. Her daughter lived near me and she was visiting her. They were out for dinner and I left a note on the door and I said, "When you come home, come up to the house, I want to tell you something." When they got home they came rushing up to my apartment and they were all excited and said "You're getting married, you're getting married." And I said "No, I'm pregnant."

I quit work on a Thursday and Lisa was born the next Thursday and I went back to work three weeks later. I've worked ever since. In the first six months of her life I didn't think I would live. I just didn't think I was going to survive with no sleep, getting up twice a night to feed her and also going from a very active life to a life that just consisted of getting up, getting dressed, going to work, fixing dinner, watching TV, and going to bed, because I had no money for babysitters. That went on for about three years. But the first six months were the hardest.

I didn't know it at the time, but I think I had a fantasy about having my own baby all by myself. We'd have one of those houses like you see on TV, with aprons and cookies baking and I'd be teaching her how to read and doing fun things with her like going to the zoo. Actually I hate going to the zoo. I hate going to Disneyland. I hate doing all that sort of stuff. If I had my way we'd go to a library for the rest of our lives. I don't know. I guess my fantasy was about all the things I had never lived with before. She was going to be a very bright child, maybe President one day. One of those. Oh dear. We would be terribly happy together and we would both have somebody to love. Somebody that's there that you can touch.

It didn't work out quite that way. That doesn't sound very good does it? It did work out that way, partly. We certainly do love each other. But you have to learn parenting just like you have to learn anything else. Everybody goes into parenting with very specific ideas of how their children are going to be raised. Mine was you teach them obedience. You will do what I say when I say it and how I say it. My mother was very much like that—and I am trying to change from that now—very take-charge and no argument at all. You just by God did it. And I did. But Lisa didn't, and she and I are still working through that. We've had a really strange couple of years. I guess it started when Lisa hit about four and started getting big enough and strong enough and verbal enough to really argue with me. I had it pretty much my own way before then and didn't realize that something was very wrong.

I did a little reading and at that time I happened to fall into MOMMA* and learned about the parent reeducation courses, about nonauthoritarian child raising. Which is very difficult for me. I'm still not doing as well as I might. Nor is Lisa for that matter. But we are both trying and I know that that's going to work out okay.

The best part of my day is crawling in bed with Lisa or if she comes in and crawls in with me. We have tickles or talk about funny things to wear that day or not wear and make up a song or something.

I'm also working on making Lisa more independent. I'm teaching her how to scramble eggs and things like that. I hate getting dragged out of bed in the morning to cook her breakfast. And she likes to do it. She really likes to do things for herself.

All these neat things I found out through MOMMA. When Lisa was almost four we moved to the west side and I happened to read in the paper the announcement of the first meeting of MOMMA. I thought I could meet some new friends because I didn't know anybody over here, so I went to a meeting. Somehow I ended up taking notes and I signed up on a couple of committees. The next thing I knew I was heavily involved in their newspaper and I did the bookkeeping for it and the typing. Now I'm involved in the national board. There are seven chapters of MOMMA by now, L.A., Valley, San Gabriel, Long Beach,

---

* MOMMA is an organization started in 1972 by and for mothers who are divorced, separated, widowed, or never married. It is based on the concept that single motherhood is more than just a stage between marriages which encourages a philosophy of self-help.

New York, Monterey Park, and one other. I have sitting on my desk requests from maybe three hundred women for instructions on how to start a local chapter.

I have made some very good friends in MOMMA. In fact most of the people I see now are involved in it. It helps to talk about things with other single mothers. One thing we all have in common is that our children don't have anybody else to go to. I suppose you could say it's also an advantage, when there's conflict between the parents and a lot of contradictions. Like if you say to the child, "No, you can't go outside and run in the sprinkler because it's sixty degrees outside and it's going to rain any minute," and she runs and asks Daddy and he says okay and she does it. At least you don't have that number.

Most of the women in MOMMA are divorced, but since I joined I have met about twenty other single mothers like me, who never got married. Most of our children are in the same age range, maybe three to six years old. It must have been a trend after 1967 or something. Maybe it was un-American before, to think of doing it all alone. I don't know. We of course are different in many ways but I think we all have something in common, in that we are all independent. I think you've really got to be a fighter in this world or you can't even consider doing a thing like that. In fact, even a lot more than I thought.

Like when you apply for a job. You can lie and not put down that you are single with a child or get grilled on that. But I think women in general have problems with jobs if they have children, whether they have been married or not. Even if you don't have children, but you're married, you have immediate plans to get pregnant, right, so you're a bad risk. And if you do have children, you are going to be out a lot when they are sick and therefore they can't hire you. And that goes in spades for a single mother. It's too bad they don't realize that probably the best workers in the world are single mothers just because we have to be, especially when we are the sole support of our children.

We all also have problems with men. There's no place to go in this world today for a single mother other than a bar or things like Parents Without Partners or Young Republicans or something like that, God help us, and certain types tend to gravitate to those places. Certainly not men who want to relate to children.

Most men who date women with children tend to deal through you to tell your kid not to make so much noise, I can't hear the football game. When she's sitting right next to him. I finally learned to tell them *you* tell her, you deal with her if you don't like something she does. They don't like it, most of the men. Very few of them that I've found are willing to stick around for these things. And they'll probably be that sort of father too.

About a half a year ago something came up that I guess I should have foreseen. Lisa began talking a great deal about her father. She knows nothing about him, not even his name, and she has never met him obviously. But when she'd get angry with me, she'd cry and say, "I want my daddy" and that just infuriated me. He has given her nothing, never even seen her. The only thing he did give her was her middle name. I realized it was not reasonable for me to be angry, she just had this overwhelming curiosity about her father, which is natural. It was just something that never occurred to me. Then I thought, of course some day she would want to know who her father was.

I found out from his brother where Bob was working and I sent a note. He was working at some country club in La Habra. I sent him a note that said I wanted to talk to him and that, be assured, it didn't have anything to do with money. I knew that if he thought I was going to ask him for money, I wouldn't hear from him.

I never had any illusions about Bob. When I told him that I was going to have the baby, we were sitting in the car in front of the house and he flat out told me if I wanted an abortion or not he didn't have any money. And I said I didn't need any money from him, I had made up my mind I was going to have the baby. And he said it was not likely he would have any money in the future either.

I had known Bob about four years, on and off. We were just friends. He was a bartender at this little place over in Burbank where a couple of my girlfriends and I would go on Friday nights to listen to the guitar player, and we'd sit around and sing.

I remember that night so well. I had gone to have my hair done and stopped by to have a drink. Bob said there was a party on that night and did I want to go and I said sure. So we went to the party which wasn't much fun and somehow we ended up in bed.

He's married now, and in the letter I said, "please tell Jackie that I've been in touch with you because I don't want her to think I'm going behind her back." I told him that I had no intention of disrupting his life or anything. I simply wanted to talk to him.

So he called me at work and we had a talk on the phone and we made arrangements for him to come a week later and we'd all go out to dinner. It was the longest, most agonizing week of my life. I kept saying, should I tell Lisa, should I not tell her. Because he's one of those people who says yes he will do something and of course he never does it. I finally decided in the end not to tell her. Just when he came, I would explain then. And thank God I didn't because he didn't come. He called me. He was supposed to be there at eight for supper. He called me at about a quarter to nine and said that Jackie, his wife, he had shown her my letter and she went into an immediate hysterical fit, and he had left the house and gone to the liquor store down the road to telephone me to say he wasn't coming. I know now that he probably did that as a rescue, because by telling Jackie about it she would get angry and wouldn't let him go.

Lisa doesn't talk about him much anymore, so maybe it was just a phase she was going through. But I worry about it. I've been thinking that one of the women in MOMMA is starting this class called co-parenting, where you have a mediator to talk between a father and mother, about how they can best co-parent their children. And I thought, boy, I would really love to get Bob and Jackie and me together with a mediator one night so that we can somehow make Jackie feel safe and make Bob realize that he has a little responsibility in this too. No money by any means, but certainly to form a relationship with Lisa.

In the olden days when two or three generations lived in the same house together there were other people besides the parents for the children. Like the Waltons on TV. You have the grandparents and the parents and the six children all living together and there's a real sense of family life there.

I've been thinking a lot about that and about the future. Before Lisa was born I really didn't have any direction to my life. But especially in the last couple of years, I've been trying to figure out how I could go back to school, how to get my bills paid off so I could work part-time and go to school part-time. And that hasn't worked because I'm in this cycle that I think a lot of single women are in. They work. They have a disaster. They get a loan to pay the disaster. They get it paid off and another disaster happens. Like yesterday the car, two hundred dollars. I'm making eight hundred dollars a month which I've made for two years without a raise because they've put a freeze on wages because the brokerage business has been so bad. It's a hell of a lot more than a lot of women make but it's still not enough, especially today, not when you have a child.

Last summer Lisa and I went to North Dakota on vacation. My aunt and uncle live there on a farm and we had sort of a semi-family reunion which was a lot of fun. I told my Aunt Jenny that I was not happy in the job I was in, I wanted very much to go to school and just could not find a way out, having to work and support Lisa and me. There's a state college there in town and I asked her if Lisa and I could come and live there for nothing so I could go back to school and she, much to my surprise, said yes, of course. They are in their mid-fifties and all their children are gone and she said they'd be pleased to have us.

We're leaving in December, Lisa and I, to move back there, to live on the farm, and Lisa can go to a country school and I can go to school, at long last. I don't know if I could have done it otherwise. You've got to have that old paycheck coming in. It's so hard to break out of the lifestyle that you're into, living with the stereo and color TV and all this stuff. I'm selling everything and I'm not taking anything with us but our bicycles and clothes. I'm not going to start that all over again. I don't ever want to get locked into all that furniture again, refrigerators and payments and all that, ever again.

Lisa is terribly excited about it. When we were there, when she saw her other little cousins calling what was really her great-aunt grandma, she was a little confused. So she went and had a talk with my aunt and uncle and said that she wanted to have a grandma and grandpa too and they said that's fine. "You can call us Grandma and Grandpa and we will be your grandma and grandpa."

That's the only thing Lisa talks about lately, how she's going to live on the farm and ride a horse to school and have a real grandma and grandpa.

She writes to them. She's just learning to write and I help her with the spelling and all that, but she knows just what she wants to say:

"Dear Grandma and Grandpa, I will bring you a present when we get there. I will be a good girl. What is the new colt's name? Does it look like Stormy? I will give you a big, big hug and I will bring you some seeds. We can plant them together on a hot day. I will water them for you. They will be raspberry trees. They will grow in the spring. I miss you.
Love, Lisa."

The route Gail N. traveled as a single mother is of course unusual. Although her path was fraught with many obstacles—social disapproval, ridicule, and scorn—she, unlike the millions of other single mothers who are divorced, deserted, or widowed, had the advantage of choosing her route.

The percentage of pregnant women who are voluntarily choosing to have their children and raise them on their own has been rising steadily during the last decade. A growing number of women are intentionally becoming pregnant by men they do not plan to marry for the express purpose of creating their own one-parent families. Perhaps the most significant development—since it is the most visible sign of an institutional acceptance of this type of family—is the official sanction of single-parent adoptions in a growing number of American states.

In California this change in adoption policy came about primarily because the number of babies exceeded the number of available two-parent homes. It was therefore decided that where two-parent placement was impossible, single-parent adoption would be allowed. However, the widespread use of effective contraceptives, the legalization of abortion, and the growing unwillingness of unwed mothers to give up their children has resulted in a shortage of adoptable children. According to adoption officials, the waiting period for healthy Caucasian babies is now two to three years; for non-Caucasian infants, who a few years ago could hardly be placed, the waiting period is now eight to ten months. Nevertheless the proportion of single-parent adoptions has continued to increase. As one adoption official explained:

> With the shortage of babies we were able, for the first time, to shift much of our focus to the placement of older children. Where in the past these children were effectively doomed to institutionalized or foster home care, today we are able to place many of them in permanent homes.
>
> We found that frequently for the older child, particularly the child over 6, a single-parent placement is the one with the best chance of success. Most of these older children are under county care because of severe family problems like alcoholism or drugs, or sudden tragedies, and they're often unwanted and neglected children who have been severely traumatized by their natural parents. They're children who've had to learn to maneuver and counter-maneuver and to turn grown-ups against each other just to deflect some of their hostility from falling on them, and in many cases it is almost impossible for them to relate to one or the other sex because a father or mother has been so brutal. So for some of these older children, a two-parent adoption is simply not possible, with the result that in the last few years we have been turning increasingly to our single applicants.[1]

Most of these applicants are women. However, the Department of Adoption is also trying to encourage men, since some children do better with a single father. L.A.'s San Fernando Valley adoptions office has launched a public information drive to encourage single people, as well as older couples who were also formerly considered ineligible, to apply. The result has been that more and more children who would otherwise grow up unwanted and unloved are finally finding homes.

As these developments demonstrate, deviations from the patriarchal family norm can be beneficial, not only to women, but to men, and to society at large. More flexible adoption policies constitute official recognition of the fact that it is the absence of sound childhood familial bonds and *not* the experience of alternative familial structures that is responsible for much of today's personal and social disorganization and violence.

An Intentional Family: Lisa T.

The most publicized contemporary experiments with alternative family structures have involved various forms of communal living. In this country, particularly among the young, an unprecedented number of people are forming intentional communities. Some, like Oregon's Cerro Gordo Community Association, are ecologically oriented and consist of a number of single individuals and households joining together to build their own town. Many are organized around the realization of a pre-formulated political or social goal, like Paolo Soleri's Arcosanti, a project to build a new type of city in the Arizona desert. Others, such as Synanon and Hilltop, include former drug addicts and alcoholics who have found that community living makes it possible for them to lead functional lives.

Some communes are simply a handful of people who have chosen to live together. Others are formally organized. Some are modeled after the Israeli kibbutz and are geared toward economic and social self-sufficiency and an egalitarian social structure. Others are patterned after the religious ashrams of the East and have as their main purpose spiritual development through meditation. There are group marriages, where sex is one of the central bonds, there are gay communities in which a number of homosexual couples live in one household, and there are elderly people living in groups of their own choice as a means of stretching meager pensions or Social Security benefits. In urban and rural locales, people of all classes, ages, and backgrounds are seeking more broadly based alternatives to the nuclear patriarchal family, which either fails to meet their needs, or as the elderly and unmarried young adult have learned, is simply not structured to include them.

Perhaps nowhere is the legal and institutional resistance to alternative familial forms as visible and pronounced as in the official response to communal living arrangements. For example, a few years ago, when the U.S. Department of Agriculture issued its 1971 food-stamp regulations, it added a provision making "unrelated individuals living together" ineligible. Many poor people who lived in crowded housing where they had to share a house or apartment with another person or family found themselves suddenly unable to get stamps. When their problems were brought to the attention of Congress, a group of legislators, including Hubert Humphrey, Henry Jackson, Edward Kennedy, Birch Bayh, Fred Harris, and Edmund Muskie, sent a memo to the U.S. Department of Agriculture:[2]

> The new law changes the definition of household from an economic unit to a group of related individuals. This change was made to specifically exclude so-called "hippie communes" from the program. Unfortunately, the language of the regulations would also exclude other eligible households as well. We, therefore, propose that the regulations clearly state an (eligible) household may not mean a "hippie commune" but that it may include household units related other than by blood or law.[3]

As legal observers immediately pointed out, the classification of "unrelated adults" already raised a number of serious constitutional questions, which the addition of "hippie commune" now made much worse. For example, on what grounds was the official discrimination against "hippies" to be justified? Who was to determine whether a household was a "hippie commune" or not? And did not such a classification lend itself to the most serious abuses in local discretion against individuals who were, for one reason or another, suspected or disliked on account of their appearance or manner of dress?

The "hippie commune" language never found its way into the law, and in 1973 the U.S. Supreme Court affirmed a federal decision in which the exclusion of "unrelated individuals" was held to violate the equal-protection clause of the Fourteenth Amendment.[4] Nevertheless, similar restrictions in zoning laws, excluding unrelated individuals from living in single-family residential neighborhoods, have been upheld, enabling residents to successfully exclude communal-living groups.[5]

In *Palo Alto Tenant's Union* v. *Morgan*, a federal court rejected the plaintiffs' argument that because "they were living together as a family" and "treating themselves and treated by others as a family unit" they were entitled to the same treatment as any other family.[6] The court reasoned as follows:

> The traditional family is an institution reinforced by biological and legal ties which are difficult, or impossible, to sunder. It plays a role in educating and nourishing the young which, far from being "voluntary," is often compulsory. Finally, it has been a means, for uncounted millenia, of satisfying the deepest emotional and physical needs of human beings.
>
> The communal living groups represented by plaintiffs share few of the above characteristics. They are voluntary, with fluctuating memberships who have no legal obligation of support or cohabitation. They are in no way subject to the State's vast body of domestic relations law. They do not have the biological links which characterize most families. Emotional ties between commune members may exist, but this is true of members of many groups. Plaintiffs are unquestionably sincere in seeking to devise and test new life-styles, but the communes they have formed are legally indistinguishable from such traditional living groups as religious communities and residence clubs. The right to form such groups may be constitutionally protected, but the right to insist that these groups live under the same roof, in any part of the city they choose, is not.[7]

The court's reasoning in denying communal groups equal legal protection under the law rests heavily on the distinction between "voluntary" and "involuntary" obligations. Although its conclusion is of doubtful constitutional validity, it is interesting that the court singled out a point that in many ways goes straight to the heart of the matter.

One of the basic weaknesses of patriarchal social organization is precisely that it is based so heavily on involuntary social and personal alternatives. As we have seen, the only legally and socially sanctioned family is the male-headed, procreation-oriented, monogamous, two-parent unit where the husband's duty of support and the wife's duty to render services are reciprocal. Although under certain circumstances men may voluntarily choose to deviate from that ideal without any undue consequences (for instance, by remaining bachelors or "playing around"), voluntary deviations by women are either strictly forbidden and severely punished, or, at the very least, socially condemned. This is not to say that there are not other family forms available to women; indeed, the patriarchal system actually demands that some women be forced to live in them. But as generations of unwed mothers and welfare families know only too well, their essential characteristic is that they are involuntary rather than voluntary alternatives. There are even some communal living arrangements that are sanctioned and required in our patriarchal society, but again, their essential characteristic is that they, too, are involuntary. Jails, mental institutions, juvenile halls, and whorehouses are examples of patriarchal institutions in which society forces together those who do not or cannot conform.

As more and more women and men try to find a way out of the rigidly hierarchical and sexually stereotyped interpersonal relationships characteristic of patriarchal social organization, many have begun to experiment with more cooperative, horizontally organized family structures.

Lisa T., a forty-one-year-old social worker, is one of these people. Here is what she has to say:

> Up until now most women have defined themselves only in terms of their relationship to a man. But it seems clear to me that today single working women, especially mothers and women over thirty-five, are discovering that these illusions aren't as available. And

when you talk about alternatives it is more on a survival level than on an exploratory one. What I would like to do sometime in the future is to create a living situation made up of women like these, who are older, who are working, who know that their possibility of finding the American dream is gone. I can see a group of women moving into a house together, with their children. They fix it up themselves. They don't call somebody. They learn how to fix a leaking roof. They learn how to fix the plumbing. They do it together. That doesn't mean that you don't relate to men, it just means that the basic definition of the source of one's life would be with a group of women and children. I mean, living collectively makes sense. It makes sense economically, it makes sense in terms of sharing responsibilities, it makes sense in terms of sharing your life with other people and to be able to do that still allows you a certain amount of privacy and a certain amount of autonomy in your life. It just seems better than anything else. So that would be what I would project, and it comes out of my own experiences.

Lisa's experiences have already included living in a commune. Before that she was a student, a social worker, and a suburban housewife.

Basically I always worked throughout our marriage. Half the time I was in school or Bill was in school, we both worked and there wasn't any sense of who earned more money. I don't think there was ever that kind of a hangup, that he was the major breadwinner. When we had children I was home for a year, but then I couldn't stand it so I went to work a few hours a day. After the kids were a little bit older I went back to work full-time.

I grew up with a sense of knowing that it was important for a woman to be financially independent. That was just an assumption I had. However, all the other assumptions existed, so that in my marriage, while I went to graduate school and got a master's degree in social work, my husband went and got a Ph.D. in education. Why he got the Ph.D. and I got a master's had a lot to do with being a woman. I even had to justify the master's on the basis that I'd be a better mother if I was working, because I'd be happier. Somehow it was okay for me to have a job, but not okay for me to be the academic person. That was what the man did because his role was obviously more important.

We had what most people considered a hip-liberal-progressive marriage. When we got divorced, people said, "God, we'd never have believed it." It certainly wasn't blatantly oppressive. Like I knew women who would say, "Oh, I can't do that. My husband won't let me." And I'd just think, "What do you mean he won't let you. It's absurd that you would be in a situation where your husband won't let you do something you want to do." In fact, I was the more dominant person in our relationship and where that became oppressive was that to be a woman who worked and to assert myself in the way that I did, I ended up not only being tagged, but internalizing that sense of being an aggressive, competitive bitch. If you're not a nice sweet housewife then you're a . . . and in a way that is as oppressive as being passive because you're always feeling guilty about who you are.

We almost separated after we had been married for two years. We had come to a point where I saw that there was no way I could be who I wanted to and be married to Bill. But we didn't separate then, and for thirteen years it was a matter of well, if we can just get over this one thing, if he gets over this anxiety, or if we get more secure about things, then it will be better. But it was the realization that it wasn't going to happen that finally. . . .

INTERVIEWER: How long ago did you separate?

LISA: Four years ago. We had just bought a large house, a very big house, and I really couldn't afford to stay in that house alone. So I guess, that's how this whole thing really started.

INTERVIEWER: How do you mean?

LISA: It just sort of evolved. My cousin was living there and helping me take care of the kids while she was going to college. And then there was a young guy who was suicidal, I guess, and he was living in a terrible place and he wanted to know if he could rent a room. I decided, well, that would help, so he rented a room. And then the daughter of someone I worked with wanted to live on the beach for a while, so she rented a room, and then a woman who I had known as a student at UCLA was in a transitionary time in her life so she came and rented a room. For about six months the five of us, plus my two children, lived there, until I went to Europe for a couple of months. When I came back only my cousin was living there and I was financially in a bad position. There was a couple I knew from UCLA who wanted to live on the beach. So they rented a room. But at that point, it began to evolve differently. Because, while they moved in initially just to rest for a little while—that was the very hectic year of Kent State and Cambodia and everything—after a while the house moved in a more political direction.

INTERVIEWER: You had been active politically before. . . .

LISA: Not really. I had been politically aware. Then at UCLA I worked closely with students who were very politically active in terms of trying to create new alternatives. They and some other people were talking about a collective to work politically in the community. I was not part of that directly, but what happened was that the house started growing in that direction. Two other people who had those ideas moved in, and the situation in the house changed. Because our concern at that time—our basic sense of how we wanted to live our lives—had to do with change and with the future. The way we related to each other came out of that basic feeling and there was a very immediate commitment to one another and to the children.

Meanwhile, my cousin was still living there and she met a guy and he moved in. So there was a group of people, some of whom belonged to a collective that was just developing and some who didn't.

You know, when you said "voluntary alternatives," I sort of laughed, because I don't know what's voluntary. You just sort of go along with what's happening. But it wasn't conscious for me. I didn't consciously say I am going to collectively do this or that. It developed. And as it developed I became part of it because it seemed the right and natural thing. There were lots of errors made, there were people who moved in who shouldn't have moved in and who moved out because it wasn't the right place to be, but over the past two years, three of us have remained constant. Initially the primary link was me, the fact that there was a physical place, that the house existed and that it had already become a symbol of some kind, and that I and my children existed and that I was someone who was part of UCLA programs that were attracting and generating new ideas, new feelings, and the ability to attempt new things. People who came to live in the house came out of that experience. I knew them enough to know that they would be good people, but I didn't really have strong relationships with any of them.

INTERVIEWER: How do you make decisions? What decisions are made as a group and what decisions are made individually?

LISA: Again, that changes. People come as individuals into the house. A lot of it was a process of developing a way in which to make decisions. Sometimes we make them more collectively and sometimes we make them individually and sometimes we mess up and we have to work on that. We have house meetings once a week. We try and talk with each other about things that are going on—what do you think's happening to this person or what should we do about this or that. We've changed about the way in which we deal about money. We've had to think about that and work on that.

INTERVIEWER: How do you deal with money?

LISA: Well right now some things we share collectively like the running of the cars and the food. . . . Some of it is on the basis of those who have give and those who need get. Then there's the basis of sharing tasks. We divide up—cooking, everybody cooks once a week, everybody does dishes once a week, everybody cleans up one room once a week, and then if there are things that have to be done, it's determined who's available to do them. Generally, you know, the way we handle the work and the money, it just gets split up. But actually that will all change, because until now I've been paying the rent because that's so huge. And I've had the most money.

INTERVIEWER: And now?

LISA: Okay, now, at this point in time, I am leaving that house. I am leaving the university. We are all leaving that house. Now everything shifts. Now it's no longer people moving into my house. Now it's a group of people making decisions together, starting fresh, starting new. So that shifts things and the center shifts. There's lots of centers now, instead of just me and the children. Part of the reason for that is also that I have a monogamous relationship now with a man, as well as within a collective situation. I see both of those as fluid.

INTERVIEWER: What kind of a situation are you moving into? You mentioned that you now have a stable, what you call monogamous relationship.

LISA: I didn't say stable. No, I don't see that as stable in the usual sense of the word. I see that as something that exists now for this period of time and I don't know how long that period of time is. That would depend on how long that relationship meets the needs that exist. Now that can be for a long time and that can be for a short time. But I don't think I really see that as something that maintains a form of necessarily living together either as a couple or in a collective.

INTERVIEWER: But he is moving north with you?

LISA: Right. There will be anywhere from three to five adults and one child that will live either together or in near proximity to each other. I think more than *collective* at this point, I would say *family*.

INTERVIEWER: One of your children, Chris, is staying in Los Angeles. Can you tell me a little more about that.

LISA: Okay. It's not an easy thing. Part of it is coming to terms with what is supposed to be a good mother, and what I feel is a good mother. My way of living, a form of life that I have chosen, involuntarily or voluntarily, is not necessarily the form of life that is best for Chris. For Toni it's very good. She loves it. She wouldn't want to live any other way. Chris needed more rooted-ness, more order. And the nuclear-family home that her father could offer provided that. There are lots of things that I am un-comfortable about in that, a lot of values that I think are being placed upon her that are not my values, but if they are her values I don't believe that I can impose mine upon her. Nor do I think that I should change my way of life in the sense of having her impose her values on me.

INTERVIEWER: What will this family commune be like, the one in Oregon?

LISA: We don't know that yet. We know who's going, but we don't know how it is going to be. All of that will get determined by so many things, by what jobs we take, by the people that we meet there. I think that, whatever situation you're in, there are some needs that aren't going to be met, so you make a choice of which needs. In a collective situation you get some needs met but you don't others. I have a need for a community, for a sense of belonging and at the same time the need to be alone and indepen-dent.

INTERVIEWER: What is the bond between the people in your collective?

LISA: We all care about the same kinds of things. First of all, there's the personal commitment. Part of that is to try to be honest and try to learn and try not to be defensive, all those idealistic things. Of course there's a political commitment in terms of common goals for society. And a big part of it is the bond with the children. I guess I represented a certain kind of stability. With other collectives you rent a house. When it starts to break up, either somebody keeps the house or you get rid of it. But with us, people could leave, but I was still going to be there with the children.

You have to be held together by something, either the work you do or the ideology that you believe in or the commitment to particular people. But I think the commitment to children has a different kind of continuity. The children have been a central aspect of the house. People just didn't live in a house by themselves. There were other lives that they had to be responsible for.

It really has to do with a focus, a center, and with having shared goals. And being willing to struggle, and to take risks, and to try something new. And now, whether that brings us closer together or disperses us, I think there will always be a bond, and in that way it is not like friends who go different ways, but like a family.

A Marriage Contract: Jennifer R. and Gregory S.

Marriage is always a contract. To the extent that the state does not permit any deviation from the contractual terms imposed through its laws, it becomes an involuntary one. According to the common-law rule of "coverture," the wife's legal identity was literally incorporated into that of her husband, with whom she was considered "one person in law,"[8] and for a long time contractual agreements between a husband and wife were legally impossible under Anglo-American law. With the passage of the Married Women's Acts which granted wives the right to contract, and the subsequent evolution of our system of jurisprudence during the nineteenth and twentieth centuries, agreements between husbands and wives gradually gained judicial recognition. Today postnuptial and antenuptial contracts are lawful as long as they are not against "the public policy of the state."

In general, courts have held that any agreement between married persons or persons contemplating marriage "to change the essential incidents of marriage" is illegal.[9] In 1928 the New York Supreme Court, in annulling a marriage in which the husband and wife had agreed to refrain from intercourse indefinitely, concluded that "marital intercourse, so that children may be born, is an obligation of the marriage contract," and "is the foundation upon which must rest the perpetuation of society and civilization" which "may not be modified by private agreement between the parties."[10] The wife's duty to follow her husband's choice of domicile has also been held an "essential incident of marriage." For example, in a 1940 case when a wife contracted with her husband to pay him a sum of money in consideration of his agreement to accompany her on her travels, a federal court held that the contract was against public policy.[11]

With regard to the contracting of property rights, courts usually permit antenuptial agreements in which couples transfer or agree to transfer property to one another, waive property rights in one another's estate, or provide for each other by will.[12] However, agreements to modify a husband's duty to support and a wife's duty to render services have been held against public policy on the ground that these reciprocal duties are "essential incidents of marriage" and because courts will not enforce contracts "in contemplation of divorce."[13]

Since public policy has been the guiding principle in rulings on marital contracts, and since public policy has, in the past, discouraged divorce, the traditional rule has been that marital-settlement agreements dealing with such matters as spousal and child support must be made *after* the parties have separated or agreed to separate. However, in light of our current, considerably liberalized divorce laws—particularly no-fault, which clearly indicates that public policy is changing—it is questionable whether the traditional rationale retains constitutional validity. Indeed, recent cases indicate that courts are now more willing to permit couples to make realistic plans for the eventuality of a marital breakdown. For example, since 1970, Florida, Illinois, Oregon, and Nevada have broken with earlier public policy and upheld nuptial and prenuptial agreements providing support in the event of separation (although a 1973 California case did not).[14]

However, the courts have yet to deal with the growing number of marriage contracts that represent a wish on the part of the parties to depart from the sexually stereotyped roles traditionally considered essential to the marital relationship—contracts in which spouses agree to share housework, to pay one spouse for domestic services, or in which they agree to retain separate names or pursue parallel careers.

Initially, the legal profession gave a very cool reception to such agreements, but in recent years a number of favorable articles have appeared in legal journals—notably Lenore Weitzman's treatise in the *California Law Review*. These articles have indicated that the increased use of contracts may be creating a shift in the "public policy" that governs the regulation of marriage in this country.[15]

Actually, egalitarian marriage contracts are far from new. Amelia Earhart and her husband had one, as did many eighteenth- and nineteenth-century feminists. In 1885, Lucy Stone and Henry Blackwell wrote that they deemed it a duty to declare that their marriage implied "no sanction or promise of voluntary obedience" of marriage laws that "refuse to recognize the wife as an independent rational being; while they confer upon the husband an injurious and unnatural superiority." A hundred years before that, William Godwin and Mary Wollstonecraft, who in 1792 published *A Vindication of the Rights of Women*, wrote that they would submit to marriage only on their own terms and in such a way as to "give the connection as little as possible the appearance of such a vulgar and debasing tie as matrimony."[16]

In 1972, when Jennifer R. and Gregory S. were married, they sent out as a wedding announcement the marriage contract I had helped them prepare. Part of the contract states:

> It is our goal in our marriage that each of us shall have complete equality of opportunity to develop our respective potentials, emotionally, intellectually, professionally, and financially; that we

shall each have our own careers; that we shall each take equal responsibility for household tasks and childcare; and that this principle of mutual respect and support for each other's individuality and integrity shall govern all aspects of our relationship and our lives. Regardless of social pressures or of sexual stereotypes we shall each do everything necessary and appropriate to secure full implementation of this goal.

"We wanted to do some consciousness raising," Gregory told me when I asked him why they decided to use their marriage contract to announce their wedding. "Making our own contract and getting married on our own terms—that seemed like a much more powerful statement than just saying we were living together."

Both Jennifer and Gregory understand that their own personal histories and personalities are responsible for the unconventional path they chose.

JENNIFER: I have always acted on instinct a lot. I don't consciously do things that are antiestablishment or antitradition. I don't really think about it that way. I'm always surprised when my parents label something as terrible, and I just did what seemed right. Before Greg and I moved to California, we went to see them and the whole visit turned into how they didn't think I should drive all the way cross-country with a man. I guess when Greg and I got married, in a way I hoped it would make things all right with my family. But of course it didn't. But the main reason for getting married was that in some emotional way it was important to me.

I still had some kind of feeling that if you really love somebody you marry him. I needed to make that statement and I also needed that statement from Greg.

It's hard for me to separate all of that from the need we both felt to get things down legally in terms of property, of mutual protection, and in terms of the decisions that we would make. We talked about it and that was when we decided to come to see you. To find out about the law. We knew we didn't want the traditional marriage, but also I don't think we set out to have a marriage contract. We set out to clarify our feelings and to get some advice from you about the legal aspects of marriage that we didn't understand very well. I think the idea of a contract actually came from you, as an answer to those needs.

In their marriage contract, Jennifer and Greg agreed to take equal responsibility for the physical, emotional, and financial care of any children they might have. They also agreed that household duties would be shared equally, that they would each have their own careers, an equal voice in choosing the marital domicile, and that Jennifer would retain her own last name. They worked out a formula whereby their regular income was to be pooled in a joint bank account from which all usual household and family expenses and acquisitions would be paid. Management and control of all jointly held earnings and property and all financial decisions regarding them were to be made jointly in accordance with certain guidelines set out in the contract. They agreed that they would devote a minimum of one hour per week "to communication of our feelings toward each other, to work through our problems, and to raise our consciousness about social and internal pressures enforcing traditional sexual roles," and that they would review the entire marital agreement once a month, and, if necessary, renegotiate it every five years.

"It is our intention that this be a primary, not necessarily an exclusive, relationship," the contract states.

> However, should one person feel deprived of the sense of a primary relationship by the activities of the other, it is our intention that this first be discussed between us and should we fail to satisfactorily resolve the problem, that we both together shall seek help from a third party mutually agreed upon. If we are unable to agree on the third party within three days, then the choice of the person who feels deprived shall govern. It is our intent and our hope that this process will enable us to focus on the underlying problems and facilitate openness, closeness, and a mutually satisfactory resolution."

Greg and Jennifer elaborated their feelings about this section of the contract:

GREG: I believe everybody should really be able to basically do what they want to do as long as it's not hurting anybody else, and that's racially or sexually or whatever way you want to live your life. I guess that's one of the main principles in our marriage contract, that we each maintain our individual identity.

I think it would make me very uncomfortable to have a traditional relationship with a woman. The idea that I would, for example, be denied cooking. Or denied cleaning. Or denied equal responsibility and expertise with children. Nor would I care to be given all the responsibility for things like business decisions or work decisions or living decisions. I don't like making decisions like that for other people. Period.

There were things that we were already doing in our lives that are not accorded recognition in the traditional kind of marriage, in terms of equality, of sharing different roles. So we began talking about that, and about how we could incorporate those things in formalizing what already was a marriage.

JENNIFER: In many ways our marriage contract just states how we get along. We share a lot of values. Like the statement that ours is a primary but not necessarily an exclusive relationship. When we first moved back to Boston there was an old friend of Greg's there from college. She came to the house and had a drink with us. It was just obvious to me that I didn't have anything in common with her. But it was also obvious that she and Greg really enjoyed being together. They made an arrangement which Greg cleared with me to go and have a couple of drinks. I guess I really never had too many thoughts about it. I know that a couple of years ago I would have, and maybe before the contract I would have. And a lot of it would have been inarticulate. I think it was partly having talked it through that helped me to look at it that way, instead of like before, feeling somehow I needed to be upset about it, even if I wasn't.

It used to be very threatening to me that somebody I cared about would want to spend time with somebody else. When I think about it now, I realize that it was just as threatening if they wanted to discuss a book I didn't know anything about or play tennis, and it didn't really have anything to do with whether they wanted to go to bed with that person or not. It was just the idea that I wasn't adequate, that they needed to be with somebody else. I don't feel that way anymore. I feel good about Greg and me, and what we share, and it doesn't really have anything to do with what we also share with other people.

GREG: The process of writing the contract, our talking to you and our thinking things through; that clarified a lot of our values, and it also set up procedures for us, so that later we could sit down and talk things over again.

We don't do the consciousness-raising every week, but it's helped us to know that it's there. I also believe that the clause that says that the person who feels something is wrong determines that need, is very good. I think it's important to recognize that we are each committed to and accepting of the subjective reality of the other person, that the other person's subjective reality is just as valid as yours. I think more and more, particularly as I work with children, that there is no such thing as rationality in relationships. I think you just have to say okay that's what you feel right now and what are we going to do about it. In so many marriages I see, if one person feels one way and the other doesn't feel that way, they might not do anything about it until they both feel that way, and at that point it's often too late.

JENNIFER: In the last few years, when we've seen a lot of our friends who are married in trouble, we realized that we have something to go to that is ours. Somehow we have an additional resource that other people don't have. If we run into problems, we can go to our contract.*

---

* Whether Jennifer's and Greg's contract is in its entirety a legally enforceable document remains to be determined. For reference, it is reproduced in full in appendix 2.

11

Family-law Reform

Despite growing popular recognition of the need for multiple family forms in our rapidly changing heterogeneous society, and despite their advocacy in the literature of the social sciences, the concept, as we have seen, has gained only the most limited acceptance in our laws. Our legal system's failure to respond to the real needs of people has enormous implications for us all. The state's imposition of a single marital form and the equation of any deviation from the patriarchal norm with familial and social disorganization also raises important constitutional questions.

In the United States we are governed by a system of constitutional law that is continually evolving as courts interpret the Constitution in the light of changing social, economic, and political conditions. It is a system that has been characterized as one of living justice, under which laws must keep up with evolving community standards. In the words of Roger J. Traynor, former Chief Justice of the California Supreme Court:

> Courts have a creative job to do when they find that a rule has lost touch with reality and should be abandoned or reformulated to meet new conditions and new moral values.... We do a great disservice to the law when we neglect that careful pruning on

which its vigorous growth depends and let it become sicklied over with nice rules that fail to meet the problems of real people.[1]

The Supreme Court of the United States is the final arbiter in determining the constitutional validity of any statute, court decision, or other governmental regulation or law. Since this function necessarily entails the evaluation of fundamental questions of social policy, the Court must continually weigh and balance the importance of governmental regulations against that of individual rights. In carrying out this task, the Court must first determine whether a governmental regulation serves any legitimate public interest, since only then is it permissible. If, however, a fundamental human right is affected, the Court has held that such regulations must meet much stricter constitutional standards and that only if the public interest at stake is so major as to involve the safety, or even survival, of the state may a basic civil right be curtailed.

Applying these principles to the field of family law, legal scholars have suggested that laws which impose the traditional patriarchal marriage as the only permissible familial form are unconstitutional, not only because they are sexually discriminatory, but also because they serve no legitimate public interest. This was the conclusion of Professor Lenore J. Weitzman in her exhaustive treatise on marriage and marital contracts:[2]

> Although the states' right to regulate marriage has long been recognized in this country, the courts have not been very explicit in setting forth the interests of the state in such regulation. A number of landmark cases merely refer to the importance of marriage as the foundation of our society.... The state's traditional interest in promoting public morality was thought to be served by requiring and regulating legal marriage. Some have argued that allowing persons to engage in sexual relationships without first going through a civil or religious marriage ceremony is conducive to a decline in public morality. While this view might have been accurate in the past, present standards of public morality are such that it is not unusual for people to have intimate relations or to

live together without marrying. . . . The state has also asserted an interest in promoting family stability by controlling marriage and divorce. Yet it is doubtful that present state control has been effective. Certainly current divorce statistics would lead one to question its effectiveness, and current norms might lead one to challenge its desirability. Further, if family stability were the main goal, then encouraging couples to contract regarding the terms of their relationship should increase rather than decrease stability. . . . A third state interest is that of securing the continued welfare of its citizens by making them legally responsible for one another. . . . While the state may be justified in requiring members of a family to bear some legal responsibility for supporting one another, laws requiring that only the husband bear this burden would be overly broad in some instances, as where the wife and children are able to support themselves, and underinclusive in others, where the husband is the one in need of support. . . . The state also has an interest in ensuring that children are properly cared for. . . . However, assuming that [the traditional method of assigning the family the responsibility for the support and care of children] is a legitimate state interest, it can be accomplished through nondiscriminatory means, without assigning responsibility for child care or child support on the basis of sex.[8]

But even if patriarchal marriage laws serve some kind of state interest, they would still be unconstitutional if they unreasonably interfere with a fundamental human right. While there is nothing in our Constitution explicitly guaranteeing the individual's right to freely enter into familial relationships as a basic human right, the whole history of constitutional law consists of the interpretation of enumerated rights to include new situations unforeseen by the founding fathers. For example, in prohibiting states from maintaining racially segregated public schools in *Bolling* v. *Sharpe*, Chief Justice Warren interpreted the constitutional guarantee to "liberty" to include the right to equal education:

> Although the Court has not assumed to define "liberty" with any great precision, that term is not confined to mere freedom from bodily restraint. Liberty under law extends to the full range of conduct which the individual is free to pursue, and it cannot

be restricted except for a proper governmental objective. Segregation in public education is not reasonably related to any proper governmental objective, and thus it imposes on Negro children of the District of Columbia a burden that constitutes an arbitrary deprivation of their liberty in violation of the Due Process Clause.[4]

Following this type of approach, a recent line of Supreme Court cases has held that the constitutionally guaranteed right of privacy is a fundamental human right which may not be interfered with by laws arbitrarily seeking to regulate intimate personal relationships and decisions relating to childbearing. In the landmark decision of *Griswold* v. *Connecticut*,[5] the Supreme Court explicitly stated that the constitutional right to privacy covers marital relationships and declared a statute forbidding the use of contraceptive devices unconstitutional. In *Eisenstadt* v. *Baird*,[6] the Supreme Court took this line of reasoning one step farther and struck down a Massachusetts statute which permitted the prescription of contraceptives to married persons, but prohibited the same to unmarried persons. In that case the Court made it clear that decisions about childbearing come under the right of privacy and that individuals possess that right, whether they are married or not:

> It is true that in *Griswold* the right of privacy in question inhered in the marital relationship. Yet the marital couple is not an independent entity with a mind and heart of its own, but an association of two individuals each with a separate intellectual and emotional makeup. If the right of privacy means anything, it is the right of the *individual*, married or single, to be free from unwarranted governmental intrusion into matters so fundamentally affecting a person as the decision whether to bear or beget a child.[7]

Continuing with this line of reasoning, laws that define the only legally sanctioned family as a procreation-oriented, two-parent, permanent, monogamous, male-headed, and male-dominated unit that can only be formed by two people of opposite sex would also have to be viewed as unwarranted governmental interference with the fundamental right of consenting adults to enter into reasonable and functional family unions which meet their individual needs.

Furthermore, by denying alternative familial forms the protection of our laws, our present system of family laws can also be said to violate the equal-protection requirements of our Constitution. Although this issue has not yet reached the Supreme Court, it has begun to be litigated at the lower-court level. In 1973 actress Michelle Marvin sued actor Lee Marvin for one-half of the assets accumulated while they lived together.[8] Ms. Marvin, who had her last name legally changed to Marvin in 1967, alleged that she and the actor began to live together in 1964, that at that time they had agreed to share all earnings and accumulations equally, that she had given up her career as a singer as part of the arrangement, and that for six years they had lived together and represented themselves as husband and wife. After she lost, her attorney, who is appealing the decision, told the *Los Angeles Times* he considered the case a divorce without a marriage. "It costs $3 to get a marriage license," he said. "I say that for a $3 license one should not have different rights than one who has the same relationship but doesn't pay the $3. I consider this unequal protection of the law."[9]

Test cases like the above could open the door for the acceptance of a variety of legally sanctioned and protected family forms which differ from the patriarchal standard. The contemporary no-fault philosophy of divorce has already established a public policy that goes beyond traditional notions of morality by simply recognizing that when individuals pool their efforts into a family unit, they acquire certain property rights and obligations that are legally enforceable, regardless of fault. The equal-protection argument advanced by Ms. Marvin's attorney is based on the constitutional maxim that similarly situated individuals must be similarly treated. Logically extended, it would require that all family associations that do not violate strong social policies be recognized under our laws.

In dealing with this issue, the Supreme Court would have to balance the social interests involved. The approach I favor would be to grant the equal protection of our laws to any familial grouping, provided that it does not violate basic human rights, fundamental principles of equity, or other compelling considerations of social policy required to protect family members, particularly children, from abuse and exploitation.

I would like to propose that a new concept of family law is in order, and that in place of those laws that arbitrarily impose only one legally sanctioned family form, we adopt new laws containing a more functional and up-to-date legal definition of *family*. In line with our evolving needs and standards, these laws would give equal protection to alternative unions, and the term *family* would include a variety of contractual units whose members take specifically defined personal, economic, and social responsibilities for each other and who perceive themselves as constituting a family. These units could be legally formed through a variety of contractual arrangements. Our family laws would regulate these contracts, but instead of limiting them to any particular form, they would be concerned with real issues of public welfare, which our present family laws sadly neglect. The state would require that these contracts abide by certain equitable standards of fairness, that they be subject to the close judicial scrutiny traditionally given agreements between persons in confidential relationships, and, like present-day marital-settlement agreements and divorce decrees, that they be subject to judicial modification under appropriate circumstances.

Such a new system of family law will require a great deal of study and creative legal work, drawing from already well-developed fields such as partnership and corporate law and new ones still to be devised, and it will require a major reevaluation and clarification of social values and goals. In the long run, such a system would decrease rather than increase the judicial load. It would require people to anticipate the possible dissolution of a union and to provide how that dissolution would proceed, thus discouraging unwise and impulsive contracts. From a social-policy standpoint, it would permit a multiplicity of familial choices that are congruent with contemporary life and at the same time provide individuals with the backing of our legal machinery for the enforcement of whatever contract is appropriate to their needs, be it a young couple wishing to have children, a group of elderly people seeking a more economic and emotionally rewarding arrangement than living alone or in an institution, a group of young people who wish to adopt and raise a child, a homosexual couple, and so on. It would apply to sexual and nonsexual familial commitments (while *not* seeking to regulate sex per se) and would recognize lifetime contracts as well as limited-time ones (as our divorce, but not our marriage laws, already do).

For the millions of children whose parents are divorced or whose families otherwise fail to meet the current social and legal norms, such a family-law system would mean a new equality, a new dignity, and the sorely needed knowledge that their families and their ways of life are as good as anyone else's. It would mean that people might stop feeling insecure because they can't seem to meet some idealized marital goal in their particular union. It would also mean that the institution of patriarchal marriage, which has for so long been the cornerstone of patriarchal society, could be replaced by more egalitarian and humane forms.

In the 1971 case of *Reed* v. *Reed*,[10] for the first time in American history, the Supreme Court struck down as an unconstitutional violation of the equal-protection clause of the Fourteenth Amendment a statute which gave a husband preference (in administering a decedent's estate) solely on the basis of his sex. By this same reasoning, the vast body of family laws giving husbands superior family status and power will also have to be struck down, a process that has already started, and which the passage of the Equal Rights Amendment will hopefully accelerate. Both the Equal Rights Amendment and the Fourteenth Amendment would also require that the system of laws I am proposing to govern multiple-choice family unions be free from any sexual discrimination. Since the state cannot constitutionally be an instrument of any such discrimination, this could also be interpreted to mean that familial contracts containing such discrimination would not be enforceable. The issue would then revolve around the question of whether contractual obligations are based on sexual stereotypes or upon a freely agreed choice of functions.

Just as the new fair-employment laws have required affirmative-action programs, so would family-law reform. In addition, all federal and state agency regulations would have to be reexamined and their application directed toward the elimination of bias. For example, under the FCC's equal-time requirements, one of the conditions governing the grant of a federal license for a television station would be proof of the elimination of programs presenting the patriarchal family as the only desirable form or portraying characters based solely on sexual stereotypes (just as racial stereotypes are today no longer condoned).

Finally, marital and sexual stereotypes would also have to be eliminated from the vast complex of nonfamily case law and legislation, ranging from taxation and welfare to education and child care, because, as we have seen, these also provide reinforcement for outdated marital and sexual modes.

I am aware that such fundamental legal and social reform is a momentous task, but I believe that in view of the alternatives, it is one we must at least attempt. Historically, when a social system has failed to adjust to the real and perceived needs of its people, existing institutional structures have had to rely on tighter social controls, and ultimately on force, to resist the pressures for change. Cycles of tyrannical dictatorships and/or bloody revolutions and counterrevolutions have always resulted. Today we can already observe the emergence of both of these phenomena in the stepped-up governmental surveillance and emphasis on internal security on the one hand and, on the other, the terrorism and lawlessness that in our inner cities almost border on civil war.

This is not to suggest that if women do not achieve equality under the law there will be rioting in the streets. Our historical conditioning has been so successful that the behavioral pattern of acceptance which characterizes women's reaction to oppression is likely to persist. However, the continuation of a repressive patriarchal approach to the wide spectrum of current social problems may precipitate increasingly violent reactions from all oppressed groups who are subject to the growing frustrations of our present social structure.

The roots of the problem lie in the very nature of patriarchal societies, which are, by definition, based on hierarchical and power-centered social institutions and human relationships for which the male-dominated family provides the basic model and socialization tool. For that reason, to bring about meaningful change, not only for women, but for all of us, the social inventions for this new postindustrial age must be nonpatriarchal, and the family must be the primary focus of social and legal change.

For women, the issues are even more immediate and direct, since their traditionally defined roles and functions as wives and mothers will inevitably be altered by the eco-population crisis and concomitant scientific developments. Until now, women's bodies have been the only containers in which the ovum is fertilized and the embryo develops and matures, but recent experiments in protein synthesis and cloning indicate that other alternatives may soon become available.[11]

Whether this redefinition of women's functions and roles will lead to greater freedom or to a further devaluation of their sex depends entirely on whether our society retains or discards its patriarchal character. This is so, because *in patriarchal societies the issue is not what women do or do not do, but the fact that it is women who do it.* In the patriarchal scale of values, it is a woman's time and efforts which are not respected. Consequently whatever women do, be it housekeeping, bank-telling, typing, or child-rearing, is never highly rewarded, economically or socially.

It is for this reason that no existing American divorce law provides payment to a woman for raising her children, and that child-support awards, like welfare payments, deal only with the expenses needed by a woman to feed, clothe, and house her children, but not with any compensation for her services. It explains why whole professions decline in status and pay as soon as women are admitted in sizable numbers, and why the massive movement of women into the general labor market has not and will not equalize the situation. That this is the value system both women and men are taught to internalize in our patriarchal society also helps to explain why it is so difficult for women to perceive their real situation and to do something about it. In this context, it is not the stereotyped male-female division of labor which is the crux of the problem, but rather the patriarchal evaluation of the roles assigned to each sex. The mechanics of this process can perhaps be better understood by examining it through the use of one of the classic tools of deductive logic: the Aristotelian syllogism.

The traditional assignment of male-female roles is based on two familiar premises: first, that women are biologically meant to do housework and child-rearing, and second, that housework and child-rearing are not gainful employment. Therefore, under the rules of deductive logic, women, who perform these functions, are not gainfully employed and what they do does not entitle them to pay.

The defect of this reasoning lies in the premises. Even assuming that for the immediate future only women will have the capacity to give birth, it by no means follows that only women can raise children. Bottles and formulas have long been in use as alternative sources of food, and although it is highly possible that the warm bodily contact inherent in breast-feeding is better for the emotional health of infants, that activity is only a very small part of the process of caring for babies. Any human, male or female, can contribute to the emotional health of a baby by holding it and cuddling it and giving it tender loving care.

As for housework, there is certainly no logical reason why the individual who washes dishes and vacuums floors and polishes shoes should also be the one who takes care of children. If the two work categories are lumped together, it is only because neither is accorded enough social value to be classified—either by patriarchal society or our indices of "economic activities"—as gainful employment which entitles those engaged in that form of work to be paid. Neither is there anything about the structure of the female body that makes it more suitable than the male's for the performance of household routines and chores.

There have always been, and still are, individual men who have assumed many of the functions of child-rearing and/or housekeeping.[12] Furthermore, according to Dr. John Money, an expert in the field of psychohormonal research, most conventional patterns of male and female behavior are learned rather than genetically determined. According to Money, there are only four imperative differences between the two sexes: women menstruate, gestate, and lactate, and men impregnate.[13]

The second premise of the syllogism—that women's work inside the home has no economic value—is also a function of social definition. The "gainfully employed" are defined in our society as those who work twenty-four hours or more per week. However, a young mother who works eighty to ninety hours per week is defined as "economically inactive." Men who design and manufacture the weapons that kill and cause massive human suffering have the right to cash wages, but women who nurture and care for children and supply the food and services without which our society would instantly collapse do not have the same right. Because society continues to view child-rearing as a woman's duty, divorce judges openly state that a man, because he gets cash wages for his work, is entitled to a decent standard of living. As a result, the court awards given women and children must necessarily be the leftovers.

The first step in the direction of changing the value system upon which such social and economic distinctions are based would be to accord economic value to the services traditionally performed by women in the home.

Ten years ago the President's Commission on the Status of Women recommended that our family laws give each spouse a legally defined right in the property and earnings of the other.[14] The Uniform Marriage and Divorce Act's concept of marital property is in line with that suggestion, although only in cases of divorce.[15] The community-property system has long incorporated that principle, both during marriage and upon divorce, but because of the past refusal and current reluctance of lawmakers and judges to give women equal management and control, the effect of such laws has more often been theoretical than practical.

Several years ago, the NOW Marriage and Family Committee suggested that homemaking be made a bona fide occupation commanding cash wages. They recommended that homemaking be treated like any other job, with minimum pay scales and individual contractual arrangements between the employer (the wage-earning spouse) and the employee (the homemaker). Such a plan would provide for normal employment benefits—Social Security, retirement, sick leave, pensions, vacations—as well as some form of job-termination protection.[16] More recently, in *Work in America*, a government-sponsored study of the economics and sociology of work and the workplace, a special HEW task force made a similar proposal:

> The clear fact is that keeping house and raising children is work, work that is, on the average, as difficult to do well and as useful to the larger society as almost any paid job involving the production of goods or services. The difficulty is not that most people don't believe this or accept it (we pay lip service to it all the time) but that, whatever our private and informal belief systems, we have not, as a society, acknowledged this fact in our public system of values and rewards. Such an acknowledgment might begin with simply counting housewives in the labor force,

assigning a money value to their work and including it in the calculation of the gross national product, and including housewives in social security and other pension systems.[17]

The HEW report asked "if the housewife is to be considered employed, who is her employer?" Their own response is interesting:

> ... one answer might be, her husband's employer, for it is the wife's labor and her support that enables her husband to do whatever he does for the man or the firm he works for. In this case, the husband and the wife would be viewed as a production unit and money for the housewife's pension plan might take the form of a payroll tax paid by the employer or shared by him and his employees. In the case of widows or other husbandless women with dependent children who do not work outside the home, they too would be "covered" workers, self-employed, and pay their own retirement premiums out of their own resources, or, if on welfare, out of their welfare checks. Alternatively, one might consider them simply public service workers and pay the premiums out of the general fund.[18]

The central argument of the opponents of such proposals has always been that from a practical standpoint such arrangements are just plain impossible, and that in any case, it is an insult to the wives and mothers of America to try to measure what they do in mere dollars and cents. It is certainly one of the great ironies of our society that wives and mothers are seen either as "just housewives" or as idealized and sublime beings whose contributions are so great as to be "beyond valuation in dollars and cents."

And yet, precise determinations of just what a homemaker's services are worth have been made by judges and juries for a long time. In *American Jurisprudence*, legal experts have set well-defined and explicit guidelines for computing the money damages to be awarded a husband for the wrongful death of his wife. While acknowledging that the monetary value of a woman's life should also realistically include what they call "extra nonhousekeeping services she renders in nursing, educating, guiding, and entertaining her family and in assisting other members in their work," they report that "in estimating the value of a woman's services in the home, the cost of replacing her with a paid house-keeper, with substitute help on the housekeeper's days off, is a currently accepted minimum."[19] According to these same guide-lines, a jury is also supposed to add the value of the deceased wife's projected Social Security benefits, and take into account her age, education, the number and age of her children, her past work history, and the income of her husband.[20]

Based on the prevailing extremely low pay scale for the services of housekeepers, and without taking into account the so-called intangibles of a wife's emotional support and encouragement, in 1973 the Chase Manhattan Bank of New York estimated that a housewife was worth $235.40 per week,[21] while economist Sylvia Porter put it at $257.53.[22]

In the public sector, the methods of calculation used for deter-mining these figures could easily serve as the basis for a minimum wage to be paid mothers who are now on welfare. This wage would not be a substitute for Aid to Families with Dependent Children (which is based on the needs and expenses of children) but would be a *salary* for an employee just as our government now pays IRS agents, passport officials, FBI agents, and other public servants—not all of whom do a good job, just as not all mothers do a good job. The immediate effect of such a program would be the easing of an untenable economic burden on today's rapidly growing numbers of mothers and children on welfare. It would also permit these families to keep their self-respect and would serve as an acknowledgment of the worth of those services traditionally performed by women.

In the private sector, partnership agreements, profit-sharing plans, and other legal and financial tools already in use in private industry could readily be adapted to define the relationship be-tween homemakers and those to whom they render their services. For those who wish dual careers, bookkeeping methods could be developed to take into account their additional contributions as outside wage earners, as well as the housekeeping contributions made by other members of the family. It would take some complicated calculating, but no more than tax returns, stock-option plans, and welfare allotments already require.

Housekeeping is one of the most time-consuming things we now do as a matter of course. In millions of kitchens around this country millions of women stand at identical sinks using identical frozen and canned ingredients making almost identical meals. They cook by themselves and they shop by themselves and they wash dishes and clothes and floors by themselves, and by themselves they perform, day in and day out, the hundreds of repetitive and routine little tasks that, as Betty Friedan pointed out over twenty years ago, "make it almost impossible for a woman of adult intelligence to retain a sense of human identity, the firm core of self, or 'I,' without which a human being, man or woman, is not truly alive."[23]

Yet, the isolation of the housewife and the manner in which these tasks are performed could be altered. According to Dr. Michael Arbib, a computer expert at the University of Massachusetts, we already have mobile machines or "robots" which could be programmed to complete given tasks and which could be mass produced for less than $1,000.[24] As dishwashers and vacuum cleaners and clothes dryers have already begun to do, these devices could take over much of the menial and repetitive tasks of the housekeeper. But as long as women continue to donate their services, there will be no reason to replace them with electronic and mechanical housekeepers, no matter how cheaply they can be produced, nor will society develop and introduce more economical methods for the distribution and preparation of food or seek more efficient and less wasteful ways of sharing consumer goods and products.

The argument which states that alternatives to the present system are not "economically feasible" is simply another way of saying that there are no real economic pressures requiring change.

One way women could exert such economic pressures would be to single out one large unionized industry and withdraw all home-support services for its workers until part of the paycheck of every man who is married to a full-time housewife is made out directly to her. This would require a great deal of organization and careful and judicious planning, and there would undoubtedly be many problems, but it would certainly direct nationwide attention to the real economic value of the services housewives provide.

Any meaningful restructuring of the household will not take place overnight, and a comprehensive plan to make homemaking a bona-fide occupation will take considerable time to study, develop, and put into effect. In the meantime, the divorce rate continues to climb, and every day thousands of women join the swelling ranks of the "unemployed" housewives who have few, if any, skills considered economically valuable. With the trend toward smaller and shorter spousal-support awards, the plight of these women and their children has become one of our nation's major social problems. What can be done? For women with small children for whom homemaking is still a full-time job, the introduction of public-service salaries could supplement or replace spousal support without much delay. Older women or women in faulty health could be included in our Social Security system, as recommended in *Work in America* and in bills already introduced in Congress.[25] For those who can and want to take nonhomemaking jobs, but whose lack of training and experience now relegates them to the most menial and underpaid tasks, occupational retraining could be provided.

The Uniform Marriage and Divorce Act states that in awarding spousal support judges should "consider the time necessary to acquire a sufficient education or training to enable the party seeking maintenance to find appropriate employment,"[26] indicating a recognition of the necessity for such retraining by lawyers and judges working with family law. But the vagueness of a concept like "appropriate employment" aside, frequently such privately funded vocational retraining for the divorced wife is not a realistic possibility since there are many divorced men who make very little money, and some who make no money at all.

After World War II this country instituted a social invention called the G.I. Bill of Rights, under which servicemen could go to school at the expense of the government. The theory underlying this program was that since these men had served their country, it was now their country's turn to serve them. In 1963 Betty Friedan suggested that a similar program be instituted for the women who have served their country by raising its children and serving and caring for its men.[27]

Unlike the welfare system's Talmage work registration and retraining program, the G.I. Bill of Rights is voluntary. This, too, must be the basis of a Homemaker's Bill of Rights, which would similarly entitle former homemakers to attend existing technical schools and universities. In addition, the program should include the development of special retraining centers partially funded by an increase in marriage-license fees (upped from the current average fee of $3.00 to say $20.00, which is not out of line considering that the average divorce filing fee is $40.00). Such centers would not only provide immediate help for women in need of special training, but would also stimulate the economy by creating a meaningful "public works" program which would in turn create new jobs. In addition to such obvious social and economic benefits, a homemaker retraining program would itself constitute an important alteration of the patriarchal character of the labor market since it would be administered primarily by women. Through its programs it would also make certain that women are not simply shifted from one "female" occupation to another.

In addition, this program could serve as a model for the mid-career retraining and renewal programs which have been proposed by a HEW task force as necessary economic tools for shifting workers from declining into growing industries and for combatting high levels of underemployment and unemployment.[28]

Writing for Washington's Upjohn Institute of Employment Research, Dr. Herbert Striner has described worker retraining as a "national capital investment" already widely accepted in other Western countries such as West Germany, where more than a quarter of a million workers go back to school each year to increase their effectiveness, productivity, and job satisfaction.[29] Similar programs in Denmark and France are proving of great social and economic value. And in Sweden, where official government policy is geared toward promoting women's entry into the general labor force as well as eliminating sexual stereotyping in all areas of life, retraining programs specifically adapted to meet the needs of women have been operating successfully for a number of years.

After *Work in America* was submitted to HEW, the government seriously considered its proposal that homemakers be included in the Social Security pension system.[30] In the end, however, the decision was to give priority to other issues considered more critical. While one may disagree with that judgment, it is nevertheless encouraging that such matters are being discussed by our public officials. It indicates public recognition of the inequities within the present system and some awareness that women who care for this nation's children deserve economic and personal security and dignity. Perhaps it also indicates a growing recognition that current social problems require the acceptance of new social inventions and their swift enactment into law.

The greatest obstacle to any meaningful redefinition of social priorities is, as Dr. Conger has pointed out, the calcification inherent in our institutionalized social inventions and the concomitant resistance to change on the part of the people who have attained positions of power within the present system. While it is true that massive shifts in social attitudes cannot be immediately legislated or otherwise brought about, we are still entitled to public officials who are well informed and free from significant prejudice and bias. In case after case the Supreme Court has ruled that governmental action must be free from prejudice and bias. Affirmative-action orders aimed at eliminating bias in government contracts and in education have been an important step toward meeting this constitutional requirement. These affirmative-action programs should be expanded to include a massive drive to reeducate public officials so that they understand the real socioeconomic problems of American women.

The field in which such a program is most urgently needed is family law, since legal disputes between spouses are, by definition, contests between members of the opposite sex. Unfortunately, it is not uncommon for family-law judges and commissioners to make blatantly sexist statements, jokes, and put-downs of women, both inside and outside the courtroom. If judges sitting in a dispute between labor and management, or between black and white persons, or between any two opponents who are members of a particular group or class were to disparage either side, they would be immediately disqualified from the case. The same principle should be applied in family law.

Since attitudes can be as much a function of irrational bias as of rational knowledge, judges and commissioners sitting in family-law cases should be required to take attitude tests like those given by the Peace Corps to weed out racists. In this case, they would be used to sift out the most virulently sexist individuals. For those who would argue that this is too strong a measure, the answer is that the principle that judges and jurors must be fair and impartial is a basic element of our system of jurisprudence. The essence of the voir-dire process is the examination of jurors to weed out those with prejudicial attitudes. If the attitudes of jurors must be scrutinized and tested, surely the same principle should apply to judges, especially in the area of family law, where judges and not jurors are the triers of fact.

Such a program would be part of a more comprehensive civil-service examination required for judges and commissioners who sit in family-law cases, as well as for public officials charged with enforcing their awards. It could also test their knowledge of family law and their understanding of social and economic realities. If these public servants had to prepare for such examinations, they would learn, for example, that over one-tenth of our families are headed by women, that the vast majority of America's poor are women and children, that older women, even more than older men, are practically unemployable, and that adequate child care is almost impossible to find. If judges knew these facts, they might no longer treat the divorced woman as an abnormality, as simply a temporary aberration en route to another marriage,[31] nor could they continue to rationalize minimal support awards as simply "interim measures." Law-enforcement officials would have no excuse for failing to enforce spousal-support orders or for refusing to take vigorous steps to collect child-support awards, not only on behalf of women on welfare, but for other mothers as well.

It is important to emphasize that this is not a problem of men versus women, but of sexist attitudes, which in patriarchal societies are internalized by both sexes. All too often women who attain positions of power, such as judgeships, bend backward in identifying with patriarchal values and prejudices to show that they are not in any way favoring their own sex. Male judges may be influenced by personal circumstances, such as problems in their own marriages, that make for unconscious biases favoring male litigants as against their wives. While a few judges are violently sexist, most are simply well-meaning people unconsciously locked into archaic and paternalistic approaches to male-female relationships.

Some feminists have suggested that if women really understood the terms of the patriarchal marriage contract imposed on them by law, they would think twice before embarking on a life's career as a wife and mother. They have suggested that people who want to get a marriage license should have to pass an examination showing that they understand the marriage and divorce laws of their particular state. We require that people pass tests to get all kinds of licenses, from driving to undertaking.

We have educational programs to help us succeed in our occupations and our hobbies. But we display a singular lack of interest in programs which might help us succeed in such fundamental activities as familial and sexual relationships and parenting. We are told that these are "natural" activities which everybody "just knows," or alternately that we know so little about them that they cannot be taught. And yet, when scientists try to gain deeper understanding in these areas, there is an instant outcry. Consider Senator William Proxmire's objection to a National Science Foundation project attempting to determine the role of psychological dependency as an antecedent to interpersonal attraction, particularly in romantic love. As reported in the *Los Angeles Times*, the senator advised the National Science Foundation to get out of "the love racket" and "leave that to Elizabeth Barrett Browning and Irving Berlin" because, as he put it, at the very top of the list of things he and two hundred million other Americans wanted to leave a mystery was "why or how or if or how long people fall in love."[32]

Despite such opposition, more and more basic research on normal (as opposed to just abnormal) human behavior is being carried on today, and we are beginning to accumulate data on such important functions as sexuality, child development, and parenting. In addition, we are beginning to see some signs of a shift in the official public policy toward child-rearing. For example, in 1967 a federally funded pilot program was established to help mothers and fathers learn to be better parents. Thirty-three Parent-Child Centers, located in almost every major U.S. urban center as well as in selected rural areas, work with the entire family. Staff members come into the home and suggest better modes of parenting. Nurseries and youth groups where mothers and fathers participate, personal and occupational counseling, a complete health service, and tutoring and educational opportunities for every member of the family are offered. The PCCs represent an attempt to break through and improve nonfunctional patterns of parenting and to prevent their transmission from one generation to the next. At present their services are confined to a small number of poor families with preschool children, but they could serve as developmental models for similar projects for other segments of society.

The establishment of the PCCs together with a federal Office for Child Development (an outgrowth of this nation's first conference dealing with rights of children held in Washington, D.C. in 1967) indicates a more enlightened public policy toward family law, particularly with regard to children. Increased respect for the rights of children and greater social responsibility for their care, growth, and development are essential components of any real family-law reform. We know that education begins at birth and that a child's first few years are critical, so it seems only logical to devote a significant part of our budget to improve our approaches to early child-rearing.

Contemporary social developments both inside and outside the family require that family-law reform include the swift development of well-equipped child-care centers supported by the government. But there is a distinction between governmental support and governmental control, and it is essential that these centers be under parental and community control.

Any real family-law reform will of course require a change in our social policy toward women. One component of that policy has been the old legal and social notion that women who deviate from any of the patriarchal norms should be punished. That this policy is beginning to change was illustrated in a recent California case. In *Cary* v. *Cary*, a lower court's decision ordering child support and an equal division of property between the parties who never legally or religiously married was upheld on appeal.[33] Under the old California law such a decision was against public policy, since if the parties knew they were not lawfully married they were guilty of living in a "meretricious" relationship which barred them from obtaining any relief through the courts. But in the *Cary* case, the court held that all of this was changed in California in 1970. The appellate court wrote:

By the Family Law Act, the Legislature has announced it to be the public policy of this state that concepts of guilt (and punishment therefor) and innocence (and rewards therefor) are no longer relevant in the determination of family property rights, whether there be a legal marriage or not and if not regardless of whether the deficiency is known to one, or both, or neither of the parties. It therefore becomes our duty to give expression to the public policy expressed by the Family Law Act. We hold as to the issue before us that the Act supersedes contrary pre-1970 judicial authority. It follows that the trial court properly disregarded evidence of the guilt of the parties to the instant action. Having done so it was obliged to divide their property evenly according to the dictate of Civil Code. . .[34]

However, this same issue was decided antithetically in another California appellate case, and at this writing it remains for the California Supreme Court to make a final determination.

More definite signs of a changing social policy toward women are the new laws requiring equal management of community property, as well as the UMDA's concept of marital property, with its explicit recognition of the wife's economic contribution as homemaker. In the sense that it views marriage as a partnership with certain economic assets which can be divided in accordance with principles of equity, no-fault divorce is also a step in the right direction. Nevertheless, until the economic and social situation of husbands and wives becomes more equal, it is essential that no-fault divorce be accompanied by the kinds of legal safeguards discussed earlier.

In those divorce cases involving little property to divide, no children, and no need for spousal support, attorneys may not be necessary, and family-law reform should incorporate appropriately simplified procedures. In California, a number of organizations have been set up to show people how to get their own divorce, but they have met vigorous opposition from the state bar and many have been prosecuted for practicing law without a license. These organizations, which charge $50 to $70 for helping people complete the required forms and which show them how to appear *in propria persona* (that is, appearing in court without an attorney), fill a real public need for low-cost divorce which is not being met by private attorneys or by government legal aid, where the wait can be as long as two years. Legislation should be enacted specifically authorizing nonattorney divorces, eliminating red tape and allowing people with no assets, no children, and no economic disputes to get their own divorce cheaply and quickly. Such a procedure would save important judicial time, and it would also provide a precedent for disentangling divorce from the adversary legal system.

There is increasing recognition among both legal and nonlegal authorities that one of the most fundamental objectives of divorce reform should be a restructuring of the very nature of the legal process. For example, in a recent article in the *California State Bar Journal*, Los Angeles attorney Phyllis Ziffren Deutsch criticized current approaches to divorce as unscientific and, in a more profound sense, unethical. "A 'beautiful decision,'" she wrote, "or a 'terrific settlement' resulting in the financial, emotional or social death of one of the parties or both or of the minor children of the alliance is not necessarily a wholesome good."[35] In making a strong case for what she called the "therapeutic divorce," she argued that to be truly effective, family-law practitioners should have sufficient insight and counseling skills to really help their clients and not just get them "the best deal." In a related effort, a young law student, Robert A. Roos, recently prevailed on the California Board of Behavioral Science Examiners to accept his recommendation that attorneys with "sufficient pertinent courses in marriage-counseling subjects" be accepted as meeting the requirements of a Masters Degree in Behavior Science for the purpose of obtaining a counseling license.[36]

These could, and hopefully will, be steps toward the eventual creation of a new and much needed practitioner of family law— the dissolution specialist, a legal or paralegal counselor with specific training and expertise in counseling, accounting, and law. Until these new practitioners appear, each state could immediately require that all attorneys now working in family law pass a special examination in both law and behavioral science.

As another immediate interim step, legislation should also be passed empowering courts to refer couples to family counselors to aid them with the dissolution of their marriage. In California, a couple will be referred to a court marriage counselor if they answer affirmatively to the question "do you think this marriage can still be saved through marriage counseling?" Those who want this kind of help should certainly have it available. Counseling should also be available to those who don't wish to save the marriage but who need help in making the transition out of wedlock, since only the well-to-do can afford private counseling.

The old dogma is that divorce is against the public interest and that therefore society should do nothing to help people get through it. We think nothing of showing movies about what to do in case of an automobile accident, although we are all agreed that such accidents are undesirable. Nevertheless, while it is the consensus of experts today that divorce is preferable to unhealthy togetherness, for the millions of women, men, and children whose lives are completely changed before, during, and after divorce, our society offers little help or guidance. If we can have driver-education films, why not divorce-education films? Why not show parents how to avoid tearing their children apart, both during and after proceedings? Why not have programs and lectures illustrating some of the common problems of divorce and ways in which they can be avoided?

Happily, such a trend has begun. In Los Angeles, a recent TV special[37] offered a free booklet listing agencies where people could get counseling help with their divorces. The YWCA has instituted a pilot "divorce retrieval" program in which women are offered free psychological and financial counseling, as well as lectures on the new divorce laws. As in so many other fields, adult university education is in the vanguard. In the past year alone, UCLA Extension has offered about half a dozen programs dealing with divorce. Some have been lectures and workshops on the law. Others have been courses on emotional adjustment and money management, to help the many women who have spent their marriages economically dependent on their husbands to learn to stand on their own two feet. Perhaps most significantly, there has been a recent mushrooming of single-parent groups and workshops, where women and men can find support and encouragement in their efforts to create better lives for themselves and their families.

Today, when the real issue is no longer whether or not a bad marriage should end, but how this can best be accomplished, a totally new social and legal approach to divorce is needed. In the long run it may be that the only way to minimize the economic and emotional conflicts in the dissolution of marriage will be to remove divorce from our adversary system of law completely. Finding and creating more viable alternatives will entail a major and concentrated program of study and development. As in other areas where institutional change is urgently needed, it will also require overcoming the resistance of the very experts who will be commissioned to study the problem. It may be that the real alternatives to outmoded methods for the dissolution of marriage, as well as to our entire antiquated system of family law, will have to come from outside our legal system, from women and men who have no vested interest in patriarchal institutions and the system of values they preserve.

12

The Equal Rights Amendment and The Future of Women

On March 22, 1972, Congress approved the Equal Rights Amendment. If the ERA is ratified by thirty-eight states (the requisite three-fourths majority) before March 22, 1979, the following provision will become a part of the United States Constitution:

> Equality of rights under the law shall not be denied or abridged by the United States or by any state on account of sex. The Congress shall have the power to enforce, by appropriate legislation, the provisions of this article. This amendment shall take effect two years after the date of ratification.[1]

As of this writing, thirty-four states have voted to ratify the ERA.[2] Thirty of these did so in the first year after its passage, but since then not much has happened. In 1974 only three states voted in its favor, and the prognosis for the future looks somewhat bleak, particularly after rejections in Georgia, Arizona, and Nevada. The Illinois senate voted to require a three-fifths rather than a simple majority for ratification.[3] In addition, the legislatures of two states, Nebraska and Tennessee, which previously approved the proposed amendment, have since voted to rescind, although the courts have ruled that Congress will have to approve any such action.

Nevertheless, it is difficult to imagine that the Equal Rights Amendment will not be adopted. For the first time in the half-century during which it has been annually introduced in Congress, it has strong support from a President's wife as well as the endorsement of the President, the AFL-CIO, the American Bar Association, and a large number of established women's organizations ranging from the National Federation of Business and Professional Clubs to Catholic Women for the ERA. The major organized opponents of the ERA, besides the John Birch Society and Phyllis Schlafly, are strongly patriarchal churches such as the Church of the Latter-Day Saints, as well as groups whose objections to the proposed amendment are similarly based on the religious dogma that the subjection of woman to men is divinely ordained (Women Who Want to be Women and Daughters Already Well Endowed).[4]

Perhaps no other proposed constitutional amendment has been as thoroughly studied as the ERA. In the forty-nine years prior to congressional approval, the ERA was the subject of extensive congressional hearings. It was debated before the House Judiciary Committee in 1948 and the Senate Judiciary Committee in 1956. It was reported on favorably by the Senate Judiciary Committee in the Eightieth, Eighty-first, Eighty-sixth, Eighty-seventh, and Eighty-eighth Congresses.[5] And in 1971, the Senate Subcommittee on Constitutional Amendments held three days of hearings during which some of the nation's leading constitutional law experts testified at length, after which it was again extensively debated on the floor of both houses before its passage.

The *Congressional Record* covering these hearings and debates contains what is known as the "legislative history" of the ERA—its sponsors' and proponents' statements about how the proposed amendment was intended to affect family, employment, military, criminal, and other areas of existing law. Since, under our rules of judicial interpretation, courts may not substitute their judgment regarding desirable social policies for that of our elected representatives, it is to this legislative intent that the courts will have to look in deciding how the ERA is to be interpreted. Because the legislative history of the ERA is so comprehensive and well documented there is today little controversy among legal scholars about the proposed amendment's proper interpretation. Nevertheless, opponents of the ERA continue to make irresponsible statements about the consequences of its ratification, resulting in a great deal of popular confusion and apprehension about the amendment's impact.

One of the arguments that is still being raised—that a special amendment dealing with sex-based discrimination is unnecessary because the Fourteenth Amendment already prohibits all discriminatory state laws and practices—has been rejected by most of the nation's leading constitutional experts. They point out that although the Fourteenth Amendment has always provided that "any person" shall be guaranteed the equal protection of our laws, in practice it was not until the case of *Reed* v. *Reed* (decided over one hundred years after that amendment was adopted) that the Supreme Court was finally persuaded to include women in that classification, and then only in a situation where sexual discrimination was so blatant that the Court found that it was totally arbitrary and wholly unrelated to the objectives of the state statute involved.[6] The conclusion of these experts, as Senator Birch Bayh has put it, is that "if given enough time the Court would eventually hold that the Equal Protection Clause of the Fourteenth Amendment demands the kind of equality between sexes which the equal rights amendment would guarantee, but that the process would take far too long."[7]

Subsequent events have borne out the second half of that conclusion. In *Forbush* v. *Wallace*, decided a year after *Reed*, the U.S. Supreme Court refused to hold that a legal classification based on sex violated the Fourteenth Amendment.[8] The Court held that an Alabama law requiring a woman to give up her own name and assume her husband's had a "rational" basis because it facilitated easy record-keeping. In so doing, the Court refused to apply to legal classifications based on sex the stricter test of construction used in civil-rights cases where race is involved, namely, that such "suspect classifications" will be given "strict scrutiny" and require proof of a "compelling state interest" to justify the discrimination.[9] In 1973, in the case of *Frontiero* v. *Richardson*, the Court was split on which of these two tests to adopt.[10] The decision struck down an Air Force rule which denied dependent benefits to husbands of female officers, while granting them to wives of male officers. Four of the justices based their decision on the ground that classifications based on sex, like those based on race, are inherently suspect, and are therefore subject to the strict "compelling-state-interest" test. However, three of the justices, while agreeing that the Air Force regulation was unconstitutional, made it clear that they considered the question of whether to apply the stricter compelling-state-interest test rather than the mild "rational-basis" test a political and not a constitutional issue. They criticized their fellow judges who had based their decision on the stricter test, arguing that they should have waited to see if the ERA was ratified first.

Since that decision, the Court seems to be moving backward. One of the biggest setbacks to any hope that the Supreme Court would act vigorously to prohibit sexual discrimination came in the case of *Kahn* v. *Shevin*.[11] Justice Douglas wrote the majority opinion holding that a Florida law allowing a property-tax exemption to widows but not widowers had a reasonable basis and was therefore not unconstitutional. Former Justice Douglas, who is renowned for his contributions to the field of civil rights, had only the day before written an extensive opinion in a case where discrimination based on race was involved. There he applied the compelling-state-interest test and asserted that the Fourteenth Amendment requires that individuals be judged on the basis of their individual capacities.[12] It is ironic that in the *Kahn* case, Justice Douglas not only applied the permissive rational-basis test, but that in so doing he based his decision not on individual capacities and circumstances, but on stereotypes about sex. He reasoned that since widows generally have more financial difficulties than widowers, the statutory classification was not arbitrary. Yet, as the dissent pointed out, the desired result of giving poor widows a tax break could have been achieved more equitably by granting the exemption to both widows and widowers whose incomes fell below a certain level. There was no real, compelling reason for the statute's sexual discrimination.[13]

To his credit, Justice Douglas apparently later changed his position. In *Geduldig* v. *Aiello*,[14] challenging the constitutionality of excluding medical expenses and work loss due to normal pregnancies from state disability insurance systems, he joined Justices Brennan and Marshall in a strong dissent, severely criticizing the majority for "singling out for less favorable treatment a gender-linked disability peculiar to women."[15] The dissenting opinion argued that the majority was in error for applying the rational-basis test and that "classifications based upon sex, like classifications based upon race, alienage, or national origin, are inherently suspect, and must therefore be subjected to strict judicial scrutiny."[16]

Despite the dissent's charge that the Court was creating a "double standard," Justices Stewart, Burger, White, Blackmun, Powell, and Rehnquist concluded that economic considerations justified the exclusion of pregnancy disability, and that in any case, there was no real sexual discrimination involved:

> There is no evidence on the record that the selection of the risks insured by the program worked to discriminate against any definable group or class in terms of the aggregate risk protection derived by that group or class from the program. There is no risk from which men are protected and women are not. Likewise, there is no risk from which women are protected and men are not. The appellee simply contends that, although she has received insurance protection equivalent to that provided all other participating employees, she has suffered discrimination because she encountered a risk that was outside the program's protection.[17]

This kind of reasoning leaves the constitutional analyst with the rather startling conclusion that the pregnancy disability exclusion has been upheld on the ground that it is not discriminatory against women, but only against that class of persons which becomes pregnant.

Geduldig v. *Aiello, Kahn* v. *Shevin,* and *Frontiero* v. *Richardson* were all decided by the Supreme Court *after* Congress had approved the ERA and during a period in which new cases or statutes seeking to correct sex-based discrimination were being reported almost daily in the press. There was no longer any real debate among legal scholars as to whether the ERA should (or even would) be adopted, and professional journals were already focusing on its legislative history and its impact on existing laws. Nevertheless, the majority of the men sitting on the highest court of our land were still wavering and hedging and waiting for a "clear mandate" before granting women and men as much constitutional protection against sex-based discrimination as is accorded persons receiving unequal legal treatment resulting from other accidents of birth such as race or national origin.

As *Geduldig* v. *Aiello* demonstrates, sex-based discrimination is so deeply ingrained in patriarchal society that it is frequently not even perceived as such. The resistance to any fundamental alteration of this reality, not only by our courts but by society at large, is extremely deep rooted and, like much of the criticism aimed at the ERA, is grounded far more in emotion than in logic or fact.

One fact that is apparently either unknown or unclear to many people is that the Equal Rights Amendment will only affect what is known as govermental action—that is, federal, state, or municipal interference with constitutional rights—and that it will *not* directly regulate personal or social relationships or even relationships between individuals and private business. The American Constitution, and particularly our Bill of Rights, was specifically designed to protect citizens from unreasonable and arbitrary governmental interference on the principle that there are inalienable human rights which are not and cannot be surrendered by "free men" when they enter into the social contract implied in our system of government, a system which is to be "for and by the people." It is only because the equal-protection clauses of the Fifth and Fourteenth Amendments have *not* been judicially construed to include women that we still have so many laws, regulations, and other governmental practices that arbitrarily differentiate between people on the basis of patriarchal sexual stereotypes. The ERA would require the legal rights, opportunities, and obligations of both men and women to be based on individual characteristics, circumstances, and needs, thereby meeting the so called "functional test" of constitutionality—and not, as some ERA critics have claimed, to "make men and women all the same."

Much of what is being editorialized about the ERA is simply not the truth. Consider the much publicized conclusion that passage of the ERA will deprive employed women of protection from state laws regulating hours, wages, and working conditions. A great deal of attention was devoted to this issue during the congressional hearings and debates. In 1971, Professor Norman Dorsen, one of the leading authorities in the field, presented a complete analysis of what he called "the crazy quilt of existing state protective laws" as well as his opinion on how the ERA would affect the situation.[18]

> First, there is no consensus (among the states) on what is needed protection for either men or women, and much of the legislation, instead of providing solutions to the real problems of women workers actually "protects" them out of jobs they are perfectly capable of fulfilling. Second, under Title VII of the Civil Rights Act of 1964 much state legislation of this type is being invalidated and will be of no long-term importance. Third, such laws that confer genuine benefits can and should be extended to men under the Equal Rights Amendment.
>
> For instance, while women are allowed chairs for rest periods in forty-five states, they are given job security for maternity leaves of absence in *no* state and maternity benefits under temporary

disability insurance in only two states. . . . In the benefit areas most people would consider most important—a minimum wage and a day of rest—men do receive substantial protection already. Only seven states have minimum wage laws for women only, but twenty-nine states, plus the District of Columbia and Puerto Rico, cover both men and women. More important, the federal minimum wage law covers both men and women at *higher* rates than all state laws except one (Alaska).

In contrast, maximum hour laws are a major area where men are not covered. Thirty-eight states cover women only, and three states cover men and women. Since the Supreme Court has upheld the validity of maximum hour legislation for both sexes since 1941, one can only suspect that unions have not pushed for maximum hour legislation, given their success in obtaining nationwide minimum wage laws for both sexes. This analysis would give credence to the EEOC and federal court decisions which have concluded that hour laws have been used as an excuse to keep women out of better-paying jobs.[19]

Professor Dorsen then analyzed the laws of eighteen states prohibiting employees from assigning night work to women and those of six states prohibiting women from working for certain periods before and after childbirth.

Women in fact do night work all the time. Nurses, telephone operators, airline reservationists, and scrub women have not been protected from night work. Pregnant women, too, often chose to work right up to the birth date. Who ever heard of a housewife being allowed time off from her housework and small children just because she was pregnant?

Weight laws also are of doubtful protection for women. There are only four states with weight limits applicable to all jobs, and these limits are set so low that, if literally applied, they would prohibit women from doing any serious labor, including carrying an unborn child. In the remaining few states with weight limits, they apply only to certain industries. In New York, for instance, women are "protected" from lifting weights only in the foundries. The theory, apparently, is that some mystical essence in foundry weight lifting will injure women, while lifting the same weight in other industries will not. Possibly it is the male workers in foundries who are being protected—from job competition.

Thus, when all the state laws applying only to women are examined closely, it becomes clear that they do not provide a coherent system of meaningful protection. Nor do they deal with the real problem for women—exploitation by being underpaid and funneled into the lowest-paying, most menial jobs of our society. State labor laws have never dealt with this problem. Furthermore, the premise that real protection can be based on legislating by sex is fallacious.

Sex is an insufficient criterion to predict with accuracy who needs what protection. If injury due to lifting weights is a problem the answer is to forbid employers to fire individuals—both men and women—who refuse to lift weights above a safe limit. If some men and some women don't want to work overtime, laws should be passed forbidding employers to fire those who refuse overtime; both men and women who do want overtime pay should not be penalized.

In short, analysis of state laws that apply exclusively to women does not establish that they protect women in any important way. In fact, these laws do not protect women in the one area clearly applicable to women only—maternity benefits and job security; they are ineffective in dealing with the exploitation of women through lower pay than men; and they are used to discriminate against women in job, promotion, and higher-pay opportunities. They do not furnish a reliable basis for opposition to the Equal Rights Amendment.[20]

State protective laws have indeed hindered women in the labor market far more than they have helped. However, for the many women confined to the nonunionized bottom layers of our work force, even the most minimal and laxly enforced protective regulations seem better than none at all. Although both sexes, as workers and human beings, should be entitled to fair and decent working conditions, it is not surprising that women, who are so disproportionately represented in the most marginal and least rewarding occupations, are frightened of an Equal Rights Amendment they have been misled to believe will deprive them of the little protection they have. The truth is that long before the ERA was passed by Congress, and even before the women's liberation movement had begun to gather momentum, many of these protective labor laws were already being dismantled. In the 1968 case of *Rosenfeld* v. *Southern Pacific Railroad*,[21] the plaintiff was a woman who had worked for the Southern Pacific Railroad for over twenty years doing the same kind of heavy physical work as men. When she applied for a promotion she was passed over for a less qualified man with less seniority, on the grounds that the higher position, which had certain hour and weight-lifting requirements, could not lawfully be performed by a woman under California's protective labor laws. Holding that she was entitled to the promotion, the district court ruled that the California protective labor laws were in conflict with Title VII of the Civil Rights Act of 1964, which prohibits employment discrimination based on sex. On appeal, the decision was affirmed and California's attorney general issued a ruling that the state's protective labor laws regulating hours and weights would no longer be enforced.

At the time of Professor Dorsen's testimony before Congress in 1971, twenty-two states and the District of Columbia had already repealed or substantially weakened protective labor laws concerning women. "It appears," he noted, "that the opponents of the amendment are trying to erect bridges which were crossed five years ago, when Title VII went into effect."[22] Today, half a decade later, the opponents of the ERA are attempting the same ploy, and the media and some public officials, who either know, or should know, better, are echoing their charges that the ERA must be stopped to protect women in the labor force. The truth is that, according to the U.S. Department of Labor Women's Bureau, all states except Nevada have already either repealed or stopped enforcing the laws regulating what hours women may work.[23]

According to its sponsors, the real effect of the ERA will be that where protective labor laws restrict employment or promotion opportunities for women (as in the cases of weight-lifting requirements, nightwork prohibition, or exclusion from certain occupations), these laws will probably have to be struck down.

However, where these laws confer benefits (such as a minimum wage and rest periods) they could easily be extended to men. As many legal scholars have pointed out, since the ERA would require that all benefits and rights stemming from government be accorded equally to women and men, the amendment should be interpreted not only as extending to women those rights and benefits already enjoyed by men, but also as extending to men those now enjoyed by women. The legislative history of the proposed amendment supports this interpretation. "The purpose of the amendment is not to cut down benefits accorded to only one sex, but to extend them to both sexes," Senator Bayh testified in support of the ERA.[24] "Where the law confers a benefit, privilege or obligation of citizenship," testified representative Martha Griffiths, another congressional sponsor of the amendment, "such would be extended to the other sex, i.e., the effect of the amendment would be to strike the words of sex identification. Thus, such laws would not be rendered unconstitutional but would be extended to apply to both sexes by operation of the amendment. We have already gone through this in the Fifteenth and Nineteenth Amendments."[25]

In interpreting a constitutional amendment, as in interpreting any other law, the courts are traditionally bound by the intent found in its legislative history. Furthermore, it is a firmly established rule of construction that wherever possible a statute or law will be interpreted so as to avoid the necessity of declaring it invalid under the Constitution. Our courts have repeatedly extended benefits and rights to a class of people that a statute unconstitutionally excluded, rather than voiding the law. In 1880, for example, the Supreme Court ruled that a state constitution limiting the right to vote to white people would not be struck down under the Fifteenth Amendment, but rather, would be extended to grant that right to blacks. The Equal Employment Opportunities Commission (the federal agency charged with interpreting Title VII of the Civil Rights Act of 1964) has similarly ruled that laws giving benefits to women should be extended as

well to men. Specifically referring to protective labor laws and
alimony, legal scholars have testified that "the ERA would result
in the general extension of certain benefits to men that now are
available only to women,"[26] and would also serve as "a constitutional guarantee against repeal of existing laws which now forbid
sex discrimination in employment."[27]

In January 1972, the presidentially appointed Citizens' Advisory Council on the Status of Women issued a report entitled
*The Equal Rights Amendment and Alimony and Child Support
Laws* which directed itself specifically to the argument that the
proposed amendment "will weaken men's obligation to support
the family and therefore, weaken the family."[28] Dismissing the
claim as erroneous, the council came to the following conclusion:

> Far from resulting in diminution of support rights for women
> and children, the Equal Rights Amendment could very well result
> in greater rights. A case could be made under the Equal Rights
> Amendment that courts must require divorced spouses to con-
> tribute in a fashion that would not leave the spouse with the
> children in a worse financial situation than the other spouse.
> The belief that alimony laws permitting alimony to wives
> would be invalidated by the courts rather than extended to men
> is not supported by any legal authority or the legislative history.
> The legislative history clearly indicates the intent of the proponent
> in Congress to extend alimony to men in those states now limit-
> ing alimony to women. Furthermore, in view of judges' preoc-
> cupation with keeping women from becoming public charges, it
> seems almost certain, should a State Legislature fail to extend to
> men a law limiting alimony to women, that a judge would extend
> the law to men rather than invalidate it. If any judge should in-
> validate the law, it is clear that legislatures' concern for keeping
> women from becoming public charges would be sufficient to enact
> a new law applying equally to men and women.
> In summary, the Equal Rights Amendment would not deprive
> women of any enforceable rights of support and it would not
> weaken the father's obligation to support the family. Because it
> would require complete equality of treatment of the sexes, it
> might be used to require that the spouses in divided families con-
> tribute equally within their means to the support of the children

so that the spouse with the children is not bearing a larger share of the responsibility for support than the other spouse.[29]

In his efforts to persuade the Senate to pass the ERA, Senator Bayh flatly stated that "the passage of the Equal Rights Amendment would not make alimony unconstitutional."[80] He pointed out that the statutes of one-third of our states have already extended that right to men, and that there is "no reason to not make all men eligible for alimony."[31] In his testimony before the Senate Judiciary Committee, Professor Dorsen pointed out that this was the approach taken by the model marriage and divorce legislation proposed by the Commissioners on Uniform State Laws. "The Uniform Marriage and Divorce Act eliminates definitions based on sex and substitutes those based on function," he said. "This is what the Equal Rights Amendment is intended to do. By passing it we will help insure more genuine protection for those who really need it, and end the many injustices women still face."[32]

The Senate Judiciary Committee's final report on the ERA went even further: "Where one spouse is the primary wage earner and the other runs the home, the wage earner would have a duty to support the spouse who stays home in compensation for the performance of his or her duties."[33] Citing this language as clear and unequivocal evidence of legislative intent, Professor Joan M. Krauskopf commented: "The report defines the duty of support under the ERA in functional terms based on factors such as each spouse's earning power, current resources, and non-monetary contributions to the family's welfare. Law would have to recognize homemaking tasks as legally a contribution to the family."[34]

Former Senator Sam Ervin is one of the most frequently cited authorities in attacks on the Equal Rights Amendment. His minority views are reported in the Ninety-second Congress's *Senate Report on the Equal Rights Amendment*,[85] wherein he quotes extensively from an article that appeared in the *Yale Law Journal* in 1971.[86] Since the amendment was passed by that Congress, the senator's arguments in opposition are not indicative of congressional intent and consequently have no real bearing on the ERA's judicial interpretation. However, this fact is rarely mentioned by ERA critics citing Ervin, or in media coverage of their attacks. Beyond that, the senator has been accused of misquoting his sources, of lifting phrases from context, "thus distorting, misconstruing or even inventing their meanings; he omits conditions, specifications and clarifications that greatly alter the area or significance of the effect under discussion; and his occasional inaccuracies or misquotations consistently err toward the negative."[37]

The Citizens' Advisory Council on the Status of Women has issued a special report documenting thirty-one specific instances of distortion and outright misquotation in Senator Ervin's statements about the ERA.[38] For example, in one passage about protective labor laws the *Yale Law Journal* article cited by the senator read as follows: "In general, labor legislation which confers clear benefits upon women would be extended to men. Laws which are plainly exclusionary would be invalidated. Laws which restrict or regulate working conditions would probably be invalidated, leaving the process of general or functional regulation to the legislatures." Senator Ervin's quotation, however, selected only the following half-sentence: "Laws which restrict or regulate working conditions would probably be invalidated."[39] Or dealing with the ERA's impact on the military, Senator Ervin cited the following quote: "The Equal Rights Amendment will greatly hasten this process and will require the military to see women as it sees men," failing to include the rest of the sentence: "... as a diverse group of individuals, married and unmarried, with and without children, possessing or desiring to acquire many different skills, and performing many varied kinds of jobs."[40]

Other opponents of the ERA have not even pretended to deal with it in logical terms. For example, in Georgia, where the legislature voted against the amendment, lawmakers argued that the ERA was "so stinking of Communism it's just pitiful to do something like this to America," that it would "lower our ladies down to the level of men," legalize homosexual marriages, and "create havoc in the prisons by preventing segregation of the sexes."[41]

Since we are all products of patriarchal socialization it is not surprising that the idea of equality between women and men should arouse a great many prejudices and fears, not only in men, but in women as well. Women's ambivalence about the ERA stems from a not unfounded, if seldom clearly articulated, perception that as long as the fundamental patriarchal character of our society is not altered, their basic situation as the powerless "second sex" will not change. However, adoption of the ERA would have great symbolic significance and would bring about some changes in attitudes. Of equal and perhaps even greater importance would be the symbolic value of its nonpassage. While the courts would probably continue to require that the sexes be treated equally in certain areas (those that constitute no real threat to the present social structure), women would almost certainly lose many of the gains they have already made, since the defeat of the ERA would undoubtedly be construed as a license to discriminate against women. While I therefore consider passage of the ERA essential, I am also aware that, just as racism has not been eliminated by three constitutional amendments, the Equal Rights Amendment will not in itself eradicate the even more deeply rooted social disease of sexism.

Just as the Thirteenth, Fourteenth, and Fifteenth Amendments were related to this nation's transition from an agrarian to an industrial economy, the proposed Twenty-seventh Amendment is part of a contemporary shift into postindustrial society, a shift which has already altered the traditional roles and social functions of women. As these continue to undergo major changes, the real issue for women is how they will be defined and by whom.

Therefore, the single most important issue concerning the ERA is *who* is to interpret and implement it. The amendment provides for a two-year "moratorium" to give the states and federal government time to revise their existing laws and enact new ones where required. State legislatures and federal agencies, bar conventions and committees, judges, lawyers, and sociologists are already gathering to decide how this is to be done. As long as these groups are controlled by men, the interpretation and implementation of the ERA will be dependent upon male analysis, despite the fact that women constitute 53 percent of our population.

The ERA offers a unique challenge to American women. They can passively sit back and let the men, who have for so long defined their world and circumscribed their part in it, do so once more. Or they can take the responsibility and the risks and insist on taking charge themselves.

While it is essential that women exert their influence at the polls by nominating and voting for only nonsexist candidates, it is not realistic to expect that massive inroads will be immediately achieved through existing political machinery. Nor can women expect to suddenly amass enough wealth to gain the economic power necessary to achieve control in the male-dominated corporate board rooms where so many social and political decisions are made. Women must therefore exert pressure along avenues that are immediately available and from which they have not been constrained by patriarchal acculturation. For example, they can use their already highly developed skills at fund-raising to finance massive lobbying and media campaigns through national women's organizations; they can make their presence felt at every legislative hearing, bar convention, and local bar-association meeting, at every family-law symposium, and at other forums where the ERA, proposals for divorce reform, and laws and measures affecting women are currently being discussed, evaluated, and interpreted. Women's organizations can hold public hearings patterned along the lines of those already held by congressional and state legislative committees. Such hearings might be entitled

to media coverage under the fairness and equal-time requirements of the FCC and would bring the real issues to the attention
of the nation.

While it is shocking that women have been enfranchised in this
country for only fifty-five years, it is even more shocking that
during this time the American political apparatus has successfully functioned to exclude them from any real participation. To
begin to correct this situation, women should demand that state
and federal governments hire qualified women to study and draft
the legislative modifications that the ERA will require. Much, if
not most, of the legislation introduced by federal and state legislators is not drafted by the elected representatives themselves,
but by paid members of their staffs, lobbyists, bar associations,
and law professors, or by special bodies such as the Commission
on Uniform State Laws, which commissioned and financed the
development of the Uniform Marriage and Divorce Act. There
are precedents in our legal system for requiring that those citizens
most directly affected by an act of the government be afforded
meaningful participation in its planning and implementation.
Federal financing for such projects as urban renewal, land-use
planning, and urban transportation is contingent on proof that
community representatives have been included in their step-by-
step planning activities, and large budgets are allocated by state
and local agencies to that end. The same rationale certainly applies to women with respect to the ERA, since they are the
citizens who will be most fundamentally affected by its passage.

One of the most promising phenomena of recent years is that
American women are overcoming one of the strongest of all patriarchal taboos—the prohibition against helping themselves. During the past decade, women have developed a number of important social inventions specifically designed to that end. The
most publicized of these, the so-called "consciousness-raising
groups," have allowed women working together to examine their
personal and social situations and to break through inner and
outer patriarchal bonds. Through the practice of "court-watch-

ing," other women's groups are systematically monitoring the legal system by going to court and recording the activities of judges and attorneys, particularly in relation to sexist practices and prejudices, and publishing their results.

But if women are to break through our ubiquitous patriarchal structure, a much more concerted and well-organized approach is required. As one step in this direction women should establish a network of institutes for the development of nonsexist social inventions. The top priority of these institutes would be the creation of improved methods for implementing desired social changes, with a crash program to create devices that would ensure the inclusion of women in the interpretation and implementation of the ERA as fully functioning, recognized, and paid participants. Such institutes could be financed by setting aside a certain portion (say 25 percent) of all punitive damages awarded in sex-discrimination cases. There are precedents for this type of approach not only in class actions where damages are collected on behalf of an entire class of aggrieved persons, but in the growing practice of using a social-reparations approach in sentencing convicted individuals. Instead of being incarcerated, convicted individuals—or groups—are organized to perform useful services for those they have harmed. For example, a group of milk-company executives found guilty of price-fixing were recently ordered to donate $175,000 to charitable organizations and to work forty-five days for community agencies that provide help for needy children. U.S. District Court Judge Carl Muecke said he was looking for a constructive alternative that would more closely compensate those injured by the milk companies' practices. "Any fine I would levy," he stated, "would go to the Government, and that would be like spitting in a blast furnace."[42]

When and if the ERA is adopted the first step in its implementation will be to examine all existing federal, state, and local laws to determine whether they contain classifications based on sex, and if so, whether these classifications are constitutionally permissible. Where a law is found to be in conflict with the Equal

Rights Amendment, the second step will be to decide whether that law should be expanded to include both sexes, nullified entirely, or, where necessary, replaced by different legislation. I believe that a third step is also desirable—the enactment of laws specifically designed to make up for the disadvantaged position in which women now find themselves.

This is not a novel approach, nor is it without precedent. For example, the U.S. Supreme Court has accepted the proposition that there are circumstances in which the law must make allowances for differences between the rich and the poor. In the landmark case of *Griffin* v. *Illinois* the Court held that state courts must provide free trial transcripts for indigents' appeals in criminal cases even though solvent defendants are required to pay for theirs.[43] And, in *Gideon* v. *Wainwright*, the Court extended that ruling to require that indigent defendants must be provided with court-appointed counsel in criminal proceedings.[44] The executive branch of our government has also adopted this approach, precisely in the area and the manner I am suggesting. Executive Order 11246, passed in 1967, prohibits private firms with federal contracts from discriminating on the basis of race, creed, national origin, or sex. In 1972 the order was amended to require private firms to develop and implement "affirmative-action programs" to secure equal employment for women and minorities. The order requires an employer to give minority groups and women preferential treatment in hiring and promotion. Since the passage of Title IX of the Higher Education Act of 1972, similar requirements also apply to college campuses receiving any form of governmental financing or aid. In business and education, active recruiting and hiring programs are now required by law to correct some of the damage caused by traditional discrimination against women.

The ERA should be interpreted in line with this reasoning. Wherever sexism in our society has created sex-based inequalities and inequities, the amendment should be interpreted to require affirmative-action legislation. It should not be used to penalize and punish women under the guise of equal treatment, as has unfortunately happened under some of the egalitarian divorce laws. In the field of family law, these affirmative-action programs could require measures designed to equalize the economic position of a homemaker unemployed by divorce with that of her former mate. Such programs could also include procedures to facilitate collection of spousal- and child-support payments through specially adapted versions of already existent garnishment and attachment laws, and they could require new tax laws, under which employed custodial parents can list child care as a legitimate business-expense deduction. In the light of contemporary social and economic realities and trends, the affirmative-action programs should also require that legislatures give priority to measures designed to minimize the social and economic imbalances and dislocations that women's transition into postindustrial society is bringing about. For example, adequate child-care facilities should be provided for both single and married parents contributing child-care services and, as in Sweden, each parent should have the option of working only four hours a day.

When in the past women have made significant gains during periods of social ferment, they have often lost them after "things settled back to normal." Whether the changes currently taking place will be more lasting and whether the ERA will be interpreted and implemented in ways that are really constructive for women is, finally, up to women themselves. Not only are there massive external obstacles, but there are also more insidious internal ones. Forced to earn their keep by being loved, indoctrinated to be weak, frail, and emotionally dependent, women have learned to suppress their self-reliance and initiative, to pay exaggerated attention to their external appearance, to become manipulative rather than self-assertive, and to be masochistic, clinging, and insecure—in short, to inhibit most of the personality traits associated with emotional maturity. As Simone de Beauvoir has pointed out, the dominance-dependency syndrome is the psychological key to all successful master-slave relationships. In our society, such relationships are subtly manifested in the "kept" woman, the use of women as sex symbols, and the equally parasitic patriarchal ideal of the wealthy housewife whose only function is to consume and to serve as an attractive and idle status symbol for her successful husband. As long as these personally and socially destructive roles continue to be accepted by both sexes as the pinnacles of feminine achievement, there can be no real improvement in the lives of either sex. The symbiotic nature of traditional male-female roles is recognized by social scientists as one of the prime causes of unsatisfactory and mutually harmful relationships between the sexes and as one of the underlying causes for many of our psychological and sociological problems.

Perhaps the most difficult internal obstacle that women must overcome is the doctrine that each woman is every other woman's enemy. This is an integral part of the economic structure of patriarchy, where women are traditionally required to compete with one another for marriage and for men, not just out of romanticism, or love, or to meet sexual needs, but for survival. It is no accident that in our society religion, myth, literature, film, TV, and every other socialization medium portrays women as treacherous, manipulative, "catty," and untrustworthy. It is this that makes it possible for female secretaries to think they relate better to male rather than female bosses, regardless of personal characteristics, and it has also been responsible for women's inability to unite as an effective political force.

Disunity among nondominant social groups is not new. Even among such an overtly oppressed group as black slaves, there was a split between "field niggers," who were treated worse than animals, and house slaves, who tended to judge the field hands by white men's standards. Lacking positive identification with anyone of their own race, the more privileged slaves identified with their masters, on whose side they sometimes actually fought in slave revolts. The split between conventional women and feminists has proceeded along similar lines. Even among women working for adoption of the ERA, those who agree with such feminist goals as equal pay and employment or freely available abortions find it necessary to qualify their position by saying that this does *not* mean they are in favor of "women's liberation."

I am not suggesting that women unite against men, but against the patriarchal institutions and systems of values which are destructive to both sexes. Patriarchal societies, whether capitalist, communist, or fascist, all closely circumscribe the life choices, not only of women, but of men, and impede close, open, and truly human relationships between the sexes by imposing rigid emotional and behavioral stereotypes and roles. Both sexes are the losers in a social organization where the male, still basically defined as the dominant "hunter-provider," dies suddenly of diseases induced by accumulated stress, and where women flock into doctors' offices suffering from the more gradually lethal physical and psychological effects of repression.

Nor am I suggesting that the solution is for women to take over the roles of men and become the "dominant sex." Such a reversal of roles would still leave us with all the underlying problems of a society where enforced conformity to rigid stereotypes distorts and confines our human potential. When I speak of equality I am speaking of equality of opportunity on an individual human level, and equality of opportunity is, by definition, impossible in a society where familial and public institutions are organized to enforce power-based relationships and systems of belief.

What I am talking about is a revolution—not the type of bloody revolution where one group wrests power from another until it again is toppled in its turn—but the kind of revolution that occurs in science from time to time. Contrary to popular misconceptions, science has not developed in an orderly, stepwise fashion by adding bits of data year by year. Rather, science moves forward through dramatic changes or revolutions which occur when accumulating data no longer fit the generally accepted view about the nature of the universe—what the noted historian of science Dr. Thomas S. Kuhn calls the existing scientific "paradigm."[45] At that point a crisis occurs, and, as Dr. Kuhn points out, unless there is a revolution or major restructuring so that a new paradigm emerges, no more productive research can take place. It has been out of such fundamental restructuring of scientific systems, and not from minor revisions of old theories, that real scientific progress has come.

The path of human history follows a similar course. As outmoded world views and social inventions fail to meet emerging social needs, crises occur. Today we are in a time of such crisis. We are already experiencing the dissolution of many of our old social institutions. We can no longer make minor changes by tacking on small improvements to the existing patriarchal system. It is the system itself that needs to be scrapped. Only when we adopt what in science Kuhn would call a completely new paradigm will new options become available, or even visible. And only then will the crisis be resolved. At this point in human history the future of our planet is at stake, and our "hard" patriarchal world view must be modified by a "softer" more "feminine" consciousness. It is of course a time of crisis, but it is also a time of opportunity: of opportunity for both women and men to join together and invent a better, more truly human future for us all.

APPENDIX

I

DIVORCE
CHECKLIST

Divorce
Checklist

Do You Need a Lawyer?
Selecting Your Lawyer
Working With Your Lawyer
Attorney's Fees
Divorce Procedures
The Division of Property
Child and Spousal Support
Child Custody and Visitation
Debts, Taxes, Insurance, Wills, Modifiability,
    and Miscellaneous

Do You Need a Lawyer?

If you have no children, little property, and don't want any
support, you are a logical candidate for a do-it-yourself divorce.

Whether that course of action is feasible depends greatly on
where you live. In most states formal pleadings (complaints and
answers) are still required. Unless you have some knowledge of
how these must be drafted to meet both the substantive and

procedural requirements of your state, the cost of your time and effort may outweigh the fee of an attorney. In those counties of California and other states where forms rather than legal pleadings are used, do-it-yourself divorces are relatively simple to obtain. The required forms are available at the local courthouse, and a number of recently published books offer instructions on how they are to be completed. Private organizations like the Wave Project and the California Divorce Council will assist in filling out these forms and will offer advice on court procedures for a nominal fee, so that substantial savings may be realized by handling your own dissolution.

However, since every divorce requires a court appearance by one of the parties, you have to be willing and prepared to go to court by yourself, or *in propria persona*. Although such *pro per* appearances are becoming more common, judges are sometimes impatient with people who are not represented by counsel, and this is another factor that has to be taken into account.

But the most important question you must consider is whether your situation is really as simple as it seems, or whether there may be some legal issues or problems of which you are not aware. *If you have any doubt at all*, I believe it is best if you consult an attorney, to get a clearer picture of what is involved. In any case, if your spouse plans to hire counsel, you will be well advised to do the same.

*   *   *

You should get an attorney if:
—your spouse has retained one
—there are children whose rights need to be protected
—you and your spouse cannot agree on the property settlement, child support, or any other terms of the dissolution
—you feel nervous about your ability to function effectively in a courtroom

You *may* not need an attorney if:
—you have no children, property or debts
—you do *not* require support
—you feel absolutely confident that the agreement you and
your spouse have made is truly equitable and will really
work

     ❈   ❈   ❈

Selecting Your Lawyer

In some locales, feminist organizations like NOW are compiling
lists of nonsexist lawyers. However, the fact than an attorney is
not a sexist does not necessarily ensure his or her competence. It
is still necessary to find out how the women and men on these
lists are screened, and to screen them yourself. While many community bar associations provide referral services, the attorneys
suggested are rarely if ever screened at all, except to see if they
meet minimal standards—ordinarily only the possession of an un-
expired or unsuspended license.

Before buying a new refrigerator or even a pair of shoes, you
shop around. You ask your friends about the various brands and
seek to discover which offers the best value for the money. You
read consumer guides, then physically inspect the appliance or
footwear before you make your choice. Picking an attorney should
be a similar process, in which you gather as much information as
you can before you come to a decision. Unfortunately it is very
difficult to come by information about professionals. For one
thing, by "gentlemen's agreement," one professional will rarely,
if ever, criticize another, no matter how incompetent she or he
may be. The best approach is to seek personal recommendations
from acquaintances and friends, and then interview the attorney
or attorneys yourself. If an organization has suggested a particu-

lar attorney, try to find someone who has used his or her services. You should try to find someone whose practice is either confined to family law or who works extensively in that field.

Although there are of course limitations of time and money, unless you are really sure about your first choice, in the long run you may be better off interviewing more than one attorney. You may not be able to evaluate a person's professional competence in one consultation, but you can tell a great deal about such matters as general intelligence, ability to listen, and willingness to inform and clarify. In addition, even one meeting will usually tell you a great deal about the very important issue of sexist attitudes and behavior.

Today a black would no longer knowingly go to a racist lawyer, or a Jew to an anti-Semite. Yet women still flock to avowedly sexist and openly patronizing attorneys, particularly in domestic-relations cases. Since divorce proceedings usually bring into question a woman's traditional status as wife and mother and her spouse's traditional status as husband and father, it is particularly important to choose an attorney who is, as much as possible, free of conscious and unconscious sexist biases and prejudices.

A prominent attorney who was speaking as counsel for a husband in a divorce proceeding expressed himself as follows: "I don't know why she's making all this fuss. He only had the use of her body for two years." His candor, not to mention his crudeness, was unusual. His attitude may not be.

It is essential when interviewing prospective counsel that women pay close attention to attitudes. The last thing a woman needs when she is getting a divorce, when perhaps for the first time in her adult life she is getting ready to stand on her own two feet, is to be made to feel incompetent. Even those attorneys who are not blatantly sexist do their clients a great disservice if they act in the patronizing and superior manner that we have come to regard as professionalism. While the "don't worry, honey," "it's going to be okay, dear" approach may initially sound comforting, in the long run it is destructive. Divorce is a time in a woman's life when she needs to feel, for herself and for her children, capable, competent, and worthwhile. She should not be treated like a dependent little old lady, or a cross between a pretty but feebleminded school girl and a sexual object.

❀ ❀ ❀

Guidelines for selecting an attorney:
—Ask your friends, find out what happened to those who are divorced.
—Choose candidates who work extensively in family law.
—Interview each candidate (it may cost money, but it's worth it).
—Evaluate candidates for intelligence, sexist attitudes, ability to relate well, understanding of the problems facing you.

❀ ❀ ❀

Working With Your Lawyer

Client and attorney, like patient and doctor, have what the law calls an agency relationship—the professional is paid by the client to *help and serve* her or him. By legal definition then, the proper role of the attorney, and every other professional, is to sufficiently educate the client so that she or he can understand each problem and its risks. It is the lawyer's job to give advice to the best of her or his training and ability, not to give orders. It is the client's job to decide what course of action to take.

A client's consideration of her or his problems encompasses much more information than she or he can ever express to an attorney. While it is true that the attorney has professional expertise, it is the client's future that is at stake. The attorney will survive the case; the client may not. Therefore it is the client who must be the final arbiter, and who, after carefully weighing the advice of the attorney, must make her or his own decision. Sometimes you can't tell whether you have the right attorney until after you have worked with her or him for a while. Lawyers and judges have faulted women for "changing attorneys as often as they change hats." While jumping from one attorney to another may not make much sense, I believe that it is equally nonsensical to stick with an attorney if you, after thinking it through carefully and realistically, have concluded that you are not being advised and/or represented adequately. However, in making that decision, it is important to keep in mind that attorneys have to function within certain outside limitations and realities. Sometimes they have a strong case. At other times they have a weak one. Attorneys, no matter how good they are, are fallible. They and their staffs are often overloaded and working under a great deal of pressure. The client who is an active participant in the case, who checks the factual information and tries to understand the legal issues involved, will naturally get the best results, since it is much easier for attorneys to do a good job if they have their client's active help.

*   *   *

Guidelines for working with your attorney:

—Be prepared to make your own decisions on the basis of evaluation of your situation by your attorney.

—Accept your attorney's legal counsel, especially with respect to reasonable expectations of probable court action, or be prepared to change attorneys.

—Cooperate with your attorney by providing concise and complete information as needed, without trying to take over conduct of your case.

*   *   *

Attorney's Fees

One of the more common mistakes women make (very often on the advice of their husbands) is deciding to economize on their attorneys. Of course one should avoid those attorneys who build what we in California call "Beverly Hills briefs," who create fee-producing problems by exacerbating interspousal and inter-attorney disagreements and hostilities, but one should not avoid the expense of a good attorney in an attempt to preserve or increase the funds that will later be distributed as part of the divorce settlement.

For most women, the subject of professional fees often triggers terror. Unaccustomed to the business and professional world, they perceive the fees normally charged by attorneys as astronomical. Also, women have been told that it is the husband's obligation to pay for the lawyer, and there is great resentment if, as is the judicial trend today, the court does not order the man to pay all the fees, a resentment that is often (perhaps unconsciously) deflected against the lawyer. But more than anything else, a great many women are so frightened of the prospect of having to stand on their own and take care of themselves economically that any expenditure is a matter of panic.

Since attorneys are a necessity, trying to economize by hiring a mediocre lawyer or none at all is simply very bad business. As a matter of fact, the wife's attorney usually has more of a job than does the husband's. The husband not only has had control of the assets, but has all the information about them. The massive effort of discovery and analysis of the financial picture, as well as the task of persuading the court of the wife's needs, falls to her attorney.

If there is any money to fight over, a wife needs a good attorney to represent her interests and that attorney will not come cheap. If there is no money there can still be a fight (for example over child custody, or over the apportionment of debts) and this is where the problem of attorneys' fees becomes really acute.

For the poor, even in those communities that have free legal-aid services, the waiting period for a divorce case can be as long as a year or more. Where a woman's husband has some property or at least a steady job, but the woman has no direct access to any of the money except for her household allowance, there are a few more options. Some bar associations have referral lists of attorneys who are willing to provide a consultation in such cases, either for free or for a very low fee. Many attorneys will take such cases without a retainer (an advance payment), in the expectation that the court will award them fees. The problem here is that, at least in California, there has been a trend toward lower fee awards; and in any case, it is sometimes impossible (or at best, very difficult) to collect from an angry ex-husband.

But even where a woman has some money of her own or where she and her husband have agreed that her attorney will be paid, there is still the question of how much. Since bar associations no longer provide fee guidelines, at present the only way to get a general picture is to ask around. In 1975, southern California hourly rates ranged from $30 to $120, and divorces averaged $500 for routine cases, with retainers for complex situations involving substantial property usually starting at $750.

To avoid misunderstandings, it is always a good idea to talk to your attorney in advance about fees. Most attorneys will require payment of a retainer before they take the case. This is usually a lump-sum payment which is intended to cover initial costs and hourly charges. Since you must pay this amount out of your own pocket, make sure that your attorney has agreed to reimburse you proportionally if the court makes an award for fees. Be sure you understand what you are being charged for, not by harassing your attorney or by requiring petty and excessive accountings, but in the same way that you would expect to be informed by anyone else who is being paid for their services.

* * *

Checklist regarding fee considerations:
- —Look out for "glamour" attorneys who charge high fees even for simple cases.
- —Be realistic about your legal needs and avoid false economy; remember that divorce is an adversary proceeding and you need adequate representation.
- —Ask your friends about reasonable fees.
- —Discuss fee arrangements with your attorney and be clear about probable costs and charges.

       ✿   ✿   ✿

Divorce Procedures

Once you have found an attorney who is legally competent, empathetic, and conscious of the problems of sexism, you will have gone a long way toward minimizing the trauma of divorce. You will also find it helpful to familiarize yourself with the steps and procedures that divorce entails, so that each new development does not come as a surprise or shock.

The materials that follow are intended as guidelines, not as substitutes for the counsel of an experienced attorney. They are designed to provide a better understanding of the legal and practical considerations involved in a divorce, thereby reducing the anxiety normally associated with the unknown. They do not offer individual advice, since specific decisions can only be made by taking individual circumstances into account.

Each state has its own divorce laws. This means that the substantive laws and the procedures governing divorce, such as grounds, length of residence required, and time before the decree becomes final vary from state to state. Many states still refer to the divorcing parties as *plaintiff* and *defendant,* requiring the former to file a complaint and the latter to file an answer. These documents are legal pleadings that will not be accepted by the courts unless they are couched in the requisite legal language, so that in most cases their drafting will require the assistance of an attorney. In California and other no-fault states that have accepted the recommendations of the Uniform Marriage and Divorce Act, plaintiffs and defendants have been replaced by *petitioners* and *respondents* who now file simpler documents called petitions and responses. In some states these are printed forms which deal primarily with statistical information, such as the date of the marriage and separation, and the number and names of children. Like the complaint, the petition also states what relief is sought in addition to the termination of the marriage, such as spousal support, child support and custody, division of property, and attorney's fees. In California, the petition lists these items, and simply provides boxes to be checked.

Upon the filing of the complaint or petition, the court issues a summons, a document by which the other spouse is ordered to appear in court at a certain hour and date. It is at this point that a divorce proceeding formally begins. The next step is that the summons plus the complaint or petition are served on the other spouse. Normally service is in person (by a marshal or another adult who is not a party to the action). Where there is no known location or where the other spouse lives out of state, there are also procedures for service by mail or publication. Proof of proper service must be filed with the court.

As in other legal proceedings, if the person summoned does not appear, the law interprets this as an admission of guilt or a decision not to contest, and a default judgment will be entered. Therefore, if you are served with a summons you must either file the necessary answer or response and appear in court at the prescribed time or, as is more usual in divorce cases, get an extension of time within which to plead. This extension will afford time to negotiate a marital-settlement agreement.

Whether the terms of a divorce are negotiated by agreement or litigated in court, the legal dissolution of a marriage requires both an appearance in court by at least one of the parties and a judgment or decree. In granting a divorce, the court will issue both *interlocutory* and *final* decrees. These terms are the source of some confusion. The divorce procedures of most states provide for a number of hearings during the course of the divorce action. The most fundamental and important of these is the interlocutory hearing, during which the marital-settlement agreement, if there is one, is approved by the judge or, if no agreement has been reached, the case is tried and the judge makes all final determinations. An interlocutory decree is then issued and for all practical purposes, unless there is an appeal or some other procedural problem, that is the end of the case. There is no final hearing. All that is left now is to wait out the prescribed period of time until a final decree can be entered. The rationale for this waiting period (six months in California, and one year in the majority of states) is to give couples time to reconcile. In content, the final decree is the same as the interlocutory, only upon its issuance the case is formally concluded and the parties are free to remarry.

The interlocutory hearing therefore is the main event in a divorce or dissolution case. It can take five minutes in a simple default case where a property-settlement agreement has been worked out in advance, or hours and even days and weeks in those cases where there is a fight over children or property or both.

In addition to the interlocutory hearing, there can be a number of other hearings in divorce and dissolution cases. One type deals with motions, usually concerning the discovery of evidence and legal maneuvering involved in matters of procedure. Discovery motions, for example, may request a court order compelling a party to answer interrogatories or to produce some concealed evidence. Sometimes a motion is also made on the ground of some procedural or technical error, for which the court can be asked to penalize the opposing party.

Another widely used procedure in a divorce or dissolution is the preliminary hearing, in California called *order to show cause* (OSC). This hearing is a device for obtaining temporary court orders, particularly relating to support, and forbidding spouses from harassing or molesting each other or from squandering the community or marital property. These hearings are primarily designed to maintain the status quo until a marital-settlement agreement can be worked out or the preparation for trial can be completed. They are very useful, since an OSC or temporary hearing will go to trial ten to fifteen days from the date of service, whereas the wait for an interlocutory hearing is usually several months.

*   *   *

The usual steps in a divorce are:
— filing of complaint or petition
— issuance of summons
— service on respondent or defendant
— filing of proof of service
— respondent or defendant filing a "responsive pleading" or obtaining from opposing counsel an extension of time within which to file
— preliminary hearing(s) if appropriate
— negotiated property-settlement agreement (division of property, spousal support, child support and custody), followed by default hearing where terms of settlement are incorporated into the interlocutory decree of divorce
or
— litigated adversary interlocutory court hearing where a judge decides the terms on which the marriage is to be dissolved
— entry of final decree (same terms as interlocutory decree) after statutory waiting period, if any

*   *   *

The Division of Property

Although in both negotiated and litigated cases all aspects of a divorce are interrelated, for the sake of simplicity they are here dealt with in different sections.

The majority of divorces involving any substantial marital property are settled by marital-settlement agreements (or as they are sometimes called, property-settlement agreements). These are not forms but are drafted by spouses' attorneys to fit the circumstances of each case. They include provisions for the division of property, child and spousal support, visitation rights, and various economic factors such as the payment of taxes, insurance coverage, trusts, and wills. Since this contract will affect your life and the lives of your children for many years, it is very important that your attorney explain every clause to you until you are sure you fully understand its meaning. Business people do not sign agreements unless they fully understand what they are getting into, and neither should you. A marital-settlement agreement is a business contract. It deals with dollars and cents, with property, with mutual responsibilities and obligations, in short, it encompasses the same subjects as any other business contract.

It is the lawyer's obligation to help the client understand an agreement. Remember that when you are represented by an attorney the law presumes you have been properly advised and that you understand what you are doing. In the absence of fraud, duress, or actual mental incapacity, it will be to no avail if you later go back to court and argue that you did not understand the document you signed.

The legal ground rules for the division of property vary from state to state. Barring some overwhelming generosity or guilt on the part of either spouse, marital-settlement agreements are usually drafted in line with local laws, taking into account the manner in which judges are commonly making awards in the community.

With regard to the legal aspects of the agreement, you can learn something about the rudiments of law in the same way that you can learn something about a disease if you are ill. You should acquaint yourself with some of the rules about gifts, inheritances, earnings, and assets acquired before and during marriage and after separation. In each state different laws will govern. In some areas you can obtain this information through university extension programs or through organizations like the YWCA. For those seeking greater depth, there are books or articles in professional journals.

In general, the rules for the division of property depend upon whether the laws of the state are based on community-property precepts or on those of the common law. In community-property states all property acquired during a marriage (except for special situations such as inheritance or gift) belongs to both spouses and is consequently subject to division, whereas separate property (property falling into one of the exceptions or owned before the marriage) is not. In common-law states, all property held in the name of a married person is her or his separate property. Unless property is held jointly (for example, in joint tenancy or tenancy in common), it is technically not subject to division in divorce proceedings. However, the laws of common-law states may include such equitable devices as constructive trusts which permit judges, if equity and fairness require, to distribute property held exclusively in one spouse's name to the other.

Where there is any dispute about the nature of the property, proof of ownership becomes a major issue. If a woman has not participated in her family's financial management, she may be ignorant of the real status of assets and liabilities, or even of their existence. Concealed assets are not unheard of in divorce cases, and it is important that your attorney make good use of the discovery tools that are available. Naturally, this will mean additional attorney's fees and also, where required, the use of accountants and other experts, but if the case warrants it, it is money well spent. In many cases it may not be necessary to go this route. Past tax returns, or quarterly profit-and-loss statements may be all that is required. Since each case is different, only a cooperative effort between client and attorney can offer the most effective and sensible course of action.

Property is more than houses, pots, pans, cars, and furniture. It includes intangibles such as rights to pension payments, copyrights, patents, life-insurance cash values, retirement benefits, income-tax refunds, and rights to future income or deferred cash or property payments. For example, if one of the spouses is an insurance agent he or she may be entitled to income from renewal rights on policies sold during the marriage for a number of years to come. Actors and television writers may have residual rights. Executives and employees of corporations may be members of profit-sharing and stock-option plans. Professionals like doctors, lawyers, and accountants may own accounts receivable (monies owed to them but not yet paid). They—and the owners of small businesses—may also have an asset called good will.

Not only a good attorney and accountant, but a professional appraiser may be needed to determine the value of the marital assets. Nevertheless, no matter how competent and responsible these people may be, they or their staffs can make mistakes. Since it is your case, not theirs, their conclusions must be thoroughly checked. Just as you check your department-store bills and the invoice from the plumber, you should continually oversee the business aspects of your settlement.

❖   ❖   ❖

Property division checklist:
　　—Identify all property owned or controlled by either party.
　　—Utilize discovery proceedings where necessary.
　　—Take all measures necessary to verify your spouse's statements of financial condition.

—Identify intangible assets.

—Determine what property elements are legally subject to division.

—Ascertain if court restraining order is needed to prevent disposal or waste of marital assets.

—Determine value of assets, using expert assistance when necessary.

❊   ❊   ❊

Child and Spousal Support

It is often difficult to determine just how much money will be needed for spousal and child support. These needs must of course be balanced by the amount of funds available. The first task is to determine what income (other than spousal and/or child support) you now have or can realistically expect, and to offset that against your present and anticipated expenses. Some states, like California, have forms (financial questionnaires) for the itemization of income and expenses. These can be very helpful in arriving at realistic figures.

On the income side, if you are employed you will of course deduct taxes, Social Security, unemployment and other payroll deductions such as medical or life insurance, retirement plans, etc. from your gross income. You should also estimate how much you will have to pay in taxes on any anticipated spousal support.

The standard expense items are usually rent or mortgage payments, property taxes and insurance, home maintenance and utility costs, payments for telephone, food, and household supplies, clothing, laundry, and cleaning expenses, medical and dental costs, professional expenses, education and child care, car payments, car insurance, gas and repairs or other transportation costs, medical-, accident-, and life-insurance payments, entertainment, travel, installment payments, and whatever incidentals or miscellaneous expenses may arise. It is easy to forget such items as replacements (towels wear out, dishes break), piano lessons, school supplies, camps, books, and other expenses for the children (as well as cosmetics for yourself), and an occasional gift for a friend. There should also be reserve funds for emergencies, should the water heater blow up or the refrigerator go on the blink.

Once you have all the expense categories, the next task is to determine their monthly amounts. A good approach is to write down what it would take to maintain your accustomed standard of living. Even though you may later have to scale this down, you do *not* want to begin negotiations with rock-bottom figures representing the minimum you can get along with. To determine current and past living expenses go through old checks or check stubs and refer to old tax returns, particularly if you have itemized deductions. Some items will have to be estimated, particularly new types of expenses called for by your present or anticipated situation, such as clothes for work, higher transportation costs in commuting, child care while at the job, etc.

In a great many families, where there was just enough income to manage one household, the fact is that there simply is not going to be enough to adequately support two. Nevertheless, by carefully and realistically figuring out your monthly expenses, you will at least provide yourself with a rational basis for your support-award demands, while gaining a more realistic understanding of your situation.

Other circumstances, such as your and your spouse's relative wealth, the length of your marriage, your health, your work training and experience, your age, and, if you are the custodial parent, the physical and mental health of your children, will also play an important part in determining the necessary amount of spousal and/or child support. Alimony is taxable to the recipient and deductible to the payer; consequently fathers can sometimes be induced to pay more total support by shifting some of the child-support monies over to alimony, since they then obtain larger tax deductions. However, in arriving at any such trade-off,

you should keep in mind that unless otherwise agreed, alimony will terminate if you remarry (as well as if you or your spouse die), whereas child support lasts until the child reaches majority (unless she or he marries first or becomes financially independent), and that in most states the child-support obligation survives the death of the noncustodial parent and can be claimed from the estate.

In addition to monthly support payments there are other components to spousal and child support. For example, if the noncustodial parent is employed, family members may be covered under some kind of health and accident insurance program through his or her job. Under most plans the coverage of minor children can be continued even after the divorce, and a spouse may be covered until the divorce is final. Fathers who can afford it have traditionally undertaken to pay all or a portion of their children's medical and dental expenses (including orthodonture and psychiatry), as well as all or part of the cost of their college education.

Since more and more states are adopting laws which make a minor an adult at the age of eighteen, if you and your spouse agree that child support should continue past that age, be sure that this is clearly spelled out.

❋   ❋   ❋

In developing an acceptable agreement
for spousal and child support:
—Prepare a detailed estimate of anticipated income, excluding spousal and/or child support, and considering tax and other deductions.
—Prepare a detailed estimate of anticipated expenses, based on accustomed standard of living, as a basis for negotiation or litigation.
—Be aware that adjustments may be required, since two households cannot live as cheaply as one.

—In addition to direct spousal- and child-support payments, keep in mind "fringe benefits" such as insurance coverage, medical expenses, and provision for college education and other special needs of the children.

* * *

Child Custody and Visitation

Child custody and visitation can, and whenever possible should, be worked out between the parents. Unless there is strong evidence that a parental agreement is against the children's best interests, judges will usually go along with it, despite the fact that, legally, child-custody matters are to be determined by the court. Since the children have no legal standing in court, once parents have made an agreement the issue of the child's best interest does not really come up unless a third party—usually a social worker—intervenes.

Clarity is the hallmark of every good agreement. If you spell out who is responsible for doing what and when, many future problems can be avoided. Unfortunately, not only the sloppy agreements, but often also those too heavily laden with legal terminology can create rather than avoid future litigation. If there is an area of possible ambiguity, be explicit, spell it out, and ask your attorney to include such clarifications in the agreement or request their inclusion in the interlocutory and final decrees.

In situations in which one or both parents have a history or tendency of fighting through their children, it may be advisable to include exact times, dates, and places for visitation. Arrangements for summer vacations and holidays should also be worked out in advance, along with any other ambiguities that may cause friction.

Custody and visitation require careful consideration not only of legal but of psychological issues. Unfortunately all too often divorcing parents are too engulfed by their own problems and/or battles with each other to really think these issues through. For example, severely limiting a noncustodial spouse's visitation rights is sometimes considered a legal and personal victory. But from a realistic standpoint, particularly in a society that already tends to define a father's relationship to his children largely in economic and disciplinary terms, it may actually end up by completely alienating a father from his children.

In some cases a child may be better off—at least temporarily—by being removed completely from any contact with a psychologically destructive parent. However, "punishing" a mother or father by depriving her or him of the parental relationship does not make much sense, since eventually children will want to know their absent father or mother (and if prevented from so doing, will often idealize that parent or feel worthless and abandoned). That is not to say that it is the custodial parent's responsibility to make the relationship between the children and the noncustodial parent work.

The reality is that where there are children, a divorce does not sever the bonds between the members of a family—it only alters them. This is why professional divorce counseling is gaining currency and also why self-help groups formed by single parents are springing up all over the country. Such services and groups can be very helpful in thinking and working through the best child-custody and visitation arrangements for a particular family (as well as providing much needed emotional support at a difficult time of personal adjustment).

If there are no fundamental disagreements about child-rearing and two divorcing parents are able to work cooperatively, joint legal custody may be possible. It has the advantage of giving each parent equal legal responsibility as well as a sense of equal personal and emotional commitment, which is bound to be helpful not only to the child but also to the parent who has physical custody for the greater part of the time. On the other hand, if you have any fears that your spouse may use the joint custody as a means of harassment through the child or that your respective value systems may be more dissimilar than they appear, it is better to seek exclusive custody in order to avoid a destructive tug of war with the child in the middle.

While your attorney can give you helpful guidelines and suggestions, it is up to the parents to try to understand and evaluate what seems best for their child and in particular what custody and visitation arrangements are best suited to the particular situation, keeping in mind that, just as during the marriage, ideal solutions may not be possible.

❊ ❊ ❊

For working out child custody and visitation rights:

—Consider all possible alternatives for child custody, whether traditional or not.

—Where parental conflicts exist, be extra clear about all details of custody and visitation.

—Rely on your own judgment, in addition to your attorney's suggestions, to define custodial arrangements.

—Resist tendencies to use custody and visitation issues as weapons in a continuing battle between divorced parents.

❊ ❊ ❊

Debts, Taxes, Insurance, Wills, Modifiability, and Miscellaneous

Do not fail to include a division of debts in the settlement agreement. Otherwise, you may find that you are obligated to pay bills you did not expect. One must also provide for the disposition of all credit-card and charge accounts.

Since the Internal Revenue Service permits spouses to file joint tax returns until their divorce is final, marital-settlement agreements sometimes contain provisions in which spouses agree to file jointly for the balance of the tax year. Where appropriate, formulas are spelled out for the apportionment of the tax burden. For example, it may be split equally or paid entirely by one spouse.

If the marital-settlement agreement is not carefully drafted, there can be unwelcome tax consequences to a divorce. For example, there are some situations in which it is to the wife's advantage to take a larger share of the property immediately in lieu of extended alimony payments. The tax rules that apply here are very technical, but their gist is that if the IRS determines that the marital-settlement agreement involved a profitable exchange or sale of property, the government will impose a capital-gains tax on the transaction. To avoid this, the advice of a good accountant or tax attorney may be required.

The advice and help of another technical expert, an insurance agent, may also be useful before the marital settlement is made final. You should find out what insurance coverage you and your children had during your marriage (house, car, medical, hospital, life, etc.) and determine what replacement coverage will be needed. This can be incorporated into the marital-settlement agreement or court decree.

In addition to providing children with medical and hospital coverage, it has been customary to name them as irrevocable beneficiaries under existing life-insurance policies, at least until they reach majority. This should also be covered in your agreement.

Where substantial alimony payments are to be made, the recipient spouse may be well advised to take out appropriate insurance on the payer spouse, since in the absence of a contrary agreement, the obligation of spousal support will terminate upon the death of the payer and there will be no basis for a claim against his or her estate.

In most states, divorce invalidates any provision of a will which leaves property to a former spouse, whether this is spelled out in the marital-settlement agreement or not. It is wise to make new wills after a divorce.

Some parents include in their marital-settlement agreements provisions by which they each undertake to leave the children of their marriage a certain percentage (otfen one-third or one-half) of their assets. These provisions come under the general heading of third-party beneficiary contracts, and if properly drafted are enforceable by their beneficiaries—the children—even though they were not parties to the contract themselves.

Marital-settlement agreements also include a variety of general clauses by which each spouse disclaims and relinquishes any further interest or claim in the other's property or earnings, and by which they agree to be responsible for their own debts and obligations.

Another important concern is the modifiability of a marital-settlement agreement after it is signed. In most marital-settlement agreements, provisions may be amended by written agreement between the parties. As a general rule, when only one of the parties wants a change, she or he can go back to court, provided there has been a real change in the circumstances of either or both parties and that the original agreement did not contain a nonmodifiability clause. However, child support is always modifiable, regardless of the agreement between the parents. Since much litigation has revolved around the modifiability of spousal support, it is essential that your agreement clearly state whether you intend this to be modifiable. As with other matters touched upon in this checklist, information about some of the criteria you may want to consider in deciding whether your situation calls for modifiability is discussed in some detail in the text of this book.

A dissolution or divorce is a transition from one legal status to another. Besides the property-settlement agreement and the court decree, it will involve other less formal matters, such as opening new bank accounts, reregistering cars, and recording new deeds of real property and declarations of homestead.

Many of these are just matters of filling in and filing forms. Some of them, like deeds and car registrations, will require reconveyances or transfers from your spouse, and you should therefore determine whether your marital-settlement agreement includes an implementation clause. Such a clause (or court order) can provide that each spouse agrees (or is ordered) to sign all appropriate papers and documents to effect the implementation of the agreement or decree. It can also provide that if a spouse defaults on that obligation or order, the county clerk or another appropriate person or agent is empowered to sign in place of the defaulting spouse.

*   *   *

In checking that your marital settlement and/or
court order takes care of all loose ends,
consider the following:

—Be sure to provide for the payment of debts incurred prior to separation.

—Review tax advantages and/or special problems which may arise in your situation, and, if necessary, consult a tax expert.

—Consider insurance-coverage changes which will occur through divorce, including replacement costs.

—Investigate effect of divorce on existing wills.

—Be sure agreement is explicit regarding modifiability, especially with respect to spousal support.

—Check agreement or order for an effective implementation clause and be sure that all practical matters such as reconveyances, changes of ownership, credit cards, etc. are taken care of.

*   *   *

APPENDIX

2

SAMPLE MARRIAGE CONTRACT

Marriage Contract

THIS AGREEMENT is made and entered into by and between Jennifer R. (hereinafter referred to as Jennifer), and Gregory S. (hereinafter referred to as Gregory), at Los Angeles, California, on October 12, 1972.

We make this agreement with reference to the following:

A. We plan to marry in Los Angeles, California, on October 15, 1972.

B. We have known each other for two and a half years and we have each made full and fair disclosure to each other of all relevant financial and biographical information.

C. There has been no undue influence, duress, or any other such inducement to either one of us to enter into this agreement.

D. We each enter into this agreement out of our own free will, our respect and love for each other, and our desire to make our own personal contract with reference to our respective marital rights and obligations toward each other and toward any children of this marriage.

In consideration of the mutual promises contained herein,

and for good and valuable consideration, we agree as follows:

1. *Goals.* It is our goal in our marriage that each of us shall have complete equality of opportunity to develop our respective potentials, emotionally, intellectually, professionally, and financially; that we shall each have our own careers; that we shall each take equal responsibility for household tasks and childcare; and that this principle of mutual respect and support for each other's individuality and integrity shall govern all aspects of our relationship and our lives. Regardless of social pressures or of sexual stereotypes we shall each do everything necessary and appropriate to secure full implementation of this goal.

2. *Name.* After our marriage, Jennifer shall retain the name of Jennifer R. for all purposes, including but not limited to use on official documents (such as driver's licenses and tax returns), instruments of commerce (such as loan applications, credit cards, letters of credit), and instruments of property (such as deeds, bills of sale, mortgages). In this connection, we specifically contemplate that we shall each continue to maintain lines of credit in our own names.

3. *Household Duties.* Household duties (including but not limited to cleaning, laundry, errands, gardening, shopping, cooking, and entertaining) shall be shared equally, both in terms of time and task. Taking into account that there may be certain times when one or the other of us may be under more personal, career, or other time pressures, it is our intent to insure that in the long run this shall be equalized. We shall sometimes alternate tasks and sometimes share them, in conformity with the underlying principle that each of us has an equal responsibility to our marriage and family, a principle that we recognize will become even more essential in the event that we have children.

4. *Careers.* It is our intent that we shall each have our own careers and we agree to support each other in achieving this goal.

   a. We acknowledge that there will be many subtle social and psychological pressures tending to emphasize Greg's career and devaluating Jennifer's and we commit ourselves to be conscious of these at all times.

b. We further acknowledge that due to the sexual biases of this society, Jennifer may need more time and effort to develop her career.

c. We value the work of childrearing and housekeeping equally with work that commands cash wages or furthers a career.

d. We reject the idea that the person who makes more money is a more valuable human being.

5. *Domicile.* We shall each have an equal voice in choosing our marital domicile. In the event of disagreement, we set forth the following as guidelines.

a. We acknowledge that the principles set forth in Section 4 hereinabove (*Careers*) are particularly applicable herein.

b. We acknowledge that each person has the right to decide what is best for her/his career and that this is a matter of individual choice.

c. We nevertheless shall each consider the personal and career needs of the other in reaching such a decision, and neither of us shall take a position in a new location unless the other can be employed in said location in a comparable and satisfactory position.

d. If one of us decides that a move will further her/his career, then the other of us shall make a commitment to honestly search for a satisfactory job in that location.

e. Notwithstanding the above, we do not completely rule out the possibility of using the principle of alternating decisions.

f. Neither do we rule out the possibility of living apart from each other for a limited period of time and commuting for weekends and holidays.

6. *Separate Property.* We acknowledge that Gregory is the owner of certain bond certificates presently held in an agency account managed by _____, and that Jennifer has an expectancy of a certain inheritance. The principal of said bonds and of said inheritance together with all income therefrom, plus any other

property or monies received by either one of us by gift or inheritance, and all income therefrom, shall remain each of our separate property. We contemplate that circumstances may arise when we may wish to amend this clause in order to utilize portions of the income and/or principal of our said separate property for joint purposes, for a limited period of time, in which event any such income or principal shall be, for said limited period, treated in accordance with the provisions set forth in Section 7 herebelow.

7. *Earnings, Expenses, Acquisitions, and Separate Accounts.* With respect to our respective earnings and income from all other sources, we agree to follow the following procedure:

a. Every month all monies shall be deposited when received into an account standing in both of our names as joint tenants.

b. All usual household and family expenses, including but not limited to rent or mortgage payments, utilities, house maintenance and cleaning services, food and household supplies, health and accident insurance, automotive expenses and insurance, childcare, ordinary educational and professional and travel expenses, entertainment, family visits, and vacations shall be paid out of this account.

c. All usual personal and household acquisitions including, but not limited to linens, towels, household furnishings, furniture, appliances, and automobiles shall be paid out of this account. Wherever a deed or bill of sale or other written instrument evidences an acquisition, title shall be held in the names of Jennifer R. and Gregory S., as joint tenants.

d. We acknowledge that we now jointly own the following property: our family home, located at _____ Los Angeles, California, legally described as follows: _____ and encumbered by a certain first trust deed; a record player; a Persian rug; a Smith-Corona typewriter; and a Ford Van automobile.

e. We shall each share equally in the management and control of all jointly held earnings and property. All financial decisions regarding said property and earnings and their use shall be made jointly by us. We set down a number of guidelines in order to facilitate the decision-making process:

(1) Each year we will plan as far as possible:

i. What we shall need to live during the following year, in the manner that we desire, and

ii. What monies shall be used to live in that manner and in what way we choose to go about getting the necessary amounts.

iii. To facilitate planning, we may want to analyze last year's budget, making allowance for a cost-of-living increase over the preceding year to arrive at our fixed expenses and subtract that from our anticipated income.

(2) The underlying principles shall be equal responsibility, trust, flexibility, and a realistic awareness of our financial position combined with respect for each other's ideas and judgment.

f. At the beginning of each month we shall discuss, plan, and establish our budget for expenses and acquisitions for the month.

g. Each month, after sufficient monies have been allocated and/or expenses and acquisitions have been paid in accordance with said budget for the month, the surplus, if any, from the joint account described in subparagraph (a) hereinabove, shall be divided equally between us, and deposited in our respective separate accounts.

8. *Children.*

a. It is our intent in this section to enter into a third-party beneficiary agreement for the benefit of any children of this marriage.

b. We agree that we shall each have the equal responsibility for the physical, emotional, and financial care of any children of this marriage. Childcare duties shall be shared equally, both in terms of time and task. Taking into account that there may be certain times when one or the other of us may be under more personal, career, or other time pressures, it is our intent to insure that in the long run this shall be equalized. We shall sometimes alternate tasks and sometimes share them, in conformity with the underlying principle that each of us has an equal responsibility to our marriage and family.

c. Our children shall bear the hyphenated name of R.-S. or S.-R.

d. We each accept equal responsibility for the financial support of our children for their food, clothing, education, shelter, and medical care in accordance with our standard of living, until each child shall reach the age of 21. Notwithstanding the above, we envision that the education of our children may go beyond the age of 21 and it is our intent, insofar as we are able, to provide the equivalent of 20 years of education for each of our children, including 8 years of college, or other growth experience. There is herein an area of conflict between us. It is Jennifer's position that the children shall be entitled to choose whatever form of educational growth experience they deem reasonable regardless of the approval or disapproval of either Gregory or herself. It is Gregory's position that the choice of the children of educational growth experience has to be somewhat congruent with his value system. To facilitate resolution of this and other possible conflicts in this area, we agree that we will review and re-evaluate the section dealing with children upon the birth of each child and then again upon each child's seventh, thirteenth, and seventeenth birthday or any other time that we may deem suitable or appropriate.

e. This section applies to any children we mutually agree to adopt.

f. Notwithstanding the above, it is agreed between us that Jennifer has a right to conceive a child of Gregory's before she is 30 years old. Should a doctor confirm that Gregory is sterile, then Jennifer has the right to conceive by other means.

9. *Primary Relationship.* It is our intention that this be a primary, not necessarily an exclusive, relationship. However, should one person feel deprived of the sense of a primary relationship by the activities of the other, it is our intention that this

first be discussed between us and should we fail to satisfactorily resolve the problem, that we both together shall seek help from a third party mutually agreed upon. If we are unable to agree on the third party within three days, then the choice of the person who feels deprived shall govern. It is our intent and our hope that this process will enable us to focus on the underlying problems and facilitate openness, closeness, and a mutually satisfactory resolution.

10. *Communication and Consciousness Raising.* We agree that we shall devote a minimum of one hour per week to communication of our feelings toward each other, to work through our problems, and to raise our consciousness about social and internal pressures enforcing traditional sexual roles.

11. *Review and Amendment.* We agree to read, review, and discuss this agreement once every month. At least once every 5 years and in the interim whenever appropriate, we shall review and, when necessary renegotiate, this agreement. This agreement, however, may not be amended except by a writing signed by both of us.

12. *Separation.* In the event that there should arise between us irreconcilable differences and that we decide to separate, it is our intent to resolve our differences by amicable means and not by an adversary method. If we are unable to reach such an amicable agreement, we shall chose a third person to act as arbitrator. If we cannot agree on a third person, then we shall each choose one person to represent each of us, and said persons shall then choose a third person to act as arbitrator. We both agree that the arbitrator's decisions shall be binding upon us. We wish, however, that the arbitrator's decisions be governed by the following principles:

a. The principles enunciated in this marriage contract.

b. The principles of fairness toward each one of us, and our children.

c. That all jointly held property shall be divided equally in accordance with the value at the time of purchase or acquisition.

d. That all separate property shall remain with the person in whose name it is held.

e. It is our desire that any decision regarding financial arrangements, child custody, childcare, and child or spousal support shall take into consideration each person's welfare, prosperity, happiness, and career.

13. *Severability.* If any portion of this agreement be illegal, unenforceable, void, or voidable, or be hereafter amended, each of the remaining sections or each of the remaining items shall, nevertheless, remain in full force and effect as a separate contract.

14. *Implementation.* Each of us agrees to execute or deliver any documents or furnish any information or perform any other act reasonably necessary to carry out the provisions of this agreement without undue expense or inconvenience.

15. *Recording.* A copy of this agreement shall be recorded with the office of the Los Angeles County Recorder. Should we at any time acquire real property in another county, a copy of our marriage contract shall be filed with the county recorder of said county.

IN WITNESS WHEREOF, we hereunto set our hands this 12th day of October, 1972, at Los Angeles, California.

_____
Jennifer R.

_____
Gregory S.

SUBSCRIBED AND SWORN TO
before me this ——— day
of October, 1972.

_____

Notes

NOTES TO CHAPTER 1

1. *Monthly Vital Statistics Report*, National Center for Health Statistics, Rockville, Md., March 4, 1976.
2. Ibid.
3. Timothy B. Walker, "Beyond Fault," 10 *Journal of Family Law* 267, p. 271, citing Max Rheinstein.*
4. Ibid., p. 272.
5. Ibid., pp. 271–273.
6. Ibid., p. 277.
7. Ibid., p. 278, quoting Gerhard Mueller.
8. Albert C. Jacob and Julius Goebel, Jr., *Domestic Relations*, Brooklyn: The Foundation Press, 1961, pp. 337–339.
9. 39 Cal.2d 858, 250 P.2d 598.
10. Ibid.
11. See *Ariz. Rev. Stat.*, Title 25-312, 25-316 (1973); *Colo. Rev. Stat.*, Sections 46-1-6, 46-1-10 (1972); *Fla. Stat.*, Sections 61.031, 61.044, 61.052 (1971), *Iowa Code Ann.*, Sections 598.5, 598.17 (1973); *Ky. Rev. Stat.*, Sections 403.140, 403.150, 403.170 (1972); *Mich. Stat. Ann.*, Section 25.86

---

* Standard legal citation form has been followed for cases, legal journals, etc., since this is the manner in which these materials are catalogued and filed in the legal libraries where they are to be found. For the lay reader who may not be familiar with this form, the number preceding the name or abbreviation for the publication is the volume of that publication. The number immediately following the name is the page on which the case or article begins. In some cases, there will be the legend "p. xxx" or "at p. xxx." This indicates the specific page referred to. Thus, note 3 means that the article "Beyond Fault" by Timothy Walker is from volume 10 of the *Journal of Family Law*, and that the article begins on page 267. Since in the text the reference is to materials on page 271 of the article, it is followed by the legend "p. 271."

(Supp. 1972); *Nebr. Rev. Stat.*, Section 42-347 (1972); *Ore. Rev. Stat.*, Section 107.025 (1971); *Wash. Rev. Code* 26, Sections 3, 4 (1973).

12. *Ala. Code* 34, Section 20 (1971 Supp.); *Conn. Laws Pub. Act*, 73-373 (1973); *Ga. Code Ann.*, Section 31-102 (1973); *Hawaii Rev. Stat.*, Sections 580-41, 580-42 (Supp. 1972); *Ind. Code Rev. Laws*, ch. 11.5 (1973); *N.H. Rev. Stat. Ann.*, Section 458.7 (Supp. 1971); *Ala. Code* 34, *Section* 20.7 (Supp. 1971); *Alaska Code Civ. Pro.*, 09.55.110; *Conn. Laws Pub. Act*, 73-373 (1973); *Del. Code Ann.* 13, Section 1522 (Supp. 1970); *Idaho Code Ann.* Sections 32-603, 32-706, 32-712 (Supp. 1972); *Kan. Stat. Ann.*, Section 60-1601(8) (Supp. 1970); *Nev. Rev. Stat.*, Section 125.010; *N.M. Stat. Ann.*, Section 22-7-1 (Supp. 1971); *N.D. Code*, Section 14-05-09 (Supp. 1971); *Okla. Stat. Ann.* 12, Section 1271(7) (Supp. 1972–1973); *Tex. Fam. Code*, Section 3.01 (1970); *V.I. Code Ann.*, Ch. 16, Section 108 (1957).

13. "Uniform Marriage and Divorce Act," approved and recommended for enactment in all states by the National Conference of Commissioners on Uniform State Laws at its Annual Conference Meeting at St. Louis, Missouri, August 1–7, 1970, as reprinted in V *Family Law Quarterly* 205 (hereinafter cited as UMDA, V *Family Law Quarterly* 205).

14. "Proposed Revised Uniform Marriage and Divorce Act," submitted by the American Bar Association Family Law Section pursuant to recommendations of its special committee, adopted by its council, November 9, 1972, as reprinted in VII *Family Law Quarterly* 135 (hereinafter cited as RUMDA, VII *Family Law Quarterly* 135).

15. UMDA, V *Family Law Quarterly* 205, at 206.

16. Doris Jonas Freed and Henry H. Foster, Jr., "Economic Effects of Divorce," VII *Family Law Quarterly* 275, p. 276, n. 6.

17. See, e.g., *West's Annotated California Code*, Section 5; *Georgia Code Annotated*, Section 30-302; *Minnesota Statutes Annotated*, Section 518; *New York Civil Practice Act*, former Section 1169.

18. *Black's Law Dictionary*, 4th Edition, St. Paul: West Publishing Co., 1951, p. 553.

NOTES TO CHAPTER 2

1. As quoted by Harry Fain in *Slicing the Dissolution Pie*, Reprint of paper presented at the California State Bar Annual Meeting, September 13, 1973, p. 10 (hereinafter cited as Fain, *Slicing the Dissolution Pie*).

2. *Hayes v. Hayes*, D700 518, Superior Court, Los Angeles, California, November 6, 1969 (hereinafter cited as *Hayes v. Hayes*, D700 518).

3. Interview with Mrs. Janne Hayes, January 25, 1975, Los Angeles, California.

4. Ibid.

5. *Financial Declaration of James Hayes*, Order to Show Cause, *Hayes v. Hayes*, D700 518, filed December 13, 1972.

6. *Financial Declaration of Janne Hayes*, Order to Show Cause, *Hayes v. Hayes*, D700 518, filed January 15, 1973.

7. "Assembly Committee Report on Assembly Bill No. 530 and Senate Bill No. 252 (The Family Law Act)," submitted by Committee on Judiciary, James A. Hayes, Chairman, on August 8, 1969, printed in *Assembly Daily*

Journal, August 8, 1969, as quoted in *Respondent's Opening Points and Authorities*, Order to Show Cause, *Hayes* v. *Hayes*, D700 518, filed December 13, 1972.

8. *Points and Authorities of Petitioner in Opposition to Opening Points and Authorities of Respondent*, Order to Show Cause, *Hayes* v. *Hayes*, D700 518, filed January 15, 1973.

9. *Financial Declaration of James A. Hayes*, Order to Show Cause, *Hayes* v. *Hayes*, D700 518, filed June 18, 1974.

10. "Hayes' Ex-Wife Seeks Welfare, Food Stamps," *Los Angeles Times*, June 6, 1975.

11. "Not Upset by Former Wife, Hayes Says," *Los Angeles Times*, June 10, 1975.

12. *Hayes* v. *Hayes*, Court of Appeal of the State of California, Second Appellate District, Division Five, 2d Civil No. 45168, October 3, 1975 (unpublished opinion).

13. Ibid., pp. 27–28.

14. "Hayes Loses Court Bid to Alter Alimony Pact," *Los Angeles Times*, March 30, 1976.

15. Telephone interview with Attorney Albert J. Corske, April 15, 1976, Los Angeles, California.

16. *Smith* v. *Lewis*, 31 Cal. App.3d 677, 7 Cal. Rptr. 95 (1973). Cited in Fain, *Slicing the Dissolution Pie*, p. 4.

17. "Uniform Marriage and Divorce Act," approved and recommended for enactment in all states by the National Conference of Commissioners on Uniform State Laws at its Annual Conference Meeting at St. Louis, Missouri, August 1–7, 1970, as reprinted in V *Family Law Quarterly* 205, Section 307, p. 231 (hereinafter cited as UMDA, V *Family Law Quarterly* 205).

18. Ibid., pp. 231–232.

19. "Proposed Revised Uniform Marriage and Divorce Act," submitted by the American Bar Association Family Law Section pursuant to recommendations of its special committee, adopted by its council, November 9, 1972, as reprinted in VII *Family Law Quarterly* 135 (hereinafter cited as RUMDA, VII *Family Law Quarterly* 135).

20. Ibid., pp. 151–153. See also "1971 Midyear Report and Recommendations of the Family Law Section to the ABA House of Delegates on the Uniform Marriage and Divorce Act," V *Family Law Quarterly* 133, pp. 179–180.

21. UMDA, V *Family Law Quarterly* 205, Section 307, p. 232.

22. See n. 20, *supra*.

23. RUMDA, VII *Family Quarterly* 135, p. 152.

NOTES TO CHAPTER 3

1. *Illinois Rev. Stat. Am.*, Ch. 40, Section 19.

2. *Iowa Code Ann.*, Section 598.21 (Supp. 1973).

3. *Michigan Stat. Ann.*, Section 25.103 (Supp. 1972).

4. 1 ALR3d.6 (1965) pp. 1–184.

5. *Bixby* v. *Bixby*, 253 Iowa 1172, 115 N.W.2d 852 (1962), reported in 1 ALR3d.178.

6. *Hicks* v. *Hicks* (1962 La. App.) 147 So.2d 750, reported in *1 ALR-3d.181.*

7. *Scanton* v. *Scanton* (1963 Fla. App.) 154 So.2d 899, reported in *1 ALR3d.90.*

8. *In re the Marriage of Rosan,* 24 Cal. App.3d 885, 101 Cal. Rptr. 295 (1972).

9. *The Equal Rights Amendment and Alimony and Child Support Laws,* Citizens' Advisory Council on the Status of Women, Washington, D.C.: Department of Labor, 1972 (hereinafter cited as *The ERA and Alimony and Child Support Laws*).

10. Ibid.

11. "Uniform Marriage and Divorce Act," approved and recommended for enactment in all states by the National Conference of Commissioners on Uniform State Laws at its Annual Conference Meeting at St. Louis, Missouri, August 1–7, 1970, as reprinted in V *Family Law Quarterly* 205, Prefatory Note, p. 207.

12. *The ERA and Alimony and Child Support Laws,* p. 7.

13. Marian P. Winston and Trude Forsher, *Nonsupport of Legitimate Children by Affluent Fathers as a Cause of Poverty and Welfare Dependence,* Santa Monica: The Rand Corporation, December 1971, pp. 15–16 (hereinafter cited as Winston and Forsher, *Nonsupport of Legitimate Children*).

14. *The ERA and Alimony and Child Support Laws,* p. 7.

15. Ibid.

16. Ibid., p. 8.

17. Id.

18. *Los Angeles Times,* January 13, 1976.

19. 1 Bl.Comm. 447.

20. *Farrah* v. *Farrah,* 102 N.V.S.2d 147 (1951).

21. *Schumm* v. *Berg,* 224 P.2d 56 (Cal. App. 1951).

22. See, e.g., *California Civil Code,* Sections 241–254.

23. *California Civil Code,* Section 73.

24. *California Civil Code,* Section 4704.

25. *Guidelines for Initial Order to Show Cause,* July 10, 1973, draft, in correspondence from Jack T. Ryburn, Supervising Judge, Family Law Department, Superior Court, Los Angeles, California, to the Los Angeles County Bar Association, Family Law Section.

NOTES TO CHAPTER 4

1. Monroe L. Inker and Charlotte Anne Perretta, "A Child's Right to Counsel in Custody Cases," V *Family Law Quarterly* 108, pp. 110–111.

2. "Uniform Marriage and Divorce Act," approved and recommended for enactment in all states by the National Conference of Commissioners on Uniform State Laws at its Annual Conference Meeting at St. Louis, Missouri, August 1–7, 1970, as reprinted in V *Family Law Quarterly* 205, Sections 401–410.

3. Carol Kleinman, "Radical Approach to Child Custody," *Los Angeles Times,* December 5, 1973.

4. Christine Winter, "Added Dimension to Divorce Trauma," *Los Angeles Times*, December 5, 1973.

5. *In re Gault*, 387 U.S. 1 (1967).

6. See, e.g., *California Welfare and Institutions Code*, Sections 600, 601, 602.

NOTES TO CHAPTER 5

1. Nicholas Tavuchis, "The Analysis of Family Roles," *The Family and its Future*, ed., Katherine Elliott, CIBA Foundation, London: J. & A. Churchill, 1970, pp. 19–20.

2. Jessie Bernard, *The Future of Marriage*, New York: Bantam Books, 1972.

3. Ashley Montagu, *The Natural Superiority of Women*, New York: Collier Books, 1970.

4. Elmer Spreitzer and Lawrence E. Riley, "Factors Associated with Singlehood," *Journal of Marriage and the Family*, August 1974, p. 533.

5. Ibid., pp. 533–541.

6. See, e.g., W. B. Blackstone, *Commentaries*, 19th London ed., Vol. I, Philadelphia: Lippincott Co., 1908, where at p. 366, after listing the many disabilities imposed on a wife under the common law, the author had this to say:

> These are the chief legal effects of marriage during the coverture: upon which we may observe, that even the disabilities which the wife lies under are for the most part intended for her protection and benefit; so great a favorite is the female sex of the laws of England.

One of the commentators to Blackstone felt compelled to add his own footnote to this, starting on page 366:

> ... I shall here state some of the principal differences in the English law, respecting the two sexes; and I shall leave it to the reader to determine on which side is the balance, and how far this compliment it [*sic*] supported by the truth.... Husband and wife, in the language of the law, are styled *baron* and *feme*; the word baron or lord attributes to the husband a not very courteous superiority. But we might be inclined to think this merely an unmeaning technical phrase, if we did not recollect, that if the baron kills his feme, it is the same as if he killed a stranger or any other person; but if the feme kills her baron, it is regarded by the laws as a much more atrocious crime; as she not only breaks through the restraints of humanity and conjugal affection, but throws off all subjection to the authority of her husband. And therefore the law denominates her crime a species of treason, and condemns her to the same punishment as if she had killed the king...

Then he goes on to several other examples, among them:

> By the common law all women are denied the benefit of clergy; and till the 3 and 4 W and Mc. 9 they received sentences of death and

might have been executed for the first offense in simple larceny, bigamy, manslaughter, etc.; however learned they were, merely because
their sex precluded the possibility of their taking holy orders, though a
man who could not read was for the same crime subject only to burn-
ing in the hand and a few months imprisonment. . . .

7. *People ex. rel. Rago v. Lipsky, et al.*, 327 Ill. App. 63, 63 N.E.2d 642
(1945).
8. *Bacon v. Boston Electric Railway Co.*, 256 Mass. 30, 152 N.E. 35
(1926).
9. *In re Kayaloff*, 9 F.Supp. 176 (D.C. 1934).
10. *Estate of Wickes*, 128 Cal. 270, 60 Pac. 879 (1900).
11. *Carlson v. Carlson*, 75 Ariz. 308, 256 P.2d 249 (1953).
12. *McGuire v. McGuire*, 157 Neb. 226, 59 N.W.2d 336 (1953).
13. Ibid.
14. Leo Kanowitz, *Women and the Law*, University of New Mexico
Press, Albuquerque, 1969, pp. 71–72.
15. Blanche Crozier, "Marital Support," 15 *B.U.L. Rev.* 28 (1915).
16. David A. Binder and Riane Eisler, "Amicus Curiae Brief," Supreme
Court of the United States, *Perez v. Campbell*, Docket No. 5175, October
Term 1970 (hereinafter cited at Binder and Eisler, "Amicus Curiae Brief,"
Perez v. Campbell).
17. *Perez v. Campbell*, 421 F.2d 619 (9th Circuit, 1970).
18. Ibid., p. 624.
19. Binder and Eisler, "Amicus Curiae Brief," *Perez v. Campbell*, p. 32.
20. *Revised Texas Family Code* 1972, Section 5.21.
21. *Revised Code of Washington*, Annotated, 1973, Title 26.
22. *California Civil Code*, Section 5125.
23. Ibid.
24. Id.
25. *California Civil Code*, Section 5127; and *California Probate Code*,
Section 201.
26. *California Civil Code*, Section 5124.
27. Arnold D. Kahn and Paul N. Frimmer, "Management, Probate and
Estate Planning Under California's New Community Property Laws," *California State Bar Journal*, November/December 1974, p. 518.
28. Ibid., pp. 519–521.
29. Interview with Professor Herma Hill Kay, Divorce Law Research
Project, Center for the Study of Law and Society, Berkeley, California, 1973.
30. Interview with Attorney Roberta Ralph, Women's Lawyer's Association, Los Angeles, California, 1973.
31. *California Civil Code*, Section 5152(e).
32. *California Civil Code*, Section 5103.

NOTES TO CHAPTER 6

1. Isabel V. Sawhill, "Perspectives on Women and Work in America," in
Work and the Quality of Life, ed., James O'Toole, Cambridge, Mass.: MIT

Press, 1974, p. 90 (hereinafter cited as Sawhill, "Perspectives on Women and Work").

2. Caroline Bird with Sara Welles Briller, *Born Female*, New York: Pocket Books, 1968 (hereinafter cited as Bird, *Born Female*).

3. Sawhill, "Perspectives on Women and Work," p. 92.

4. Valerie Oppenheimer, "The Female Labor Force in the U.S.," Institute of International Studies, Population Monograph No. 5, University of California, Berkeley, 1970, pp. 187–188.

5. Bird, *Born Female*, ch. 4.

6. *Underutilization of Women Workers*, Women's Bureau, U.S. Department of Labor, Washington D.C., 1971 (revised) (hereinafter cited as *Underutilization of Women Workers*). See also *1969 Handbook on Working Women*, U.S. Department of Labor, Women's Bureau, Bulletin No. 294, p. 15 (hereinafter cited as *1969 Handbook on Working Women*).

7. *Underutilization of Women Workers*, p. iii.

8. Ibid. On p. iv, Elizabeth Duncan writes:

Occupationally women are more disadvantaged, compared with men, than they were 30 years ago. . . . Many women hold jobs far from commensurate with their abilities and educational achievement. For example, in March 1969, 19 percent of the working women who had completed 4 years of college were employed in nonprofessional jobs as clerical, sales, or service workers or as operatives, mainly in factories.

9. Sawhill, "Perspectives on Women and Work," p. 95. For a detailed analysis of the rise in labor force participation of women see *1969 Handbook on Working Women*, particularly chapter 1.

10. Interview with Dr. James O'Toole, University of Southern California, Los Angeles, California, 1975.

11. Dennis Little, "Post-Industrial Society and What It May Mean," *The Futurist*, December 1973, p. 259.

12. Ibid. For a detailed study, see also Daniel Bell, *The Coming of the Post-Industrial Society: A Venture in Social Forecasting*, New York: Basic Books, 1973.

13. *Los Angeles Times*, February 8, 1975.

14. *Work in America*, Report of a Special Task Force to the Secretary of Health, Education and Welfare, Cambridge, Mass.: MIT Press, 1973, p. 64 (hereinafter cited as *Work in America*).

15. James O'Toole, *The Reserve Army of the Underemployed, A Policy Agenda for the Next Decade*, Center for Future's Research, Graduate School of Business Administration, University of Southern California, November 1974, p. 3.

16. Ibid., p. 9.

17. Ibid., p. 20.

18. Ibid., pp. 4, 11.

19. *Work in America*, pp. 121–152.

20. Ibid., p. 63.

21. Dennis Gabor, *The Mature Society*, New York: Praeger Publishers, 1972, p. 92.

264   NOTES

22. Ibid., pp. 113–114.
23. Ephesians 5:22–23.

NOTES TO CHAPTER 7

1. Brandwein, Brown, and Fox, "The Social Situation of Divorced Mothers and Their Families," *Journal of Marriage and the Family*, August 1974, p. 501 (hereinafter cited as Brandwein, Brown, and Fox, "The Social Situation of Divorced Mothers").
2. "Can Affluent America End Poverty?" *U.S. News and World Report*, August 4, 1972, p. 23.
3. Ibid.
4. Dorothy O'Conner, "The Fap Fizzle or Poverty and the Single Mother," *MOMMA*, March 1973, p. 1.
5. *California Women*, A Report of the Advisory Commission on the Status of Women, 1971, p. 1.
6. Marian P. Winston and Trude Forsher, *Nonsupport of Legitimate Children by Affluent Fathers as a Cause of Poverty and Welfare Dependence*, Santa Monica, The Rand Corporation, December 1971, p. 3.
7. Ralph Nader, "How You Lose Money by Being a Woman," *McCall's*, January 1972, p. 65.
8. Daniel P. Moynihan, *The Politics of Guaranteed Income*, New York: Random House, 1973.
9. Brandwein, Brown, and Fox, "The Social Situation of Divorced Mothers," p. 500.
10. Ibid.
11. Ibid., p. 501.
12. Lee Rainwater, "Work, Well-Being, and Family Life," in *Work and the Quality of Life*, ed., James O'Toole, Cambridge, Mass.: MIT Press, 1974, pp. 361–378.
13. Ibid., p. 368.
14. Ibid., p. 369.
15. *Underutilization of Women Workers*, Women's Bureau, U.S. Department of Labor, 1971 (revised), p. iv.
16. "Can Affluent America End Poverty?" *U.S. News and World Report*, August 4, 1972, p. 23.
17. Thomas C. Thomas, "Work and Welfare," in *Work and the Quality of Life*, ed., James O'Toole, Cambridge, Mass.: MIT Press, 1974, pp. 379–394 (hereinafter cited as Thomas, "Work and Welfare").
18. *California Women*, A Report of the Advisory Commission on the Status of Women, 1971, p. 2.
19. *Day Care and Child Development Reports*, Washington, D.C., February 17, 1975.
20. "Goodwill Toward Women," *The New Republic*, December 25, 1971.
21. Ibid.
22. Thomas, "Work and Welfare," p. 381.
23. *In re Cager*, 251 Md. 473, 248 A.2d 384 (1968).
24. *State* v. *Plummer*, 241 A.2d 198 (1967).

25. *Parrish* v. *Civil Service Commission of the County of Alameda,* 66 Cal.2d 260, 57 Cal.Rptr. 623 (1967).

26. See, e.g., *White* v. *Department of Social Services,* 174 N.W.2d 315 (Mich. Ct. App. 1969).

27. See, e.g., *James* v. *Goldberg,* 303 F.Supp. 935 (S.D., N.Y. 1965).

28. *Wyman* v. *James,* 27 L.Ed. 408, 91 S.Ct. 381 (1971).

29. Ibid., pp. 410–419.

30. Ibid., pp. 426–432.

31. Ibid., pp. 419–424.

NOTES TO CHAPTER 8

1. *State Social Welfare Board Position Statement, Issue: Illegitimacy,* State of California Human Relations Agency, Department of Social Welfare, March 1972.

2. Ibid., p. 11.

3. Ibid., pp. 4–19.

4. See also Ruby R. Leavitt, "Women in Other Cultures," in *Woman in Sexist Society,* eds. Vivian Gornick and Barbara K. Moran, New York: Basic Books, 1971, for a survey of the status of women in some matrilineal societies where children trace descent, not through the father, but through the mother and her clan. Among the Arizona Hopi, for example, the social unit is the clan, consisting of groups of families headed by older women. Here, according to Leavitt, "the clan collectively owns the springs, gardens, and farm land, but the children, the house, the food, and furnishings belong to the group of women within the clan," and "children are benevolently guided by their parents, siblings, and their many aunts and uncles." (Ibid., pp. 280–281).

5. On a recent trip to the Middle East, journalist Georgie Anne Geyer reported that the official penalty for a woman who commits adultery in Saudi Arabia is still public stoning until death; that in many areas of Egypt "the girl's clitoris is removed either at birth or in barbaric operations at about age 9"; and that just several years ago a young woman accused of a sexual breach, was, according to custom, knifed to death in public by her brothers while running along Beirut's cosmopolitan seafront. Geyer, "Women's Lib a Distant Goal in the Arab World," *Los Angeles Times,* December 16, 1973.

6. Albert C. Jacobs and Julius Goebel, Jr., *Domestic Relations,* Brooklyn: The Foundation Press, 1961, p. 839.

7. *Ibid.,* pp. 839–840.

8. 92 S.Ct. 1208, 405 U.S. 645 (1972).

9. *Levy* v. *Louisiana,* 391 U.S. 68 (1968).

10. *Roe* v. *Wade,* 410 U.S. 113 (1973).

11. Rose De Wolfe, "Illegitimacy: The Law Leans a Little," *Los Angeles Times,* September 10, 1972.

12. Cyril C. Means, Jr., "The Law of New York Concerning Abortion and the Status of the Foetus, 1664–1968; A Case of Cessation of Constitutionality," 14 *N.Y.L.F.* 411 (1968).

13. Garrett Hardin, "Parenthood: Right or Privilege?" *Science*, July 31, 1970, editorial page (hereinafter cited as Hardin, "Parenthood").

14. Ibid.

15. Id.

16. Id.

17. Mary Petronowich, unpublished letter to the editors of *Science*, September 30, 1970, citing study by Westoff and Bumbass, Princeton's Office of Population.

18. Ibid. I am very indebted to Petronowich for much of the information and many of the ideas regarding population and birth control contained in this chapter.

19. Hardin, "Parenthood."

NOTES TO CHAPTER 9

1. For a comprehensive analysis of the history and function of social inventions, see D. Stuart Conger, *Social Inventions*, Saskatchewan: Saskatchewan New Start, 1970, and D. Stuart Conger, "Social Inventions," *The Futurist*, August 1973, pp. 149–158. I am very indebted to Dr. Conger for much of this chapter's discussion about social inventions.

2. *The Future Report*, September 24, 1973, p. 6.

3. George Orwell, *Nineteen Eighty-Four*, New York: Harcourt Brace, 1949.

4. Jacques Ellul, *The Technological Society*, New York: Alfred A. Knopf, 1964.

5. *Monthly Vital Statistics Report*, National Center for Health Statistics, Rockville, Md., March 4, 1976.

6. *Monthly Vital Statistics Report*, National Center for Health Statistics, Rockville, Md., April 30, 1976.

7. Fred Bruning, "How to Put Your Man on a Pedestal," *Los Angeles Times*, July 13, 1972.

8. For a sociological study of the family see William J. Goode, *The Family*, Englewood Cliffs: Prentice-Hall, 1964. Also, for a thought-provoking critique of the reluctance of social scientists to validate new family forms that may be at odds with the status quo, see Nicholas Tavuchis, "The Analysis of Family Roles," in *The Family and Its Future*, ed., Katherine Elliott, CIBA Foundation, London: J. & A. Churchill, 1970, pp. 19–20.

9. See, e.g., Robin Fox, "Comparative Family Patterns," in *The Family and Its Future* (n. 8), particularly the discussion on p. 10.

10. *California Women*, A Report of the Advisory Commission on the Status of Women, 1971, p. 3.

11. "Can You Survive Divorce?" KTTV, Los Angeles, October 7, 1973.

12. Public opinion poll of 303 randomly selected divorced people conducted for Los Angeles television station KTTV in February 1972.

13. *Female Family Heads*, July 1974, U.S. Department of Commerce, Bureau of the Census, p. 6.

14. See, e.g., Glasser and Navarre, "Structural Problems of the One-Parent Family," *Journal of Social Issues* 21 (January 1965), pp. 98–109.

15. Brandwein, Brown, and Fox, "The Social Situation of Divorced Mothers and Their Families," *Journal of Marriage and the Family*, August 1974, p. 508.

16. Ibid., p. 507.

17. Ibid., p. 506.

18. *Section 214 of the Internal Revenue Code of 1954*, as amended in 1971.

19. *Section 1a, U.S. Internal Revenue Code of 1954.*

20. "Uniform Marriage and Divorce Act," approved and recommended for enactment in all states by the National Conference of Commissioners on Uniform State Laws at its Annual Conference Meeting at St. Louis, Missouri, August 1–7, 1970, as reprinted in V *Family Law Quarterly* 205, Section 211.

21. "1971 Midyear Report and Recommendation of the Family Law Section to the ABA House of Delegates on the Uniform Marriage and Divorce Act," V *Family Law Quarterly* 133, pp. 157–159.

NOTES TO CHAPTER 10

1. Interview with Los Angeles County adoption official, 1974.

2. *Nutrition and Human Needs, Hearings Before the Select Committee on Nutrition and Human Needs of the United States Senate, Ninety-Second Congress*, Part 3, Food Stamp Regulations, April 29, 30; May 14, 1971, Washington, D.C.: Government Printing Office, 1971, pp. 985–988.

3. Ibid.

4. *Moreno v. United States Department of Agriculture*, 345 F.Supp. 310 (D.D.C. 1972) *affmd.* 413 U.S. 528 (1973).

5. See, e.g., *Village of Belle Terre v. Boraas*, 94 S.Ct. 1536 (1974); and *Palo Alto Tenant's Union v. Morgan*, 321 F.Supp. 908 (N.D. Cal. 1970).

6. *Palo Alto Tenant's Union v. Morgan*, 321 F.Supp. 98 (N.D. Cal. 1970).

7. Ibid.

8. W. B. Blackstone, *Commentaries*, 19th London ed., Vol. I, Philadelphia, Lippincott Co., 1908, p. 442.

9. See, e.g., *Restatement of Contracts*, Section 587; and Lenore J. Weitzman, "Legal Regulation of Marriage, Tradition and Change," 62 *Cal. Law Review* 1169, at 1259 (hereinafter cited as Weitzman, "Legal Regulation of Marriage, Tradition and Change").

10. *Miller v. Miller*, 132 Misc. 121, 228 N.Y.S. 657 (Sup. Ct. 1928).

11. *Graham v. Graham*, 33 F.Supp. 936 (E.D. Mich. 1940).

12. Weitzman, "Legal Regulation of Marriage, Tradition and Change," at 1262. This treatise provides an extremely comprehensive and interesting discussion of the subject of marriage contracts.

13. Ibid., pp. 1260–1264.

14. Ibid., pp. 1266–1269.

15. Ibid.

16. Susan Edmiston, "How to Write Your Own Marriage Contract," *Ms.*, Spring 1972, p. 66.

NOTES TO CHAPTER 1J

1. Roger J. Traynor, "Law and Social Change in a Democratic Society," 1956 *U. Ill. L.F.* 220, at 232, 236.

2. Lenore J. Weitzman, "Legal Regulation of Marriage, Tradition and Change," 62 *Cal. Law Review* 1169.

3. Ibid., pp. 1241–1245.

4. *Bolling* v. *Sharpe* 347 U.S. 497 (1954).

5. 381 U.S. 479 (1965).

6. 405 U.S. 438 (1972).

7. Ibid.

8. *Marvin* v. *Marvin*, No. C 23303, Superior Court of the State of California, the County of Los Angeles, 1971.

9. Myrna Oliver, "Judge May Kill Ex-Singer's Suit to Share Lee Marvin Property," *Los Angeles Times*, December 5, 1973.

10. 404 U.S. 71 (1971).

11. See, e.g., Gordon Rattray Taylor, *The Biological Time Bomb*, New York: Signet, 1968.

12. There has been an increase in male-female role differentiation studies by scholars who are more conscious of built-in sexist biases (such as male anthropologists interviewing only men in the subject tribe and their attribution of patriarchal motives to observed cultural patterns, e.g., the classification of any payment of money to a bride's family as a bride-price). Two recent papers on the subject are: Ethel M. Albert, "The Roles of Women: A Question of Values" in *The Potential of Woman*, eds., Seymour M. Farber and Roger H. Wilson, New York: McGraw-Hill, 1963, pp. 105–115, and Nancy Chodorow, "Being and Doing: A Cross-Cultural Examination of the Socialization of Males and Females," in *Woman in Sexist Society*, eds., Vivian Gornick and Barbara Moran, New York: Basic Books, 1971, pp. 173–197.

13. John Money, as quoted in *Time*, January 8, 1973, p. 34. See also Robert J. Stoller, *Sex and Gender*, New York: Science House, 1968, where on pp. viii–ix Dr. Stoller differentiates between sex and gender as follows:

> The word *sex*, in this work will refer to the male and female sex and the component biological parts that determine whether one is a male or a female; the word *sexual* will have connotations of anatomy and physiology. This obviously leaves tremendous areas of behavior, feelings, thoughts and fantasies that are related to the sexes and yet do not have primarily biological connotations. It is for some of these psychological phenomena that the term *gender* will be used.

"In the absence of complete evidence," writes Dr. Stoller, "I agree in general with Money, and the Hampsons who show in their large series of intersexed patients that gender role is determined by postnatal forces, regardless of the anatomy and physiology of the external genitalia," (p. 48).

14. *American Women*, Report of the President's Commission on the Status of Women, October 1963, p. 47.

15. "Uniform Marriage and Divorce Act," approved and recommended for enactment in all states by the National Conference of Commissioners on

Uniform State Laws at its Annual Conference Meeting at St. Louis, Missouri, August 1–7, 1970, as reprinted in V *Family Law Quarterly* 205, Section 307 (hereinafter cited as UMDA, V *Family Law Quarterly* 205).

16. *Report of the Marriage and Family Committee of the National Organization for Women, Suggested Guidelines in Studying and Comments on the Uniform Marriage and Divorce Act 2*, 1971.

17. *Work in America*, Report of a Special Task Force to the Secretary of Health, Education and Welfare, Cambridge, Mass.: MIT Press, 1973, p. 179 (hereinafter cited as *Work in America*).

18. Ibid., pp. 179–180.

19. *American Jurisprudence, Proof of Facts, Annotated*, Vol. 16, San Francisco: Bancroft-Whitney, 1965, p. 857.

20. Ibid., p. 855.

21. *The Idaho Statesman*, July 24, 1973.

22. Carol McMillen Benson, "I Protest," *Glamour*, October 1972.

23. Betty Friedan, *The Feminine Mystique*, New York: Norton & Co., 1963, p. 305 (hereinafter cited as Friedan, *The Feminine Mystique*).

24. Dr. Michael Arbib, "Intelligent Machines," part of the lecture series "The Next Billion Years," University of California at Los Angeles, 1973.

25. Legislation introduced by Martha Griffiths (R-Mich.) and Barbara Jordan (D-Tex.) would permit homemakers Social Security coverage if they contribute to the fund. Bella Abzug's bill would use general revenues to give coverage to women who work in the home.

26. UMDA, V *Family Law Quarterly* 205, Section 308.

27. Friedan, *The Feminine Mystique*.

28. *Work in America*, pp. 121–134.

29. Ibid., citing Herbert E. Striner, *Continuing Education as a National Capital Investment*, Washington, D.C.: W. E. Upjohn Institute, 1972.

30. Ibid., pp. 179–180.

31. For a well-documented legal and sociological debunking of the traditional concept that divorce should be seen "only as a readmission ticket to the 'freedom of the marriage market,'" see Herma Hill Kay, "Book Review: Making Marriage and Divorce Safe for Women," 60 *California Law Review* 1683, November 1972, where Professor Hill Kay reviews *Marriage Stability, Divorce and the Law*, a 1972 book by Max Rheinstein which still ponders the legal and moral pros and cons of more liberal divorce laws and which also assumes "that the very purpose . . . a divorce law ought to pursue [is] that of facilitating remarriage." Rheinstein as quoted by Hill Kay, 60 *California Law Review* 1683, at p. 1685.

32. Robert Barkdoll, "Love Research Turns Proxmire Off," *Los Angeles Times*, March 12, 1975.

33. *Cary* v. *Cary*, No. 158872, Superior Court of the State of California, the County of San Mateo, 1971.

34. Ibid.

35. Phyllis Ziffren Deutsch, "The Family Law Practitioner as Legal Psychiatric Worker," *California State Bar Journal*, March–April 1973, p. 158, at p. 201.

36. Robert A. Roos, "How to Change the Law, or the Lawyer as a Marriage, Family and Child Counsellor: A Case Study," *Los Angeles Bar Bulletin*, October 1972, p. 481.

37. "Can You Survive Divorce?" KTTV, Los Angeles, October 7, 1973.

NOTES TO CHAPTER 12

1. *H.R.J. Res.208, 92nd Cong., 2nd Sess.* (October 12, 1971); *S.J. Res.8, 92nd Cong., 2nd Sess.* (March 22, 1972).

2. *Los Angeles Times*, March 7, 1975.

3. Ibid.

4. *Time*, January 6, 1975.

5. *Congressional Record*, Vol. 117, No. 6, Washington, D.C., January 28, 1971, p. S-469-2 (hereinafter cited as *Congressional Record*).

6. *Reed v. Reed*, 404 U.S. 71 (1971). The state statute struck down provided that in determining the relative rights of competing applicants for letters of administration of decedent estates, "males must be preferred to females."

7. *Congressional Record*, p. S-469-2.

8. 92 S.Ct. 1179 (1972).

9. For a discussion of these two different constitutional tests, see, e.g., Kenneth L. Karst, "'A Discrimination So Trivial': A Note on Law and the Symbolism of Women's Dependency," 49 *Los Angeles Bar Bulletin* 499 (October 1974); and Joan M. Krauskopf, "The Equal Rights Amendment: Its Political and Practical Contexts," 50 *California State Bar Journal* 79 (March/April 1975) (hereinafter cited as Krauskopf, "The Equal Rights Amendment").

10. 411 U.S. 677 (1973).

11. 94 S.Ct. 1734 (1974).

12. *DeFunis v. Washington*, 94 S.Ct. 1704 (1974).

13. 94 S.Ct. 1734, at p. 1740.

14. U.S. Supreme Court, No. 73-640, June 17, 1974; 42 USLW 4905.

15. Ibid.

16. Id., quoting from *Frontiero v. Richardson*.

17. Id.

18. *Congressional Record*, p. S-472.

19. Ibid.

20. Id.

21. 293 F.Supp. 1219 (1968).

22. *Congressional Record*, p. S-472.

23. *Chart of Selected State Laws Affecting Women in Private Industry*, Women's Bureau, Washington, D.C. (1975 Draft).

24. *Congressional Record*, January 28, 1971, at S-469-2.

25. Ibid., at p. 470.

26. Ibid., pp. S-471–S-472.

27. Krauskopf, "The Equal Rights Amendment," at 138.

28. Citizens' Advisory Council on the Status of Women, *The Equal Rights Amendment and Alimony and Child Support Laws*, Washington, D.C., January, 1972.

29. Ibid., pp. 10–11.

30. *Congressional Record*, p. S-471.

31. Ibid.

32. Id.

33. U.S. Congress, Senate, *Senate Report 92-689*, 92nd Congress, 2d Session, p. 12.

34. Krauskopf, "Equal Rights Amendment," pp. 139–140.

35. U.S. Congress, Senate, *Senate Report* 92-689, 92nd Congress, 2d Session.

36. Brown, Emerson, Falk, and Freedman, "The Equal Rights Amendment: A Constitutional Basis for Equal Rights for Women," 80 *Yale L.J.* 871 (1971).

37. *The Equal Rights Amendment—Senator Ervin's Minority Report and the Yale Law Journal*, Citizens' Advisory Council on the Status of Women, July 1972, Introduction.

38. Ibid.

39. Ibid., p. 11.

40. Ibid., p. 1.

41. Rep. Dorsey Matthews, as quoted in the *Los Angeles Times*, January 29, 1974.

42. *Time*, February 24, 1975.

43. 351 U.S. 12 (1956).

44. 372 U.S. 335 (1963).

45. Thomas S. Kuhn, *The Structure of Scientific Revolutions*, Chicago: University of Chicago Press, 1962.

INDEX

RIANE TENNENHAUS EISLER is a pioneer in women's rights. She founded the Los Angeles Women's Center Legal Program, accredited by the University of Southern California School of Law, and was the first woman lawyer to address the California State Bar Convention on the Equal Rights Amendment. She has lectured widely about marriage and divorce in the United States and Europe, and was instrumental in introducing non-sexually-stereotyped marriage contracts into England. She has taught courses on the social and legal status of women and children at UCLA and Immaculate Heart College, and has made guest appearances on CBS, NBC, and the BBC. She is an honor graduate from the UCLA School of Law and has written articles for both legal and nonlegal journals. Ms. Tennenhaus Eisler is divorced and has two teenage daughters.